T0068775

EQUITY & TRUSTS
CONCENTRATE

New to this edition

New coverage includes:

- ***Grondona v Stoffel & Co*** [2021] AC 540
- ***Khan v Mahmood*** [2021] EWHC 597 Ch
- **Cohabitation Rights Bill 2021 HL**
- ***Knipe v British Racing Drivers' Motor Sport Charity & Others*** [2020] EWHC 3295
- ***Group Seven Limited & Ors v Notable Services LLP & Ors*** [2019] EWCA Civ 614
- ***Re Y Trust*** [2019] WTLR 335
- ***North v Wilkinson*** [2018] 4 WLR 41

EQUITY & TRUSTS CONCENTRATE

Iain McDonald
Senior Lecturer in Law,
University of the West of England

Anne Street
Visiting Lecturer, SOAS,
University of London

EIGHTH EDITION

OXFORD
UNIVERSITY PRESS

OXFORD
UNIVERSITY PRESS

Great Clarendon Street, Oxford, OX2 6DP,
United Kingdom

Oxford University Press is a department of the University of Oxford.
It furthers the University's objective of excellence in research, scholarship,
and education by publishing worldwide. Oxford is a registered trade mark of
Oxford University Press in the UK and in certain other countries

© Oxford University Press 2022

The moral rights of the authors have been asserted

Fifth Edition 2016
Sixth Edition 2018
Seventh Edition 2020

Impression: 1

All rights reserved. No part of this publication may be reproduced, stored in
a retrieval system, or transmitted, in any form or by any means, without the
prior permission in writing of Oxford University Press, or as expressly permitted
by law, by licence or under terms agreed with the appropriate reprographics
rights organization. Enquiries concerning reproduction outside the scope of the
above should be sent to the Rights Department, Oxford University Press, at the
address above

You must not circulate this work in any other form
and you must impose this same condition on any acquirer

Public sector information reproduced under Open Government Licence v3.0
(http://www.nationalarchives.gov.uk/doc/open-government-licence/open-government-licence.htm)

Published in the United States of America by Oxford University Press
198 Madison Avenue, New York, NY 10016, United States of America

British Library Cataloguing in Publication Data
Data available

Library of Congress Control Number: 2022934490

ISBN 978–0–19–286563–2

Printed in the UK by
Bell & Bain Ltd., Glasgow

Links to third party websites are provided by Oxford in good faith and
for information only. Oxford disclaims any responsibility for the materials
contained in any third party website referenced in this work.

Contents

Table of cases vii

Table of legislation xv

1 The history and development of equity 1

2 The nature of a trust 16

3 The three certainties 25

4 Constitution 42

5 Formalities 59

6 Charitable trusts 75

7 Non-charitable purpose trusts 100

8 Secret trusts 110

9 Implied trusts 125

10 Variation of trusts 145

11 Trustees' duties and powers 157

12 Remedies for breach of trust 180

13 Equitable remedies 202

Exam essentials A1

Outline answers A3

Glossary A9

Index A13

Table of cases

Abbott v Abbott [2007] UKPC 53 . . . 144

Abou Rahma v Abacha [2006] EWCA Civ 1492 . . . 188

Abrahams v Trustees of the Property of Abrahams [1999] All ER (D) 780 . . . 130

Adams and Kensington Vestry, Re (1884) 27 Ch D 394 . . . 27, A3

Agip (Africa) Ltd v Jackson [1990] Ch 26 . . . 187, 189, 199

AIB Group v Mark Redler & Co Solicitors [2014] UKSC 58 . . . 182

Air Jamaica v Charlton [1999] UKPC 20 . . . 130

Allen v Jambo Holdings Ltd [1980] 1 WLR 1252 . . . 208

Allen v Snyder [1977] NSWLR 685 . . . 14

Aluminium Industrie Vaasen BV v Romalpa Aluminium Ltd [1976] 1 WLR 676 . . . 189

American Cyanamid Co v Ethicon Ltd [1975] AC 396 . . . 207, 208, 209, 210, 212, 214, A8

Ames Settlement, Re [1946] Ch 217 . . . 127

Angove's Pty Ltd v Bailey [2016] UKSC 47 . . . 134

Anton Piller KG v Manufacturing Processes Ltd [1976] Ch 55 . . . 210, 214

Appleby Corporate Services (BVI) Ltd v Citco Trustees (BVI) Ltd [2016] WTLR 373 II . . . 170

Armitage v Nurse [1998] Ch 241 . . . 182

Artistic Upholstery Ltd v Art Forma Ltd [1999] 4 All ER 277 . . . 107

Ashburn Anstalt v Arnold [1989] Ch 1 . . . 134, 135

Aspden v Elvy [2012] EWHC 1387 (Ch) . . . A3

Astors ST, Re [1952] Ch 534 . . . 101

Atkinson's Will Trust, Re [1978] 1 WLR 586 . . . 79

Attorney-General for Hong Kong v Reid [1994] 1 AC 324 . . . 21, 163

Attorney-General v Blake [2001] 1 AC 268 . . . 5, 213

Attorney-General v Charity Commission for England and Wales [2012] WTLR 977 . . . 78, 81, 82, 88, 97, 98

Attorney-General v Ross [1986] 1 WLR 252 . . . 80, 90

Attorney-General v Times Newspapers Ltd [1992] 1 AC 191 . . . 211

Attorney-General v Zedra Fiduciary Services (UK) Ltd [2020] EWHC 2988 . . . 95

Baden, Delvaux and Lecuit v Societé Générale pour Favoriser le Développement du Commerce et de l'Industrie en France [1989] BCLC 325 . . . 186

Baden's Trust (No 1), Re [1971] AC 424 . . . 32, 35, 36, 37, 38, 40, 106, A3

Baden's Trust (No 2), Re [1973] Ch 9 . . . 32, 34, 35, 36, 40, 41, A3

Bahin v Hughes (1886) 31 ChD 390 . . . 183

Baillie, Re (1886) 2 TLR 660 . . . 121

Bainbridge v Bainbridge [2016] EWHC 898 (Ch) . . . 212

Ball's ST, Re [1968] 1 WLR 899 . . . 150, 151, 155

Bank of Cyprus UK Ltd v Menelaou [2015] UKSC 66 . . . 185

Barclays Bank v Quistclose [1970] AC 567 . . . 128, 129, 142

Barlow Clowes International v Eurotrust International [2005] UKPC 37 . . . 188

Barlow Clowes v Vaughan [1992] BCLC 910, CA . . . 197

Barlow's WT, Re [1979] 1 WLR 278 . . . 33

Barnes v Addy (1874) LR 9 Ch App 244 . . . 186

Basham, Re [1986] 1 WLR 1498 . . . 51

Bateman's WT, Re [1970] 1 WLR 1463 . . . 115, 116, 119

BCCI SA (No 9), Re [1994] 3 All ER 764 . . . 212

BCCI v Akindele [2000] 4 All ER 221 . . . 6, 134, 187, 198, 199

Beaumont, Re [1902] 1 Ch 889 . . . 49

Beckford v Beckford (1774) Lofft 490 . . . 131

Behnke v Bede Shipping Co Ltd [1927] 1 KB 649 . . . 204

Belmont Finance Corp v Williams Furniture Ltd (No 2) [1980] 1 All ER 393 . . . 187

Beloved Wilkes' Charity, Re (1851) 2 Mac & G 440 . . . 170

Benjamin, Re [1902] 1 Ch 723 . . . 173
Bennet v Bennet (1879) 10 ChD 474 . . . 131
Best, Re [1904] 2 Ch 354 . . . 79
Besterman's Will Trusts, Re 21 January 1980, unreported . . . 82
Bishopsgate Investment Management Ltd v Homan [1995] 1 All ER 347 . . . 193
Blackwell v Blackwell [1925] All ER Rep 498, CA . . . 112, 113
Blackwell v Blackwell [1929] AC 318, HL . . . 115, 119, 120, 122
Boardman v Phipps [1967] 2 AC 46 . . . 162, 164, A8
Boles and British Land Company's Contract, Re [1902] 1 Ch 244 . . . 163
Borden UK Ltd v Scottish Timber Products Ltd [1981] Ch 25 . . . 189
Boscawen v Bajwa [1996] 1 WLR 328 . . . 185, 197
Boyce v Boyce (1849) 16 Sim 476 . . . 30
Boyes, Re (1884) 26 Ch D 531 . . . 114, 118, 119, 120
Bray v Ford [1896] AC 44 . . . 162, 178
Breakspear v Ackland [2008] EWHC 220 (Ch) . . . 172
Bristol and West Building Society v Mothew [1996] 4 All ER 698 . . . 161, 176
British School of Egyptology, Re [1954] 1 WLR 546 . . . 82
Bryant v Hickley [1894] 1 Ch 324 . . . 174
Bucks Constabulary Widows & Orphans Fund Friendly Society (No 2), Re [1979] 1 WLR 936 . . . 128, 1107
Bulmer v Bolinger [1977] 2 CMLR 625 . . . 209
Burns v Burns [1984] 1 All ER 244 . . . 139
Buttle v Saunders [1950] 2 All ER 193 . . . 163

Caffoor v Income Tax Commissioner [1961] AC 584 . . . 84
Cain v Moon [1896] 2 QB 283 . . . 48, 54, 56, A4
Cameron, Re [1999] 2 All ER 924 . . . 131
Cannon v Hartley [1949] Ch 213 . . . 53
Carl Zeiss Stifung v Herbert Smith [1969] 2 Ch 276 . . . 133
Caus, Re [1934] Ch 162 . . . 87
Cayne v Global Natural Resources plc [1984] 1 All ER 225 . . . 208
Chapman v Chapman [1954] 2 WLR 723 . . . 147, 148, 149, 154
Chappell v Times Newspapers Ltd [1975] 1 WLR 482 . . . 9
Chappell v UK (1990) 12 EHRR 1 . . . 215
Chase Manhatten Bank NA v Israel-British Bank [1981] Ch 105 . . . 134
Chief Constable of Kent v V [1983] QB 34 . . . 191
Choithram International v Pagarani [2001] 2 All ER 492 PC; [2001] 1 WLR 1 . . . 49, 54, 57, 122, A3
City of Westminster Properties Ltd v Mudd [1959] Ch 129 . . . 213
Clark v Mandoj [1998] EWCA Civ 505 . . . 132
Clayton's Case (1817) 1 Mer 572 . . . 196, 197, 198
Clitheroe's ST, Re [1959] 1 WLR 1159 . . . 152
Clough v Killey [1996] 72 P&CR D22 . . . 140
Co-operative Insurance Society Ltd v Argyll Stores Ltd [1988] AC 1 . . . 204, 214
Cocks v Manners (1871) LR 12 Eq 574 . . . 103
Cole, Re [1958] Ch 877 . . . 91
Cole, Re [1964] Ch 175 . . . 46, 55, A4, A4
Coles v Trecothick (1804) 9 Ves 234 . . . 164
Colin Cooper, Re [1939] Ch 811 . . . 120
Comiskey v Bowring-Hanbury [1905] AC 84 . . . 9, 27
Commissioners for Special Purposes of Income Tax v Pemsel [1891] AC 531 . . . 78, 79
Conservative and Unionist Central Office v Burrell [1982] 1 WLR 522 . . . 103
Cook's ST, Re [1965] Ch 902 . . . 53
Coombes v Smith [1986] 1 WLR 808 . . . 51
Cornish v Brook Green Laundry [1959] 1 QB 391 . . . 206
Coulthurst, Re [1951] Ch 661 . . . 80
Cowan v Scargill [1984] 2 All ER 750 . . . 168, 176
Cowcher v Cowcher [1972] 1 WLR 425 . . . 130, 135
Coxen, Re [1948] Ch 747 . . . 80
Craddock Bros v Hunt [1932] 2 Ch 136 . . . 213
Cross v Cross (1983) 4 FLR 235 . . . 8
Crossco No 4 Unlimited v Jolan [2011] EWHC 803 (Ch) . . . 136
Curley v Parkes [2004] EWCA Civ 1515 . . . 135
Curtis v Pulbrook [2011] EWHC 167 (Ch) . . . 50, 52

Dadourian Group Int v Sims [2006] EWCA Civ 399 . . . 212
Dawson-Damer v Taylor Wessing LLP [2020] EWCA Civ 352 . . . 172

De Francesco v Barnum (1890) 45 Ch 430 . . . 205
Dean, Re (1899) 41 Ch D 552 . . . 102
Denley's Trust Deed, Re [1969] 1 Ch 373 . . . 106, 107, 108, 109, A6
Derby & Co Ltd v Weldon [1990] Ch 48 . . . 212
Diggles, Re (1888) LR 39 ChD 253 . . . 27
Dillon, Re (1890) 44 Ch D 76; 59 LJ Ch 420 . . . 48
Dingle v Turner [1972] AC 601 . . . 81, 83, 84, 97
Diplock, Re [1948] Ch 465 . . . 127, 172, 191, 197
Dodsworth v Dodsworth (1973) 228 EG 1115 . . . 141
Don King v Warren [1998] 2 All ER 608 . . . 53
Downshire Settled Estates, Re [1953] Ch 218 . . . 149
Drake v Whipp [1996] 1 FLR 826 . . . 140
Druce's ST, Re [1962] 1 WLR 363 . . . 153
Dudman, Re [1925] 1 Ch 553 . . . 48
Duke of Norfolk's ST, Re [1982] Ch 61 . . . 160
Dupree, Re [1945] Ch 16 . . . 82

Earl of Oxford's case (1615) 1 Rep Ch 1 . . . 1, 3, 13
Ebrand v Dancer (1680) 22 ER 829 . . . 131
El Ajou v Dollar Land Holdings [1994] 2 All ER 685 . . . 21
Ellenborough, Re [1903] 1 Ch 607 . . . 53, 112
EMI Ltd v Pandit [1975] 1 WLR 302 . . . 210
Endacott, Re [1960] Ch 232 . . . 101, 102, 103
Erlanger v New Sombrero Phosphate Co (1873) 3 App Cas 1218 . . . 213
Erskine's ST, Re [1971] 1 WLR 162 . . . 174
Eurotrust v Barlow Clowes [2006] 1 All ER 333 . . . 199
Evans, Re [1999] 2 All ER 777 . . . 173
Evans v BBC and IBA (1974), The Times, 27 February . . . 210
Eves v Eves [1975] 1 WLR 1338 . . . 137, 138, 142
EVTR Ltd, Re [1987] BCLC 646 . . . 129

Falke v Gray (1859) 62 Eng Rep 250 . . . 53
Farepak Foods and Gifts Ltd (in administration), Re [2006] EWHC 3272 (Ch) . . . 12
Federal Republic of Brazil v Durant International Corporation [2015] UKPC 35 . . . 193
Fellowes & Son v Fisher [1976] QB 122 . . . 209
FHR European Ventures LLP v Cedar Capital Partners LLC [2014] UKSC 45; [2015] AC 250 . . . 134, 163, 177, 189
Finger's WT, Re [1972] Ch 286 . . . 95
Fletcher v Fletcher (1844) 4 Hare 67 . . . 53
Foskett v McKeown [2001] 1 AC 102 . . . 189, 191, 193, 199
Fowkes v Pascoe (1875) 10 Ch App 343 . . . 132
Freeland, Re [1952] Ch 110 . . . 47, A4
Fry, Re [1946] Ch 312 . . . 49, 55
Fry v Tapson (1885) 28 Ch 268 . . . 170, A7
Fuller v Evans [2000] 1 All ER 636 . . . 174
Funnell v Stewart [1996] 1 WLR 288 . . . 85

Garden Cottage Foods Ltd v Milk Marketing Board [1984] AC 130 . . . 208
Gardener v Rowe (1828) 5 Russ 258 . . . 62
Gardner (No 2), Re [1923] 2 Ch 230 . . . 121
Gavin-Mack v Gavin-Mack (1993) . . . 130
Geary v Rankine [2012] EWCA Civ 555; [2012] 2 FCR 461 . . . 139
Giles v RNIB [2014] EWHC 1373 (Ch) . . . 213
Gillett v Holt [2001] Ch 210 . . . 51, 54, 141
Gillingham Bus Disaster Fund, Re [1959] Ch 62 . . . 173
Gilmour v Coats [1949] AC 426 . . . 86, 97, 103
Gissing v Gissing [1971] AC 886 . . . 11, 136, 138, 139, 140
Glaister-Carlisle v Glaister-Carlisle (1968) unreported . . . 46
Golay's WT, Re [1965] 2 All ER 660 . . . 31
Gonin, Re [1977] 2 All ER 720 . . . 47, 55, A4
Goulding v James [1997] 2 All ER 239 . . . 154, 155
Grainge v Wilberforce (1889) 5 TLR 436 . . . 70
Grant v Edwards [1986] 3 WLR 114; [1986] Ch 638 . . . 21, 137, 138
Grant's WT, Re [1980] 1 WLR 360 . . . 103, 105, 107, 108
Greasley v Cooke [1980] 1 WLR 1306 . . . 52
Grey v IRC [1958] Ch 375 . . . 70
Grey v IRC [1960] AC 1 . . . 65, 66, 72, A5
Grondona v Stoffel & Co [2021] AC 540 . . . 9
Group Seven Limited v Notable Services LLP [2019] EWCA Civ 614 . . . 188
Grove-Grady, Re [1929] 1 Ch 557 . . . 91
Guild v IRC [1992] 2 All ER 10 . . . 93
Guinness v Saunders [1990] 2 AC 663 . . . 134

Gulbenkian's Settlement, Re [1970] AC 508 . . . 32
Gwyon, Re [1930] 1 Ch 255 . . . 82

Hadley v Baxendale (1854) 9 Ex Ch 341 . . . 52
Hallets, Re (1880) 13 Ch D 696 . . . 193, 194, 198, A8
Hanchett-Stamford v Attorney General [2008] 4 All ER 323 . . . 107
Harries v Church Commissioners [1992] 1 WLR 1241 . . . 168
Hartigan Nominees Property Ltd v Rydge (1992) NSWLR 405 . . . 172
Harvard Securities Ltd (in liquidation), Re [1998] CC 567 . . . 30
Harwood, Re [1936] Ch 285 . . . 95
Havelock v Havelock (1881) 17 Ch D 807 . . . 148
Hay's Settlement Trusts, Re [1982] 1 WLR 202 . . . 22, 37, 38, 39
Hendy Lennox Ltd v Grahame Puttick Ltd [1984] 1 WLR 485 . . . 189
Hetherington, Re [1990] Ch 1 . . . 87, 103
Hilton v Cosnier [2018] EWHC 2728 (Ch) II . . . 27
Hodgson v Marks [1971] Ch 892 . . . 130
Holder v Holder [1968] Ch 353 . . . 164
Holt's ST, Re [1968] 1 WLR 899 . . . 153
Hooper, Re [1932] 1 Ch 38 . . . 102
Hopkins, Re [1965] Ch 669 . . . 82
Hopkinson, Re [1949] 1 All ER 346 . . . 89
Hubbard v Pitt [1976] QB 142 . . . 209
Human Dignity Trust v Charity Commission for England and Wales [2014] WLUK 340 . . . 89
Hunter v Moss [1994] 1 WLR 452 . . . 29, 30, 39
Hussey v Palmer [1972] 1 WLR 1286 . . . 139, A3

IDC v Clark [1992] 1 EGLR 186 . . . 135
Imageview Management Ltd v Jack [2009] 2 All ER 666 . . . 161
Incorporated Council for Law Reporting v Attorney-General [1972] Ch 73 . . . 82
Independent Schools Council v Charity Commission for England and Wales [2011] All ER (D) 198 (Oct) . . . 77, 78, 79, 83, 88, 97, 98
Inland Revenue Commissioners v Baddeley [1955] AC 572 . . . 92
IRC v Bernstein [1961] Ch 399 . . . 175
IRC v Broadway Cottages Trust [1955] Ch 20 . . . 32, 35
IRC v Educational Grants Association Ltd [1967] Ch 123 . . . 84
IRC v McMullen[1981] AC 1 . . . 82
Isaac v Isaac [2005] EWHC 435 (Ch) . . . 160
Ivey v Genting Casinos [2017] UKSC 67 . . . 188

Jackson, Re (1882) 21 Ch D 786 . . . 148
Jaffa v Taylor Gallery Ltd (1990) The Times 21 March . . . 46
James, Ex p (1803) 8 Ves 337 . . . 163
James, Re [1935] Ch 449 . . . 47
Jennings v Rice [2002] EWCA Civ 159 . . . 52, 141
JIH v News Group Newspapers Ltd [2011] 2 All ER 324 . . . 11
Jones v Kernott [2011] UKSC 53 . . . 135, 139, 140, 142, A3
Jones v Lock (1865) LR 1 Ch App 25 . . . 28, 46, 50, 55, 61, 72
Jones v Stones [1999] 1 WLR 1739 . . . 207
Joseph Rowntree Memorial Trust Housing Association Ltd v Attorney-General [1983] 2 WLR 284 . . . 91
Jubber v Jubber (1839) 9 Sim 503 . . . 29

Kasperbauer v Griffith (2000) 1 WLRT 333 . . . 113, 118
Katherine, Duchess of Suffolk v Herenden (1560) . . . 111
Kayford Ltd (in liquidation), Re [1975] 1 WLR 279 . . . 12, 28
Keech v Sandford (1726) Sel Cas Ch 61 . . . 21, 134, 162, 176
Keeling v Keeling [2017] EWHC 1189 (Ch) . . . 48
Keen, Re [1937] Ch 236 . . . 114, 115, 116, 119, 123, A6
Kekewich v Manning (1851) De GM & G 176 . . . 64
Kelly, Re [1932] IR 255 . . . 103
Kenson Contractors Ltd v Haringey LBC [2019] EWHC 1230 II . . . 208
Khan v Mahmood [2021] EWHC 597 Ch . . . 50
King (Don) v Warren [1998] 2 All ER 608 . . . 53
King v Dubrey [2015] EWCA Civ . . . 48
Kinloch v Secretary of State for India (1882) 7 App Cas 619 . . . 27

Knight v Knight (1840) 3 Beav 148 . . . 26, 39
Knipe v British Racing Drivers' Motor Sport Charity [2020] EWHC 3295 . . . 94
Knocker v Youle [1986] 1 WLR 934 . . . 152
Koettgen, Re [1954] Ch 252 . . . 84
Kolb's WT, Re [1961] 3 All ER 811 . . . 29

Lambe v Eames (1871) 6 Ch App 597 . . . 26, 27, 39
Lassence v Tierney (1849) 1 Mac 7 G 551 . . . 28
Lazard Bros v Fairfield Property Ltd (1977) 121 SJ 793 . . . 206
Leaf v International Galleries [1950] 2 KB 86 . . . 9, 212
Leahy v AG for New South Wales [1959] AC 457 . . . 104, 108
Ledgerwood v Perpetual Trustee Co Ltd (1997) 41 NSWLR 532 . . . 116
Letterstedt v Broers (1884) 9 App Cas 371 . . . 160
Lillingston, Re [1952] 2 All ER 184 . . . 48
Llpinski's WT, Re [1976] Ch 235 . . . 107
Lipkin Gorman v Karpnale [1991] 2 AC 548 . . . 134, 184, 185, 197, 199
Lister & Co v Stubbs (1890) 45 Ch D 1 . . . 163
Lloyds Bank v Rosset [1991] AC 107 . . . 135, 136, 137, 138, 139, 141, 142, A3
Locabail International Finance v Agroexport [1986] 1 WLR 657 . . . 210
Lock International plc v Beswick [1989] 1 WLR 1268 . . . 211, 214
Lohia v Lohia [2001] 1 WTLR 101 . . . 130
London Wine Co, Re [1986] PCC 121 . . . 29, 40, A4
Londonderry's Settlement, Re [1965] Ch 918 . . . 171
Long v Lloyd [1958] 2 All ER 402 . . . 212
Lopes, Re [1931] 2 Ch 130 . . . 82
Lord and Fullerton's Contract, Re [1896] 1 Ch 228 . . . 158
Lowther v Bentinck (1874) LR 19 Eq 166 . . . 175
Luke v South Kensington Hotel Co (1879) 11 Ch D 121 . . . 161
Lysaght, Re [1966] Ch 191 . . . 96

McAlpine v Panatown [2001] EWCA Civ 485 . . . 53
McCormick v Grogan (1869) LR 4 HL 82 . . . 111, 122
Macduff, Re [1896] 2 Ch 451 . . . 79
McGovern v Attorney-General [1982] Ch 321 . . . 89, 97, A5
McGrath v Wallis [1995] 2 FLR 114 . . . 130, 131
McPhail v Doulton (Re Baden's Trust (No 1)) [1971] AC 424 . . . 23, 32, 35, 36, 37, 38, 40, 106, A3
McPhail v Doulton (Re Baden's Trust (No 2)) [1973] Ch 9 . . . 32, 34, 35, 36, 40, 41
Maddock, Re [1902] 2 Ch 220 . . . 120
Mara v Browne [1895] 2 Ch 69 . . . 186
Mara v Browne [1896] 1 Ch 199 . . . 134
Mareva Compagnia Naviera SA v International Bulk-carriers SA [1975] 2 Lloyd's Rep 509 . . . 211
Marley v Rawlings [2014] UKSC 2 . . . 113, 116
Martin v City of Edinburgh District Council [1988] SLT 329 . . . 168
Mascall v Mascall (1984) 49P & CR 119 . . . 49
Matharu v Matharu (1994) 26 HLR 648 . . . 51
Mead, Re (1880) 15 Ch D 651 . . . 49
Mettoy Pensions Trustee v Evans [1990] 1 WLR 1587 . . . 23
Midland Bank v Cooke [1995] 4 All ER 562 . . . 140
Mills v Shields [1948] IR 367 . . . 48
Milroy v Lord (1862) 4 De GF & J 264 . . . 43, 45, 49, 55, A3
Ministry of Health v Simpson [1951] AC 251 . . . 197
Montagu's Settlement, Re [1987] 1 Ch 264 . . . 187
Morice v Bishop of Durham (1804) 9 Ves Jr 399; (1805) 10 Ves 522 . . . 76, 101
Morning Star v Express Newspapers [1979] FSR 113 . . . 208
Moss v Cooper (1861) 4 LT 790 . . . 114, 117, 119, 122
Murphy v Murphy [1999] 1 WLR 282 . . . 171
Mussett v Bingle [1876] WN 170 . . . 102
Mussoorie Bank Ltd v Raynor (1882) 7 App Cas 321 . . . 31

National Anti-Vivisection Society v Inland Revenue Commissioners [1948] AC 31 . . . 89
Nelson v Greening & Sykes (Builders) Ltd [2007] EWCA Civ 1358, CA . . . 71
Nestlé v National Westminster Bank plc [1993] 1 WLR 1260 . . . 165, 169, 176, A7
Neville Estates v Madden [1962] Ch 832 . . . 85

Neville v Wilson [1996] 3 All ER 171; [1997] Ch 144 . . . 65, 72, 73, 74

New, Re [1901] 2 Ch 534 . . . 147, 148

Niyazi's Will Trusts, Re [1973] 3 All ER 785 . . . 81

North v Wilkinson [2018] 4 WLR 41 . . . 27

Ntuli v Donald [2010] EWCA Civ 1276 . . . 11

Oatway, Re [1903] 2 Ch 356 . . . 194, 195, A8

O'Donnell v Shanahan [2009] EWCA Civ 75 . . . 176

O'Kelly v Davies [2014] EWCA Civ 1606 . . . 139, 140

Ong v Ping [2017] EWCA 2069 II . . . 62

Oppenheim v Tobacco Securities Trust Co [1951] AC 297 . . . 83, 84, 97, A5

O'Rourke v Darbishire [1920] AC 581 . . . 171, 176

Osaba, Re [1978] 2 All ER 1099 . . . 128

OT Computers Ltd (In Administration) v First National Tricity Finance Ltd [2003] EWHC 1010 (Ch) II . . . 32

Ottoway v Norman [1972] 2 WLR 50 . . . 113, 117, 118, 121, 123

Oughtred v IRC [1960] AC 206 HL . . . 65, 72

Oxley v Hiscock [2004] 3 All ER 703 . . . 140, 142, A3

P & P Property v Owen White & Catlin LLP [2018] 3 WLR 1244 . . . 183

Pain, Re [1919] 1 Ch 38 . . . 64

Palmer v Simmonds (1854) 2 Drew 221 . . . 29, 41

Paradise Motor Co, Re [1968] 1 WLR 1125 . . . 131

Paragon Finance v Thakerar [1999] 1 All ER 400 . . . 186

Partington, Re (1887) 57 LT 654 . . . 183

Pascoe v Turner [1979] 1 WLR 431; [1979] 2 All ER 945 . . . 50, 51, 141

Patel v Ali [1984] Ch 283 . . . 205

Patel v Mirza [2016] UKSC 42; [2017] AC 467 . . . 8, 9, 13, 132, 133, 142

Paul v Constance [1977] 1 WLR 527 . . . 28, 61

Pauling's ST, Re [1964] Ch 303 . . . 175, 183

Peachdart Ltd, Re [1984] Ch 131 . . . 189

Pearse v Green (1819) 1 Jac & W 135 . . . 171

Pearson v Lehman Brothers Finance SA [2010] EWHC 2914 (Ch) . . . 30

Peck v Halsey (1720) 2 PW 387 . . . 29

Penn v Lord Baltimore (1750) 1 Ves Sen 444 . . . 7

Pennington v Waine [2002] EWCA Civ 227; [2002] 1 WLR 2075 . . . 12, 50, 52, 55, 57, 187, A3

Pettitt v Pettitt [1970] AC 777 . . . 130, 131, 138, 139

Phillips v Brooks [1919] 2 KB 243 . . . 212

Pilkington v IRC [1964] AC 612 . . . 175

Pinion, Re [1965] Ch 85 . . . 88

Pitt v Holt [2013] AC 108 . . . 213

Polly Peck International plc (in administration) No 2 [1998] 3 All ER 812 . . . 134

Posner v Scott-Lewis [1987] Ch 25 . . . 205

Potters-Ballotini Ltd v Weston-Baker [1977] RPC 202 . . . 209

Printers and Transferrers' Amalgamated Trades Protection Society, Re [1899] 2 Ch 84 . . . 128

Pullan v Koe [1913] 1 Ch 9; (1913) 82 LJ Ch 37 . . . 53, 65

R (on the application of Hodkin) v Registrar General of Births, Deaths and Marriages [2014] AC 610 . . . 86

R v District Auditor, ex parte West Yorkshire Metropolitan County Council (1986) 26 RVR 24 . . . 37, A4

Racal Group Services Ltd v Ashmore [1995] STC 1151 . . . 213

Ralli's WT, Re [1964] Ch 288 . . . 47, 55

Ramsden v Dyson (1866) LR 1 HL 129 . . . 50

Rawstron v Freud [2014] EWHC 2577 (Ch) . . . 113, 117

Reading v Attorney-General [1951] AC 507 . . . 161

Recher's WT, Re [1972] Ch 526 . . . 103, 106, 107, 108

Remnant's ST, Re [1970] 2 All ER 554 . . . 153, A7

Resch, Re [1969] 1 AC 514 . . . 88, A5

Richards v Delridge [1874] LR 18 Eq 11 . . . 45, 55

Ridgewell v Ridgewell [2007] EWHC 2666 (Ch); [2008] STC 1883 . . . 150

Rochefoucauld v Boustead [1897] Ch 196 . . . 63, 71, 72, 73, 121

Roper-Curzon v Roper-Curzon (1871) LR 11 Eq 452 . . . 175

Roscoe v Winder [1915] 1 Ch 62 . . . 195, 196

Rose, Re [1952] Ch 499; [1952] 1 All ER 1217 . . . 49, 50, 55, 57, A3

Roussel-Uclaf v GD Searle & Co Ltd [1977] FSR 157 . . . 209
Royal Brunei Airlines Sdn.Bhd. v Tan [1995] 3 All ER 97 . . . 187, 188
Royal Choral Society v IRC [1943] 2 All ER 101 . . . 88
Rymer, Re [1895] 1 Ch 1 . . . 95, A5

Sanders, Re [1954] Ch 265 . . . 80, 81
Santander UK plc v RA Legal Solicitors [2014] EWCA Civ . . . 183
Satterthwaite's WT, Re [1966] 1 WLR 277 . . . 94
Saunders v Vautier (1841) 10 LJ Ch 354 . . . 39, 67, 106, 147, 154
Scarisbrick, Re [1951] Ch 622 . . . 78, 81, 97
Schmidt v Rosewood Trust [2003] 3 All ER 76 . . . 23, 171, 172, 176
Scottish Burial Reform and Cremation Society Ltd v Glasgow Corpn [1968] AC 138 . . . 88
Scottish Equitable v Derby [2000] 3 All ER 793 . . . 185
Seager v Copydex Ltd [1967] 1 WLR 923 . . . 5, 13
Segelman, Re [1996] Ch 171 . . . 81, 82
Sen v Headley [1991] Ch 425; [1991] 2 All ER 636 . . . 48, 56, A4
Series 5 Software Ltd v Clarke [1996] 1 All ER 853 . . . 209
Shalson v Russo [2005] Ch 281 . . . 195, 197, 213
Shaw's WT, Re [1957] 1 WLR 729 . . . 83
Shepherd Homes v Sandham [1970] 3 All ER 402 . . . 208, 210
Shepherd v Cartwright [1955] AC 431 . . . 131, 132, 142
Sigsworth, Re [1935] Ch 89 . . . 21
Silverwood v Silverwood (1997) 74 P & CR 453, CA . . . 131
Sinclair Investments (UK) Ltd v Versailles Trade Finance Ltd (in administration) [2011] EWCA Civ 347 . . . 163
Sinclair v Brougham [1914] AC 398 . . . 192, 196
Sky Petroleum v VIP Petroleum [1974] 1 All ER 954 . . . 203
Slevin, Re [1891] 2 Ch 236 . . . 96
Snowden, Re [1979] Ch 528 . . . 118
Society of Lloyd's v Robinson [1999] 1 WLR 756 . . . 146
South Place Ethical Society, Re [1980] 1 WLR 1565 . . . 85, 97
Southwell v Blackburn [2014] EWCA Civ . . . 141
Southwood v Attorney-General [2000] WL 877698 . . . 90
Speight v Gaunt (1881) 22 Ch D 727 . . . 167
Speight v Gaunt (1883) 9 App Cas 1 . . . 182
Springette v DeFoe [1992] 2 FCR 561 . . . 137, 140
Stack v Dowden [2007] UKHL 17; [2007] 2 WLR 831 . . . 126, 136, 139, 140, 141, 143, A3, A7
Staden v Jones [2008] EWCA Civ 936 . . . 27
Staniland v Willott (1852) 3 Mac & G 664 . . . 49
Starglade v Nash [2010] EWCA Civ 1314 . . . 188
Stead, Re [1900] 1 Ch 237 . . . 114, 119, A6
Steed's WT, Re [1960] Ch 407 . . . 150, 154, 155
Stephenson (Inspector of Taxes) v Barclays Bank Trust Co Ltd [1975] 1 All ER 625 . . . 147
Stewart, Re [1908] 2 Ch 251 . . . 47
Strong v Bird (1874) LR 18 Eq 315 . . . 42, 47, 55, 56, 71
Styles v Guy (1849) 19 LT Ch 185 . . . 182
Suffert, Re [1961] Ch 1 . . . 152

Tamplin v James (1880) 15 Ch D 215 . . . 205
Target Holdings Ltd v Redferns [1995] 3 All ER 785 . . . 182
Taylor v Plumer (1815) 3 M&S 562 . . . 189
Thomas v Fuller-Brown [1988] 1 FLR 237 . . . 137, 139
Thomas v Times Book Co [1966] 2 All ER 241 . . . 46
Thompson, Re [1934] Ch 342 . . . 103
Thompson v Hurst [2012] EWCA Civ 1752; [2013] 1 FCR 522 . . . 139
Thomson, Re [1930] 1 Ch 203 . . . 164
Thorner v Major [2009] UKHL 18; [2009] 3 All ER 945 . . . 51, 52, 56, 134, 135, 141
Thornton v Howe (1862) 31 Beav 14 . . . 85, 87
Tilley's WT, Re [1967] ChD 2279 . . . 194
Timpson's Executors v Yerbury [1936] 1 KB 645 . . . 64
Tinsley v Milligan [1994] 1 AC 340 . . . 8, 20, 130, 132, 133, 142
Tollemache, Re [1903] 1 Ch 457 . . . 148
Tribe v Tribe [1996] Ch 107 . . . 133

Trust of the Abbott Fund, Re the [1900] 2 Ch 326 . . . 128

T's ST, Re [1963] 3 WLR 987 . . . 151, 153

Tuck's ST, Re [1978] Ch 49 . . . 36, A4

Turner v Jacob [2006] EWHC 1317 (Ch); [2008] WTLR 307 . . . 195

Twinsectra v Yardley [2002] 2 All ER 377; [2002] 2 AC 164 . . . 126, 129, 134, 187, 188, 199, 200, A3

Union Eagle Ltd v Golden Achievements Ltd [1997] AC 514 . . . 206

United Scientific Holdings Ltd v Burnley Borough Council [1978] AC 904 . . . 4

Vandervell v IRC [1967] 1 All ER 1; [1967] 2 AC 291 . . . 20, 67, 71, 72, 73, 127

Vandervell v IRC (No 2) [1974] Ch 269; [1974] 3 All ER 205 . . . 68

Venables v News Group Newspapers [2001] Fam 430 . . . 207, 212

Wallgrave v Tebbs (1855) 2 K & J 313 . . . 114, 117, 119

Walsh v Lonsdale (1882) 21 Ch D 9 . . . 4, 10, 13

Ward v Snelling (1994) unreported . . . 131

Warner Bros Pictures Inc v Nelson [1937] 1 KB 209 . . . 205, 207

Wayling v Jones [1995] 2 FLR 1029 . . . 51

Wedgewood, Re [1915] 1 Ch 113 . . . 91

West, Re [1900] 1 Ch 84 . . . 127

West Sussex Constabulary's Widows, Children and Benevolent Fund (1930) Trusts [1971] Ch 1; [1970] 1 All ER 544 . . . 108, 128

Westdeutsche Landesbank Gironzentrale v Islington LBC [1996] 2 All ER 961 . . . 20, 133, 134, 189, 191

Weston's ST, Re [1969] 1 Ch 223 . . . 153, 155

Whitely, Re (1887) 12 App Cas 727 . . . 167

Wilkes v Allington [1931] 2 Ch 104 . . . 48, A4

William Brandts' Sons & Co v Dunlop Rubber Co [1905] AC 454 . . . 64

Williams v Barton [1927] 2 Ch 9 . . . 162

Williams v Central Bank of Nigeria [2014] UKSC 10 . . . 183, 186

Williams WT, Re [1953] Ch 138 . . . 175

Williers v Joyce [2016] UKSC 43 . . . 44, 188

Wilson v Turner (1883) 22 Ch 9 . . . 174

Woodard v Woodard [1995] 3 All ER 980 . . . 48, A4

Woodhams, Re [1981] 1 WLR 493 . . . 96

Wright, Re [1954] Ch 347 . . . 96

Wright v Morgan [1926] AC 778 . . . 163

Wrightson, Re [1908] 1 Ch 798 . . . 160

X AG v A Bank [1983] 2 All ER 464 . . . 209

X v A [2005] EWHC 2706 (Ch) . . . 175

Y Trust, Re [2019] WTLR 335 . . . 153

Yaxley v Gotts [2000] Ch 162 . . . 140

Yeoman's Row v Cobbe [2008] UKHL 55; [2008] 4 All ER 713 . . . 51, 56, 135, 141

Young, Re [1951] Ch 344 . . . 120

Z Ltd v A-Z and AA-LL [1982] QB 558 . . . 211

Table of legislation

Table of Statutes

Administration of Estates Act 1925 . . . 20

Charities Act 2006 . . . 75, 81, 88, 93, 97, 98
Charities Act 2011 . . . 75, 77, 98, 99
s 1(1)(a) . . . 77, 80
s 3 . . . 78
s 3(1) . . . 77
s 3(1)(a) . . . 81
s 3(1)(a)-(c) . . . 78
s 3(1)(b) . . . 82, A5
s 3(1)(c) . . . 82, 85
s 3(1)(d) . . . 83, 88, A5
s 3(1)(d)-(m) . . . 78, 87
s 3(1)(f) . . . 83, 88
s 3(1)(g) . . . 89
s 3(1)(h) . . . 89
s 3(1)(i) . . . 91
s 3(1)(j) . . . 91
s 3(1)(k) . . . 91
s 3(1)(m) . . . 92
s 3(1)(m)(i) . . . 92
s 3(1)(m)(ii)-(iii) . . . 92
s 3(2)(a) . . . 86, 97
s 3(2)(d) . . . 89
s 4 . . . 77
s 4(2) . . . 79, 87
s 5 . . . 89, 92, 93, A5
s 5(1) . . . 93, A5
s 5(2) . . . 93, A5
s 5(3)(a) . . . 93, A5
s 5(3)(b)(i) . . . 93, A5
s 5(3)(b)(ii) . . . 93
s 14 . . . 77
s 17 . . . 77, 98
s 17(5) . . . 77
s 46 . . . 77
s 62 . . . 92
s 76 . . . 77
s 79 . . . 77
Civil Liabilities (Contribution) Act 1978 . . . 183
Civil Procedure Act 1997
s 7 . . . 211
Companies Act 1985 . . . 45, A4
Contract (Rights of Third Parties) Act 1999 . . . 53
s 1 . . . 53
Equality Act 2010
s 199 . . . 132
Human Rights Act 1998 . . . 11, 93, 207, 210
Inheritance and Trustees' Powers Act 2014
s 8 . . . 173
s 9 . . . 175
Insolvency Act 1986 . . . 129
Judicature Acts 1873-1875 . . . 1, 3, 4, 6, 13
Land Registration Act 2002 . . . 49
s 27 . . . 45, A5
Law of Property Act 1925
s 52 . . . 45, 55, 63, A5
s 53 . . . 60
s 53(1) . . . 65, 72, 74
s 53(1)(b) . . . 26, 61, 62, 63, 66, 71, 73, 113, 121, A6
s 53(1)(c) . . . 46, 62, 65, 66, 67, 68, 69, 70, 71, 72, 73, 105, A5
s 53(2) . . . 65, 72, 113, 130, A6
s 60(3) . . . 130
s 136 . . . 45, 64
s 175 . . . 174
s 205(1)(x) . . . 65
Law of Property (Miscellaneous Provisions) Act 1989
s 1 . . . 45
Limitation Act 1980 . . . 9
s 21 . . . 183
s 21(1)(a) . . . 183

Perpetuities and Accumulations Act 1964 . . . 102, A11
s 18 . . . 102
Perpetuities and Accumulations Act 2009 . . . 104, A11
Provisions of Oxford 1258 . . . 2
Recreational Charities Act 1958 . . . 92
Sale of Goods Act 1979
s 20A . . . 29
Senior Courts Act 1981
s 37 . . . 211
s 49 . . . 4
Statute of Charitable Uses 1601
Preamble . . . 77, 78
Statute of Frauds . . . 72
Statute of Westminster . . . 2
Stock Transfer Act 1963 . . . 45, A4
Supreme Court of Judicature Act 1873
s 25 . . . 4
Trade Union and Labour Relations (Consolidation) Act 1992
s 236 . . . 204
Trustee Act 1925
s 27 . . . 173
s 31 . . . 173
s 31(1)(i) . . . 173
s 31(1)(ii) . . . 174
s 31(3) . . . 174
s 32 . . . 174, 175
s 32(1) . . . 175
s 32(1)(a) . . . 175
s 32(1)(b) . . . 175
s 32(1)(c) . . . 175
s 33 . . . 18, 153, A10
s 36 . . . 158
s 36(1) . . . 159
s 36(1)(a) . . . 159
s 36(1)(b) . . . 159
s 36(6) . . . 158
s 36(6)(a) . . . 158
s 36(6)(b) . . . 158
s 39 . . . 159
s 40 . . . 161
s 41 . . . 158, 160
s 53 . . . 149, 173, 174
s 57 . . . A7
s 57(1) . . . 149
s 61 . . . 183
s 62 . . . 183
Trustee Act 2000 . . . 23, 157, 165, 166, 169, 177
s 1 . . . 166, 170, 182, A7
s 3 . . . 22, 166
s 4 . . . 166, 168
s 4(2) . . . 169
s 4(3) . . . 168, A7
s 4(3)(a) . . . A7
s 4(3)(b) . . . A7
s 5 . . . 166, 168
s 5(1) . . . 169
s 5(3) . . . 169
s 5(4) . . . 169
s 8 . . . 166, 168, A7
s 11 . . . 166, 169, A7
s 11(2) . . . 169
s 13(2) . . . A7
s 15 . . . 166, 169, A7
s 15(1) . . . 170
s 15(2)(a) . . . 170
s 15(2)(b) . . . 170
s 15(5) . . . 170
s 22 . . . 166, 170, A8
s 23 . . . 166, 170
s 29 . . . 146, 160
s 31 . . . 160
Sch 1, para 3 . . . 170
Trustee Investments Act 1961 . . . 165, 168
Trusts of Land and Appointment of Trustees Act 1996 . . . 20
s 19 . . . 158, 160, A8
s 19(1)(a) . . . 159
s 19(2)(a) . . . 159
s 19(3) . . . 159
s 20 . . . 158

Variation of Trusts Act 1958 . . . 145, 149, 150–154, A7
s 1 . . . 149, 150
s 1(1)(a) . . . 150, 152, 153, A7
s 1(1)(b) . . . 150, 152, 153, A7
s 1(1)(c) . . . 150, 151, 152, 153, 154
s 1(1)(d) . . . 153
Wills Act 1837 . . . 10, 61, 110, 111, 112, 113, 116, 124, A9
s 9 . . . 47, 61, 111, 115
s 15 . . . 120
s 25 . . . 121

Table of Statutory Instruments

Civil Procedure Rules 1998 (SI 1998/3132)
Practice Direction . . . 211

Table of International Treaties and Conventions

European Convention on Human Rights . . . 11, 215
Art 8 . . . 11

The history and development of equity

1

KEY FACTS

- Equity tackles injustice caused by a strict application of the common law rules or unconscionable behaviour.
- Equity was originally dispensed by the King. However, this role was soon delegated to the Lord Chancellor and the Court of Chancery.
- Equity and the common law were originally administered by separate courts. The two court systems coexisted uneasily until the ***Earl of Oxford's Case*** (1615), when the King finally held that equity prevailed over the common law in the event of a conflict.
- The administration of equity and the common law was unified by the **Judicature Acts 1873–75** with the result that all judges could apply both equitable and common law rules and responses.
- It is still debated today whether the **Judicature Acts** 'fused' equity and the common law into a unified body of rules. While the two systems have become closer over time, the distinction still remains of importance in some areas.
- Equity benefits from a number of equitable maxims which can guide the courts in the exercise of their discretion.

The history of equity

REVISION TIP

It is unlikely that you will be asked simply to discuss the history of equity in an examination. It is more common for questions to reference some aspect of the development of equity as a basis for discussing the operation of equity today. Try to think about the themes which characterize equity's development and their significance to modern equity.

The legal system of England and Wales began to emerge in the twelfth century. However, as the common law began to emerge, so too did instances of injustice and unfairness. These situations were brought about by both:

- the operation of the legal system itself; and
- the strict application of common law rules.

Problems with the early common law system

The early common law system was complex and expensive. Legal actions were based on writs, which had to be spoken precisely in Latin. Consequently, cases were often lost on a technicality due to mistakes being made in their delivery. This problem was compounded by the **Provisions of Oxford 1258** and the **Statute of Westminster**, which limited the number of writs and sometimes precluded a legal action simply because there was no legal writ which covered it—no remedy without a writ.

The strict application of common law rules could also lead to injustice. For example, where someone built a home on land on the understanding that ownership of the land parcel would be transferred to him on completion, if the landowner refused to carry out this promise the builder of the home would have no action under the common law as *legally* the land did not belong to him. Moreover, the remedy of damages available at common law was not always appropriate. For example, if someone trespassed upon your property, an award of damages would not prevent the defendant from repeating their actions.

The origins of equity

Alongside the common law system, it was possible for individuals to appeal directly to the King's conscience. As the number of these appeals rose, the King delegated this role to the Lord Chancellor. Originally, the position of Lord Chancellor was held by high-ranking religious officials, and the justice dispensed was rooted in the religious morality of the times. Over time, a separate court of equity, the Chancery Court, was established in the fifteenth century, and equity as a rival system of law began to take shape. This process was continued during the sixteenth century as the position of Lord Chancellor gradually came to be held by lawyers, rather than religious officials.

Conflict between equity and the common law: the *Earl of Oxford's Case*

The laws of England and Wales therefore became the sum of the common law rules and the equitable decisions of the Court of Chancery. Where the common law courts would apply their legal rules, the Court of Chancery acted as a check upon these rules, ensuring that their application did not lead to a manifest injustice. However, this relationship was not a settled one and judges in the common law courts would frequently reach decisions based on the common law rules, despite knowing that the Court of Chancery would reach a different result. This created confusion and expense for claimants, who would have to mount two separate actions to reach a satisfactory conclusion. Moreover, these differences led to resentment that equity was interfering with the certainty of the common law. John Selden famously attacked the discretionary nature of equity by comparing it to the length of 'a Chancellor's foot'—insinuating that it was a random standard that would change from Chancellor to Chancellor. This conflict came to a head in the ***Earl of Oxford's Case*** (1615):

EARL OF OXFORD'S CASE **(1615) 1 REP CH 1**
A defendant appealed against a judgment in the common law courts on the ground that the judgment had been obtained through fraud. The Lord Chancellor, Lord Ellesmere, agreed and issued a 'common injunction' restraining the claimant from enforcing the judgment. These 'common injunctions' were seen as a direct challenge to the authority of the common law courts as they effectively deprived the recipient of the ability to pursue a remedy from the common law courts. However, the Lord Chancellor argued that there was no conflict between the two courts, as equity did not interfere with the operation of the common law. Instead, it acted *in personam*, meaning against the conscience of the recipient. Therefore, the common law decision was left undisturbed; equity only acted to compel the recipient to act according to good conscience. This dispute was finally resolved by King James I in 1616, when he declared in favour of the Court of Chancery. This gave birth to the equitable maxim that where the law and equity conflict, equity prevails.

Reform of the administration of common law and equity

With the primacy of equity now confirmed, the Court of Chancery continued to grow—but so too did delays and corruption. However, the existing legal system underwent major reform in the nineteenth century through two Acts, commonly referred to as the **Judicature Acts 1873–75**:

- The previous dual system, comprising courts of common law and equity, was merged into a single Supreme Court, comprising the High Court and the Court of Appeal.
- The jurisdiction of judges in the new Supreme Court was 'fused' so that all judges were able to use the whole range of common law and equitable rules. This meant that litigants

no longer faced the delays and expense of pursuing two separate actions at common law and equity.

- **Section 25 Supreme Court of Judicature Act 1873** gave statutory authority to the principle that where the common law and equity conflicted, equity prevailed. (This was later re-enacted by **s 49 Senior Courts Act 1981**.)

The 'fusion' debate

The reforms introduced by the **Judicature Acts 1873–75** mark the birth of the modern legal system of England and Wales. While it is clear that the **Judicature Acts** fused the *administration* of common law and equity (see Figure 1.1), there is continuing debate over whether the Acts, in fact, created a *unified system of rules*:

Figure 1.1 The fusion of equity and the common law

There are three main positions regarding the fusion debate:

The Judicature Acts only unified the administration of the law

This position argues that the **Judicature Acts** only created a unified *court system*. Ashburner in *Principles of Equity*, 2nd edn (1933), eloquently expressed this viewpoint when he likened the common law and equity to two streams running alongside one another, but never mingling their waters.

The Judicature Acts effected a more substantive fusion of equity and the common law

In ***Walsh v Lonsdale*** (1882), Jessel MR argued that 'There are not two estates as there were formerly, one established at common law … and an estate in equity … There is only one Court and the equity rule prevails in it'. More explicitly, in ***United Scientific Holdings Ltd v Burnley Borough Council*** [1978], Lord Diplock argued that Ashburner's metaphor of the two parallel streams had become 'mischievous and deceptive' and that the 'streams' of equity and the common law had long since mingled together.

It is clear that the rules and remedies of equity and the common law have moved closer together:

SEAGER V COPYDEX LTD **[1967] 1 WLR 923**

The claimant had been involved in negotiations with Copydex Ltd regarding the marketing of a new type of carpet grip. While these negotiations did not come to anything, the defendants later unwittingly used confidential information received from the claimant on how his idea could be improved to develop their own product. Breach of confidence is only protected in equity and Seager sought an injunction to prevent their use of this information. He also argued that the equitable remedy of account of profits (see chapter 12) would be inadequate. The Court of Appeal agreed and awarded the claimant common law damages which could more readily take into consideration the loss of the claimant's ability to exploit his invention.

The House of Lords also proved willing to grant equitable remedies more flexibly in respect of the breach of a *legal* right in exceptional circumstances:

ATTORNEY-GENERAL V BLAKE **[2001] 1 AC 268**

George Blake, an infamous spy who had defected to Russia, entered into a contract to publish a book about his experiences, for which he was to receive £150,000. The memoirs contained sensitive information which he had contracted with the state not to reveal. The usual remedy of damages for breach of contract would be inadequate as the government had an interest in discouraging its servants from breaching their commitments. Therefore, the Attorney-General sought a different *equitable* remedy, account of profits, to ensure that Blake would not be allowed to benefit any further from this breach.

As the information contained in the book was no longer confidential, it was difficult to argue that there was a continuing **fiduciary** obligation towards the state which would enable such a remedy to be granted. However, the court noted that the existence of more commonplace equitable remedies for breach of contract, such as specific performance or injunctions, was based on the idea that normal damages may be inadequate. Therefore, in exceptional circumstances, it was prepared to award an account of profits to protect the state's legitimate interest in discouraging such conduct.

These cases suggest only an incremental and, often, exceptional coming together of equity and the common law. Indeed, there are many more examples of how the law has retained a distinction between common law and equity. For example, the concept of the trust still relies on the distinction between legal and equitable ownership (see chapter 2) and the rules for tracing property into the hands of third parties differ at common law and equity (see chapter 12).

Moreover, equity and the common law also perform different functions:

- Common law—establishes general rules which provide certainty. This allows individuals to plan ahead and promotes commercial efficiency.
- Equity—acts as a check upon the common law. This remedies hardships which may arise from a strict application of the common law. Equity restrains the full exercise of legal rights where this would be **unconscionable**.

TERMINOLOGY TIP

Unconscionability—describes conduct which goes against good conscience. While the early Lord Chancellors restrained unconscionable behaviour on moral grounds, common examples of 'unconscionable behaviour' gradually hardened into the rules of equity (see JH Baker, *An Introduction to English Legal History*, 4th edn (2002), p 106). Today, it is no longer correct to assume that equity will restrain all immoral conduct. As equity has always attempted to respond to changing social conditions, 'unconscionability' remains a flexible device through which the court may choose to intervene. However, the inherent flexibility of 'unconscionability' also brings a degree of uncertainty as to how the actions of a party will be evaluated. See, for example, ***BCCI v Akindele*** [2004], discussed in chapter 12.

While it is difficult to argue that equity and the common law have been fully fused, the **Judicature Acts** have encouraged the development of a more *supportive* relationship between the two systems.

Equity and the common law should be fused

This third position accepts that while equity and the common law have become closer, there is a pressing need to complete the unification of the two systems. Sarah Worthington, in her book, *Equity*, 2nd edn (2006), argues that as equity and the common law continue to develop, each increasingly encroaches on the other's usual territory. This creates the risk that like cases will not be treated alike and that the ability of judges to make clear and principled decisions will be clouded.

Worthington convincingly argues that equity and the common law have always borrowed from one another and that neither system now occupies a distinctive conceptual position. A good example of this is the parallel development of **undue influence** in equity and **economic duress** by the common law, both of which look to questions of knowledge and unconscionability, but approach similar factual situations through increasingly difficult factual distinctions.

LOOKING FOR EXTRA MARKS?

You will need to do additional reading if you are to do well on a question about the fusion debate. Sarah Worthington's book, *Equity*, 2nd edn (2006), manages to be both detailed and accessible. The main thrust of her argument can be found in the first and last chapters. These chapters also provide useful cross-references to the more detailed discussions which make up the remainder of the book.

The maxims of equity

During the nineteenth century, a number of general rules of thumb began to emerge from the court's exercise of its equitable jurisdiction. These are known as the maxims of equity. They do not have their own authoritative value but operate at the level of broad general principles which can guide the court in the exercise of its equitable discretion.

REVISION TIP

Trusts and equity cover a diverse range of situations and it can sometimes be very difficult to get a sense of how these areas of law operate. Having a good knowledge of the maxims of equity can provide you with an effective template to discuss both the successes and problems of many different areas of equity and trusts. This type of question is common in examinations and to perform well it is important not just to know what the equitable maxims are, but also to be able to provide illustrations of their application.

Maxims concerning the nature of equity and its jurisdiction

Equity will not suffer a wrong without a remedy

Equity does not intervene in respect of every *moral* wrong. It will only intervene to prevent an *unconscionable* reliance upon legal rights. Three examples illustrate this principle well:

- In a trust, the trustees hold the legal title to the trust property. Should they claim the property for themselves the beneficiaries have no *legal* right to enforce. It is equity which recognizes the beneficiaries' equitable entitlement to the property. In an express trust, the legal ownership of trust property is only transferred to trustees on the basis that they will hold it for the benefit of the beneficiaries. Therefore, for the trustees to claim the property for themselves would be unconscionable.
- In *constructive* trusts of the family home, it would be unconscionable for a legal owner to insist upon their full legal rights due to an agreement to share the property combined with detrimental reliance on that agreement (see chapter 9 on implied trusts).
- Search orders—injunctions are typically awarded only after a court has heard arguments from both parties. If the claimant has to inform the suspected person of their action, it is likely that the defendant could hide or destroy the stolen documentation, thus making it impossible for the claimant to prove their case and depriving them of a remedy. Search orders are a type of **interim injunction**, which is awarded **ex parte** (ie without notice to the defendant), allowing the defendant's premises to be searched, thus preventing normal court procedures from frustrating the claimant's action (see chapter 13 on equitable remedies).

Equity acts in personam

This maxim describes how equity acts against an individual to prevent them from acting unconscionably. There are a number of consequences which flow from this:

- Failure to comply with an order is punishable by **contempt of court**.
- As equity acts against the individual *personally*, it does not matter if the property in dispute is outside the jurisdiction of the court: ***Penn v Lord Baltimore*** (1750).

- By acting personally against a defendant, equity does not interfere with common law decisions.
- This aspect of equity's operation is also sometimes expressed as the maxim, 'Where equity and the law conflict, equity prevails'. Equity prevails over the common law not because it destroys the common law right but because it imposes limits on the extent to which those rights can be enjoyed.

Equity follows the law

Equity supplements common law rules to ensure fairness; it does not replace them. Equity may prevail over the common law in the event of a conflict but the maxim 'Equity follows the law' reminds us that the relationship between the two bodies of rules is respectful. Equity will only intervene when there are exceptional reasons for doing so—typically, the prevention of unconscionable behaviour. However, the general common law rule will still remain as the starting point for any future disputes.

Maxims concerning the conduct expected of claimants

He who comes to equity must come with clean hands

Equitable remedies are discretionary in nature and are granted following a full consideration of the particular circumstances of a case. The court will consider the *past* conduct of a claimant to decide if it is appropriate for equity to intervene:

- If a claimant has themself breached an obligation or otherwise acted inequitably, an equitable remedy will not be granted: ***Cross v Cross*** (1983). This is because equity cannot be seen to favour one party if both are in breach of their obligations.
- If a claim is affected by illegal conduct on the part of the claimant, the court will use its discretion to decide whether a claim can be enforced: ***Patel v Mirza*** [2016].

PATEL V MIRZA **[2016] UKSC 42**

The claimant, Patel, transferred £620,000 to the defendant with the intention that he would use this money to bet on the changes in the share price of the Royal Bank of Scotland plc, based on the illegal use of insider information. However, this information was never received and so the plan did not go ahead. When the claimant asked for his money to be returned, the defendant refused. Patel sued for breach of contract and unjust enrichment, but the defendant argued that he was prevented from recovering his money as, following the House of Lords' decision of ***Tinsley v Milligan*** [1994], he was prohibited from relying on his own illegal actions to establish his claim.

The Supreme Court rejected the approach taken in ***Tinsley v Milligan*** and held that the claimant was entitled to recover his money. In reaching this conclusion, Lord Toulson argued that the previous approach had often produced arbitrary and unsatisfactory results. Instead, the court should use its discretion to consider (i) the effect of denying a claim on the policy which made the conduct illegal; (ii) the impact of denying a claim on other public policies; and (iii) whether denying a claim would be a proportionate response to the illegal actions of the claimant. The court considered that as the plan had not gone ahead, to deny the claimant's action would be punitive and disproportionate, and would provide an unjustifiable windfall to the defendant.

The broader policy-based approach to illegality taken in ***Patel v Mirza*** demonstrates that the maxims of equity must not be treated as fixed rules and that equity may no longer require a claimant's hands to be spotless. In ***Grondona v Stoffel & Co*** [2021], the respondent's knowing involvement in a mortgage fraud did not prevent her from obtaining a remedy against her solicitors who had negligently failed to register her title to the mortgaged property with the Land Registry. The Supreme Court focused on the need for the law to be applied consistently rather than preventing the claimant from profiting from her wrongdoing. Denying her claim for illegality would not help to deter mortgage frauds and could suggest that solicitors need not always perform their duties diligently and professionally.

He who seeks equity must do equity

Equity looks to do justice *between* the parties. Equity scrutinizes not just the claimant's prior conduct, but also their *future* behaviour in respect of the claim. Therefore, if a claimant is unwilling or unable to fulfil their own future obligations to the defendant, equitable relief will not be granted.

In ***Chappell v Times Newspapers Ltd*** [1975], following selective industrial action, the defendant threatened to terminate the employment contracts of *all* union members unless they returned to work and agreed not to take further action. Several members of the trade union who had not been involved in the strike sought an interim injunction to prevent their employer from taking this action. However the claim failed as they would not agree not to take part in any future action.

Delay defeats equity

This maxim expresses the doctrine of *laches* which prevents a claimant who has delayed from obtaining equitable relief. This principle again illustrates how equity tries to do justice between the parties. It would be inequitable to allow a claim for equitable relief on an issue which the defendant has long since considered settled. In ***Leaf v International Galleries*** [1950], an attempt to rescind a contract for a painting which the vendor had innocently misrepresented to be the work of Constable failed for delay as the action took place five years after the purchase.

Note: as equity follows the law, statutory limitations such as those in the **Limitation Act 1980** will displace any equitable jurisdiction to decide whether or not a claim is too late.

Maxims concerning the circumstances in which equity will operate

Equity looks to intent, not form

This maxim provides another example of how equity tends to assess the whole circumstances of a case, rather than applying broad and generalized rules. For example:

- Certainty of intention—in considering whether a settlor intended to create a trust, the use of the word 'trust' is not essential and the court will consider the whole circumstances of the case (***Comiskey v Bowring-Hanbury*** [1905]). (See chapter 3 for more detail.)

- Constructive trusts—this maxim explains the recognition of implied trusts whereby the court may find that the circumstances of the case, including discussions between the parties or certain types of contribution, demonstrate the intention to create a resulting or constructive trust. (See chapter 9 for more detail.)

Equity will not permit a statute to be used as an instrument of fraud

Equity follows the law and will not interfere with situations governed by statute. However, equity can also act to ensure that statutory provisions are not abused. Therefore, equity will intervene if a claimant seeks to rely unconscionably on a lack of statutory formalities.

This maxim explains the enforceability of fully secret trusts (considered in chapter 8). In a fully secret trust, the testator leaves property to a legatee without mentioning their intention that the legatee should hold the property as trustee for someone else. Property disposed of by a will must satisfy the requirements of the **Wills Act 1837**. However, secret trusts do not comply with these requirements and therefore, on a strict reading of statute, cannot be valid. This would mean that the trustee could claim the property for themself. However, as the property was only left to the trustee on the basis that they would hold it for another, to allow the trustee to rely on the formalities required by the **Wills Act** would be to permit the statute to be used as a device to commit a fraud against the testator. Therefore, equity recognizes the validity of the fully secret trust.

Equity sees as done that which ought to be done

If an equitable remedy *can* be granted, equity will act as if this has already occurred. For example:

- A contract for the sale of land is specifically enforceable as it is a unique type of property for which monetary damages would be inadequate (see chapter 13 on equitable remedies). Therefore, on the completion of such a contract, the vendor is taken to hold the equitable interest on trust for the purchaser until the transfer is formally completed.

WALSH V LONSDALE **(1882) 21 CH D 9**

A landlord agreed in writing to lease a mill to a tenant. The agreement stated that rent was to be payable in advance if requested. However, such leases required a **deed** and none was ever made. The tenant entered the property and began to pay rent quarterly. When he fell into arrears, the landlord demanded a year's rent in advance and, when the tenant resisted, the landlord sought to use the remedy of distress (which allows the landlord to seize and sell the tenant's property in order to recover the rent). The tenant sought an injunction against the distress on the basis that there was no valid lease *in law* and therefore no provision to allow rent to be demanded annually in advance. The court refused this application, arguing that by allowing the tenant to enter the mill and pay rent, the agreement to lease the mill would have been specifically enforceable. As equity sees as done that which ought to be done, the tenant was to be considered an equitable lessee of the mill *on the terms of the original agreement* and, therefore, the action for distress was legal.

Equity is equality

If more than one person claims to be interested in the same property and there is nothing to suggest what their shares should be, equity will assume that they are to have equal shares.

REVISION TIP

A good discussion of the equitable maxims will recognize that they are not fixed rules but *starting points* for analysing a legal problem. This means that they are not always followed. For example, the maxim, 'Equity will not assist a volunteer', discussed more fully in chapter 4, may be said to have generated more exceptions than applications! While this has often led academics to be sceptical of their value, equity has always resisted the application of general rules in favour of a more thorough consideration of all the relevant facts.

Equity today

While equity began life as the King's conscience, it has now become a highly developed body of legal rules which continues to constrain unconscionable behaviour and provides relief from the hardships caused by the strict application of common law rules. Together, equity and its most famous invention, the trust, have continued to develop flexibly and creatively to respond to society's changing needs:

- Search orders and freezing orders allows claimants to search for documentation relevant to their claim and to freeze the defendants' assets if there is a real risk that the failure to do so will deprive them of an adequate remedy (see chapter 13 on equitable remedies).
- Similarly, in light of the incorporation of the **European Convention on Human Rights (ECHR)** into UK law through the enactment of the **Human Rights Act 1998**, the courts have further developed the use of the interim injunction (through anonymized and 'super-injunctions') to provide legal protection for individuals' private and family life under **Article 8 ECHR**. Anonymized injunctions prevent notified persons from identifying the parties involved or information about them considered private and confidential. 'Super-injunctions' go further and prohibit reporting on the existence of court proceedings and any order made. While these injunctions have proven controversial, the judiciary has been careful to develop a principled approach to their use that emphasizes doing only the minimum necessary to satisfy such claims (see, eg, ***JIH v News Group Newspapers Ltd*** [2011], ***Ntuli v Donald*** [2010], and also chapter 13 on equitable remedies).
- The recognition of constructive trusts of the family home in ***Gissing v Gissing*** [1971] and subsequent case law has provided financial relief for claimants who do not have legal title. The continuing development of this area of law has been particularly important in the face of the continued reluctance of Parliament to intervene (see chapter 9 on implied trusts).

- The development of *Quistclose*-type resulting trusts has provided the possibility of protecting the money of innocent customers from the creditors of an insolvent company (see ***Re Kayford Ltd (in liquidation)*** [1975] and, less happily, ***Re Farepak Foods and Gifts Ltd (in administration)*** [2006]).
- The increasingly flexible approach taken to formality requirements, as illustrated by the 'unconscionability' approach adopted in ***Pennington v Waine*** [2002], highlights that a lack of statutory formalities should not be used officiously to defeat agreements (see chapter 4 on constitution of the trust).

REVISION TIP

Exam questions on this area will invariably be essays. To do well in an essay you must address the terms of the question. Make sure you read the question carefully to identify precisely what it is asking you to discuss—a shorter but tightly focused essay will always be marked higher than a longer general essay on 'everything I know about the history and development of equity'!

Whereas once equitable relief was entirely discretionary (leading to accusations that it was subjective), many forms of equity have now hardened into equitable rights, so that where the relevant criteria are satisfied, equity *will* intervene. The acceptance that beneficiaries have certain rights under a trust, rather than simply at the discretion of the court, is perhaps the most pertinent example here.

While the discretion inherent in equity is no longer unfettered, a continuing debate on the development of equity and trusts is the *extent* of that discretion. Where equity and the common law once clashed over the ideals of fairness and certainty, arguably this battle now continues to be waged *within* equity itself. In all but the first example listed above, each development has been accompanied by great debate over whether the decision can be justified within existing equitable principles. For all that equity has matured into a substantial and detailed body of rules, it seems that it is the underlying impulse towards fairness over a rigid adherence to principle that continues to drive equity today.

REVISION TIP

It is tempting to think of trust law as neatly divided into different topics. However, as you can see, there are many links between different topics. While this chapter discusses major themes and developments in trusts and equity, you should use your knowledge of other topics to build on the basics set out here.

KEY CASES

CASES	FACTS	PRINCIPLE
Earl of Oxford's Case (1615) 1 Rep Ch 1	Concerned a dispute over a lease and the question of which court prevailed in a conflict.	Equity prevails over the common law in the event of a conflict.
Seager v Copydex Ltd [1967] 1 WLR 923	Claimant sought common law damages in respect of a breach of confidence (which is only protected in equity).	Common law damages awarded as the equitable remedy of account would not be adequate. This case demonstrates the closer relationship of equity and the common law today.
Patel v Mirza [2016] UKSC 42	The appellant argued that the respondent's involvement in an insider dealing plot prevented him from recovering money paid to the appellant to exploit this information through betting on changes to the price of Royal Bank of Scotland shares.	The maxim that *one must come to equity with clean hands* is not to be applied simplistically. The court will use its discretion to consider whether it is proportionate or required by relevant public policy that a claim based on illegal actions should be denied.
Walsh v Lonsdale (1882) 21 Ch D 9	Concerned whether the claimant could enforce a *legal* remedy in respect of an equitable lease.	*Equity regards as done that which ought to be done*—the equitable lease was specifically enforceable on the same terms as the legal lease. This case also provides support for the idea that equity and the common law were fused by the **Judicature Acts**.

KEY DEBATES

Topic	Did the Judicature Acts do more than fuse the administration of equity and the common law?
Academic/author	Worthington/Mason
Viewpoint	There is evidence of an increasing willingness to employ both equitable and common law remedies in hitherto unorthodox ways in order to do justice in a given case.
Source	Worthington, *Equity*, 2nd edn (2006). For a more detailed account of Commonwealth developments, see Mason (1994) LQR 238.

Topic	Should more be done to fuse equity and the common law?
Academic/author	Worthington/Burrows
Viewpoint	It can be argued that neither equity nor the common law now occupies distinctive positions of principle in relation to how they exercise their jurisdiction. However, this increasing closeness runs the risk of creating more confusion than clarity. Therefore, the time is right to consider further unification.
Source	Worthington, *Equity*, 2nd edn (2006), ch 10 offers a useful critique of the argument that equity and common law remain distinctive systems of rules. This book and Burrows (2002) 22(1) OJLS 1 offer a helpful analysis of how the two systems could be more closely reconciled.

Topic	What is the role of equity today?
Academic/author	Watt
Viewpoint	Equity operates in an increasingly wide range of contexts.
Source	Watt, *Trusts and Equity*, 9th edn (2020), chs 1 and 2 offers a very clear and accessible account of the foundations of equity and the uses of the trust.

EXAM QUESTIONS

Essay question

> It is inevitable that judge-made law will alter to meet the changing conditions of society. That is the way it has always evolved. But it is essential that new rules should be related to fundamental doctrine. If the foundations of accepted doctrine be submerged under new principles, without regard to the interaction between the two, there will be high uncertainty as to the state of the law, both old and new (Glass JA in ***Allen v Snyder*** [1977]).

Discuss.

Essay question

> The maxims of equity are unreliable. Though rarely completely meaningless or false, they have a tendency to obscure and mislead, and to stand in the way of analysis of the real principles and policies which shape the law (Webb and Akkouh, *Trusts Law*, 3rd edn (2013), p 14).

Discuss.

Online resources

For an outline answer to this essay question, as well as multiple choice questions and interactive key cases, please visit the online resources.

C Concentrate Q&As

For more questions and answers on equity and trusts, see the *Concentrate Q&A: Equity & Trusts* by Rosalind Malcolm.

Go to the end of this book to view **sample pages**.

2 The nature of a trust

KEY FACTS

- Trusts arise when the legal and equitable interests in property are divided.
- Trusts are either express or implied.
- Trusts create obligations and rights.
- A variety of different interests can exist in trust property.

Introduction

It would be difficult to find absolute agreement on the definition of a trust, but in the simplest terms a trust relationship can be identified when the legal title is owned by one person (*the trustee*) and the beneficial interest is held by another (*the beneficiary*). They can be the same people, such as in trusts for land. A key skill to understanding trust law is to visualize the ownership of *all* property as being potentially divided. In chapter 1 you looked at the development of equity, a fundamental feature of which is the trust. The trust provides for a legal owner to be able to deal with property for the benefit of those who cannot or do not want to deal with it themselves. This is commonly expressed as in Figure 2.1.

Figure 2.1 The structure of a trust

$$\textbf{S (settlor)} = \frac{\textbf{T (trustee)}}{\textbf{B (beneficiary)}}$$

Categories of trusts

As a basic introduction, trusts can be broadly categorized as falling into two types: express trusts and implied trusts. This chapter is intended merely to be an introduction and the topics looked at here will be dealt with in more detail in later chapters.

Express trusts

An express trust can be either private or public. Private trusts are created for the benefit of private individuals or classes of individuals. Public trusts are trusts which will benefit members of the public and will be looked at when we consider charitable trusts in later chapters (see Figure 2.2).

Express trusts are trusts which are made expressly by a **settlor** (the person making a trust). Express trusts can be **inter vivos** (made during the lifetime of the settlor) or **testamentary** (made through the settlor's will to take effect upon his or her death). After death, the settlor is referred to as the testator/testatrix.

Figure 2.2 Basic categories of trusts

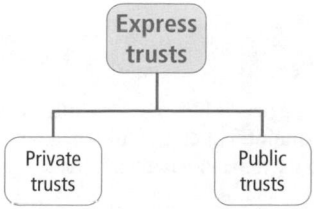

Fixed or discretionary express trusts

In a fixed trust, the beneficiaries and their interests under the trust are clearly specified. For example, 'to my two children Luke and Katie I create a trust of £20,000'. They each have £10,000 held on trust, as equity presumes equality (application of the equitable maxim).

In a discretionary trust, the property is held on trust by the trustee who has some discretion (choice) over who, within the specified class (see chapter 3), is to benefit, what their share of the trust property will be, or both. For example, 'a trust of £20,000 to my two children, Luke and Katie, as the trustee shall decide', would be a discretionary trust in which there is a discretion as to the share of the property. Under this trust, neither Luke nor Katie has anything more than an expectation in the trust; only when the trustee exercises that discretion will they have a clear interest. However, as this is a trust, the children can require the trustee to exercise that discretion. This is an important distinction between trusts and powers.

An example of a trust in which there is a discretion to choose who is to benefit would be, '£20,000 to be held on trust for such of my nieces and nephews whom my trustee selects'. The beneficiaries are identified as being part of a class who may benefit.

Bare trusts and protective trusts

Bare trusts

Bare trusts are when property is left on trust and the trustee has no discretion or **contingencies**. The trustee's only duty is to hold the property for the beneficiary. The beneficiary of a bare trust will be a sole beneficiary who is ***sui juris***: adult and of mental capability. A simple example is a stockbroker who holds the shares on behalf of another.

Protective trusts

Protective trusts are trusts aimed at preventing an irresponsible beneficiary from wasting trust property. **Section 33 Trustee Act 1925** simplifies the method by which the beneficiary is given a **life interest** which is **determinable** (can be forfeited) on given events, for example bankruptcy or sale. At this point, the protective trust ends and the property is then held on a discretionary trust for the beneficiary, their spouse, and children, or those who would inherit had the beneficiary died. (See the online resources for further discussion.)

Classifications of interest under a trust

An important point to understand is that trusts can contain different types of interests. Interests can be either **vested** or contingent.

REVISION TIP

Understanding what type of interest a person has under the trust is important when considering the powers trustees have in relation to **maintenance** and **advancement**, which are explored in chapter 11. Make sure that you understand the difference between a vested interest and a contingent interest.

An interest under a trust is said to vest in the beneficiary when the beneficiary has a present right over the trust property. However, this vested interest can be to either a present right to a present interest, or a present right to a future interest. It is important as a vested interest is owned by the beneficiary. This means that if the intended beneficiary dies this interest will pass with his or her estate.

EXAMPLE 1

'I leave my home Heath Farm to my husband Dell for life then to my son Luke.' Dell's interest is a *present* right to a *present* interest; it is said to be *vested in possession*. He has the property for his lifetime. This is particularly important when we look at trustee powers. Luke's interest is a *present* right to a *future* interest; it is said to be *vested in remainder*. Luke has the home when Dell dies, but at this time he has the right to expect the trustee to ensure that he has a home (or its value) to take possession of.

This must be distinguished from a contingent interest. A contingent interest is one that is conditional.

EXAMPLE 2

'I leave my home Heath Farm to Dell for life and then to Sumita should she reach 25.'

Dell's interest is the same as in Example 1 but Sumita's interest is contingent. She has no interest until she reaches 25.

Note: students often mistake Luke's interest as contingent. But death is something that will happen, and this is not a contingent interest. Sumita may not reach 25, so her interest is conditional.

Implied trusts

Implied trusts are those which are not expressly created. There are three broad types of implied trusts: resulting, constructive, and statutory (see Figure 2.3).

Most courses on trusts will spend a lot of time on implied trusts. This chapter only introduces the broad differences between different types of trusts. You should refer to chapter 9 for a more detailed account of implied trusts and their operation.

Figure 2.3 Categories of implied trusts

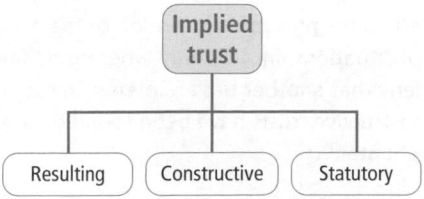

Statutory trusts

In certain circumstances statutory provisions impose a trust. For example, a trust for land is created under the **Trust of Land and Appointment of Trustees Act 1996** where joint owners hold the legal title on trust for themselves.

Another area of statutory implied trusts is in dealing with intestate estates—when a person dies without leaving a valid will. The **Administration of Estates Act 1925** provides for **settlement** of the estate to family members on the assumed intention of the deceased. The deceased person's **personal representative** will be appointed by the courts; they are called administrators, not executors.

Resulting trusts

Resulting trusts arise either when:

- there has been a failure to validly create a trust, ie it is a failed formalities trust: ***Vandervell v IRC*** [1967]. This situation has been called an automatic resulting trust because it happens regardless of the intention of the settlor. Indeed, in ***Vandervell v IRC*** a resulting trust arose contrary to the express intention of the settlor to give away property; or
- property is voluntarily transferred to another or purchased (either wholly or partly) in the name of another: ***Tinsley v Milligan*** [1994]. This category is based on the presumed intention of the resulting beneficiary. Lord Browne-Wilkinson said in ***Westdeutsche Landesbank Girozentrale v Islington LBC*** [1996] that resulting trusts were based on the intention of the parties.

LOOKING FOR EXTRA MARKS?

There is much academic discussion on the nature of resulting trusts. Read the approach taken by Birks and Chambers, compared to that of Swadling (see the online resources for more details of this further reading and judicial approaches to the issue).

Constructive trusts

Constructive trusts are based on the presumed intention of the parties. This intention is found by the courts in a variety of situations, increasingly where they feel that it would be unconscionable for a person to deny that another has an interest in the property. Table 2.1 provides some examples of when constructive trusts have been found by the courts. This subject is considered in further detail in chapter 9.

Table 2.1 Situations where a constructive trust may arise

FACTUAL SITUATION	CASE
Breach of a fiduciary duty	*Keech v Sandford* (1726): the special relationship as trustee between the claimant and respondent meant that any benefit was held for the claimant
Unauthorized profit	*Attorney-General for Hong Kong v Reid* [1994]: where the receipt of bribes which arose from a position of responsibility was found to be held on constructive trust for the state
Receipt of property belonging to another	*El Ajou v Dollar Land Holdings* [1994]: when property is transferred to another without consideration then it was held that the recipient holds the property on constructive trust for the real owner
Immoral receipt	*Re Sigsworth* (1935): receipt by killing
Family home	*Grant v Edwards* [1986]: where the home is held in the name of one party where the other contributes to the home on the express/implied understanding that they have an interest in the home

Distinguishing trust, fiduciary, and mere powers

A trust creates a legally enforceable right for the beneficiary and a legally enforceable obligation for the trustee. However, a power provides for the **donee** of the power to use property in a certain way but this power is not legally enforceable. The language of this area of law leads to confusion as textbooks will talk of a trust power, fiduciary powers, and mere powers.

REVISION TIP

Identifying the difference between these categories of interests will be clearer once you have understood the three certainties. However, there is no clear line between them and it is better to see the distinction as a gradual move from having no obligations to having fixed obligations.

Trust powers

A trustee has powers given to them within the trust, such as the power to invest. There are also dispositive powers, meaning that the trustee can give (appoint) property to beneficiaries from the trust property.

EXAMPLE 3

Luke is the trustee of a discretionary trust. He holds £10,000 on trust for such of the settlor's grandchildren that need financial help.

In this situation, Luke has the power to invest the money to generate a greater income for the beneficiaries. It is important that the trust fund works for the trust. He could appoint an agent to look after the money, perhaps a stockbroker or accountant. These are powers under the **Trustee Act 2000**. He also has the power to appoint (give) money to any of the grandchildren he thinks needs it. As the trust is for the grandchildren, the power must be exercised for a beneficiary in that class. Each potential beneficiary can enforce the exercise of the power of appointment but may not receive anything once exercised. This is a power of appointment within the trust—a power to select who shall benefit. This is distinct from the powers discussed in the following paragraphs.

Fiduciary powers

Fiduciary powers are powers in a different sense. They are not part of a trust but a 'mere' power, ie something that can be done but does not need to be done; something valid but unenforceable. The person who may benefit from the power cannot make the fiduciary exercise the power but can make sure that the fiduciary considers exercising the power, and the donee of the power must not act unreasonably in making the decision to exercise the power (***Re Hay's Settlement Trusts*** [1982]). A fiduciary power is a power that is held by a person who is in a fiduciary position, such as a trustee. It is the status of the donee of the power that makes it a fiduciary power.

EXAMPLE 4

Katie makes the following bequest:

> To Dell, my family solicitor, I give my shares in Bestbits plc in the hope that he uses them to help my nieces, Sofia and Lauren; but if he fails to do so then the shares should go to Luke.

There is no clear intention to create a trust but there is a wish (power) that Dell use it in a certain way. The gift over to Luke means that if the power is not exercised then Luke will take the shares absolutely. But should Dell decide to give all the shares to Sofia and/or Lauren then he is acting within his power and there is no breach should there be no shares for Luke to benefit from. Sofia and Lauren cannot make Dell give them any benefit. What they can do is ask him to prove that he has reasonably considered making the appointment. The presence of the gift over is a good indication that it is intended as a power and not a trust.

Mere/bare power

This is a **power of appointment** given to a person who has no fiduciary obligation. If, in the previous example, Dell had only been Katie's friend, then the power is entirely without an obligation to act reasonably in making the decision, unless it is a moral one. In that case it will be a matter for Dell's conscience but not for the law.

Powers can be further complicated by the range of objects that are within the class of potential people who may benefit from the exercise of the power. A general power can be exercised to anyone in the world, including the donee and donor. This is very similar to a gift in practice and is rarely seen. A special power is exercisable for anyone within a defined class (see chapter 3 for a discussion on this) which is identifiable by the 'is/is not' test. A hybrid power is one which is exercisable except for a class of people.

LOOKING FOR EXTRA MARKS?

The distinction between trusts and powers is not always clear. In ***McPhail v Doulton*** [1971] the High Court and the Court of Appeal considered the provision to be a power of appointment, whereas the majority of the House of Lords found it to be a trust. This is important as under a power the 'objects' of the power cannot enforce the obligation, but by making the disposition a trust the objects (beneficiaries) can ensure the obligation is carried out. This is a move from the beneficiary being both the owner of trust property and the enforcer of the trust obligation to just being the enforcer of the trust. This distinction may be further blurred by the decisions in ***Mettoy Pensions Trustee v Evans*** [1990] where Warner J saw no reason why the fiduciary power could not be enforced in the same way as a discretionary trust (perhaps because the decision was capricious) and also in ***Schmidt v Rosewood*** [2003] where it did not seem essential that a person had a proprietary interest to be able to enforce a trust obligation.

Conclusion

Understanding the nature of trusts is a question of becoming familiar with the language of trust law. Good trust lawyers will think of property rights in relation to who holds the interest at law and in equity. It is important in reviewing this chapter that you see this as an introduction to the ideas which will be developed in later chapters. Ensure that you feel comfortable with the different types of trust which can be created and the different types of interest which can exist within a trust. The language of trusts can often confuse and therefore overcomplicate the subject; understanding the terms and what they mean will pay dividends.

KEY CASES

CASES	FACTS	PRINCIPLE
McPhail v Doulton [1971] AC 424	Money was left for the provision of grants to a large class of objects, including ex-employees and their relatives and dependants.	The test for certainty of objects of a trust required a list (see chapter 3) and it was unclear if all relatives could be so listed. The test for a power required conceptual certainty only, that there were relatives. Lord Wilberforce felt that the nature of this disposition was more akin to a power than a fixed trust so the given postulant ('is/is not') test could be applied and the trust was valid. There are dissenting judgments that should be read to understand the blurred lines between trusts and powers.

KEY DEBATES

Topic	The nature of equitable obligations
Academic/author	Pearce and Barr
Viewpoint	A clarification and discussion of the relevant duties and rights of trustees and beneficiary or objects of a power.
Source	Pearce and Barr, *Pearce & Stevens' Trusts and Equitable Obligations*, 7th edn (2018), ch 21.

Key cases and key debates in other areas will be discussed in detail in later chapters.

Online resources

For multiple choice questions and interactive key cases, as well as bonus material, please visit the online resources.

Concentrate Q&As

For more questions and answers on equity and trusts, see the *Concentrate Q&A: Equity & Trusts* by Rosalind Malcolm.

Go to the end of this book to view **sample pages**.

The three certainties

3

KEY FACTS

- All trusts must satisfy the three certainties (but charitable trusts do not need to satisfy the certainty of objects requirement).
- Certainty of intention is a question of fact and the courts will consider the whole context of the case.
- Certainty of subject matter requires certainty as to what property is held on trust and the beneficial interests involved.
- Complicated issues arise concerning trusts of part of a bulk of unascertained goods—the approach taken by the courts depends on whether the property is tangible or intangible.
- A fixed trust will be certain as to its objects if a complete list of beneficiaries can be compiled.
- A discretionary trust will be certain as to its objects if it can be said with certainty that any given individual is or is not a member of the class.

Introduction

Every trust (except for charitable trusts, see chapter 6) must satisfy the three certainties of intention, subject matter, and objects: ***Knight v Knight*** (1840) (see Figure 3.1).

Figure 3.1 The three certainties

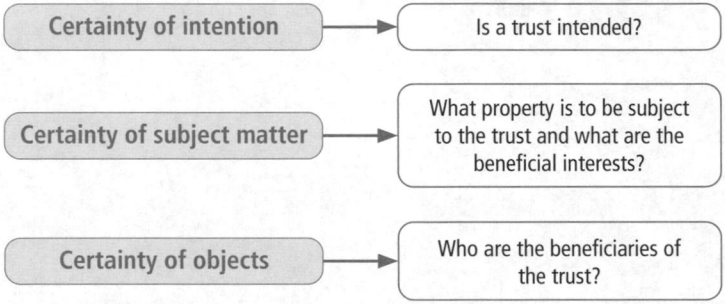

It is important that a trust satisfies the three certainties for two reasons:

- Trustees must know what their obligations are under the trust—remember that trustees will be liable for breach of trust if they fail to carry out their obligations correctly. The three certainties therefore provide a trustee with a degree of protection by ensuring that their obligations are clear.
- Satisfying the three certainties ensures that, if necessary, the court itself will be able to administer the trust.

REVISION TIP

Trusts can be declared orally or in writing. While the three certainties apply to all but charitable trusts, you should remember that every trust will also have to satisfy the formality requirements in respect of the type of property involved. So, for example, a trust of land may satisfy the three certainties. However, if the trust does not comply with **s 53(1)(b) Law of Property Act 1925** by being written or evidenced in writing, it will still be unenforceable.

Certainty of intention

Intention is established by considering *all* the circumstances of the case—*equity looks to intent rather than form*. In working out what was intended, there are a number of indicators of intention that you should look out for.

Imperative or precatory language?

Since the case of ***Lambe v Eames*** (1871), the courts have generally made a distinction between the use of precatory and imperative words.

- Precatory words express a hope, a wish, or a moral obligation. The use of precatory words typically indicates that a gift is intended (see Table 3.1).
- Imperative words express a command—a duty to do something. The use of imperative words indicates that a trust (or power) is intended.

Table 3.1 Case examples of precatory wording

CASE	PRECATORY WORDING
Lambe v Eames (1871)	'to be at her disposal in any way *she may think best*, for the benefit of herself and her family'
Re Adams and Kensington Vestry (1884)	'*in full confidence* that she would do what is right'
Re Diggles [1888]	'*it is my desire* that [my daughter] allows Anne an annuity of £25 during her life'

While the courts will be guided by the language used, remember that just as there is no magic in the use of the word 'trust' (***Kinloch v Secretary of State for India*** (1882)), the presence of precatory words will not necessarily prevent the court from finding that a trust exists, as long as it is satisfied that this was the intention of the donor:

COMISKEY V BOWRING-HANBURY **[1905] AC 84**

The **testator** left his wife the whole of his estate 'in full confidence that she will make such use of it as I should have made myself and that at her death she will devise it to such one or more of my nieces as she may think fit . . . '. These words sound precatory and would suggest a gift. However, the will continued, ' . . . in default of any disposition by her thereof by her will or testament I hereby direct that all my estate . . . shall at her death be equally divided among the surviving said nieces'. When read as a whole, the court concluded that the testator had intended a trust, under which the wife held a life interest.

- The court may also take into account surrounding evidence which sheds light on the intentions of the parties. In ***Staden v Jones*** [2008], the Court of Appeal used a solicitor's covering letter to conclude that an arrangement by which a divorcing wife waived her interest in the family home, on the basis that their daughter would ultimately be entitled to her share, amounted to a constructive trust. Similarly, in ***Hilton v Cosnier*** [2018], a man promised his former partner that she could remain in a property for the rest of her life but that the property was to go to his grandchildren on her death. It was held that there was no intention to declare a trust in favour of the grandchildren, only an intention to clarify that he was not giving the house to his former partner outright. This conclusion was supported by the fact that he did not discuss the existence of a trust with anyone and acted inconsistently with such an intention by transferring the property to his daughter some years later. In a more commercial context, in ***North v Wilkinson*** [2018], an investor argued that a 'Contract of Agreement' drawn up between himself and an inventor demonstrated an intention to create a trust which would have entitled him to a share of damages the inventor had subsequently received from another business which had adopted his inventions without his permission. However, the agreement had been drawn up without legal advice and the Court of Appeal concluded that it lacked any evidence of such an intention, not least because it did not set out how such an arrangement would practically operate.

Conduct

An intention to create a trust can also be inferred from the conduct of the donor.

PAUL V CONSTANCE **[1977] 1 WLR 527**

When Mr Constance died, a dispute arose regarding whether his wife (from whom he was separated but not divorced) or his new partner, Mrs Paul, was entitled to money held in a bank account in his sole name. During their relationship, Mr Constance had made arrangements for Mrs Paul to be able to withdraw money with his written permission. Only Mr Constance withdrew money, which was split evenly between himself and Mrs Paul, and he often told Mrs Paul that the money was 'as much yours as mine'. In addition, they had also paid some joint winnings from bingo into the account. It was held that these actions were sufficient to infer that Mr Constance had made a declaration of trust of the money in the bank account and Mrs Constance was entitled to his half of the account under intestacy.

A similar approach has been taken in some commercial contexts. For example, in ***Re Kayford Ltd (in liquidation)*** [1975], the separation of customers' money in a different bank account was deemed sufficient to demonstrate an intention to create a trust.

However, not all conduct can lead to the inference to create a trust: see, for example, ***Jones v Lock*** (1865).

The effect of lack of certainty of intention

If there is no intention to create a trust (or power), the **donee** will take the property absolutely, as a gift (***Lassence v Tierney*** (1849)).

Certainty of subject matter

There are two elements to certainty of subject matter:

- it must be clear what property is held on trust; and
- the beneficial interests must be clear.

The property held on trust must be certain

Vague or general descriptions of the trust property

It must be clear what property is to be held on trust or the trust will be void as the trustees, beneficiaries, and, ultimately, the court will be unable to determine what is held on trust (see Table 3.2).

Table 3.2 Case examples of uncertain descriptions of property

CASE	UNCERTAIN DESCRIPTION OF PROPERTY TO BE HELD ON TRUST
Palmer v Simmonds (1854)	'the bulk' of the testatrix's estate
Peck v Halsey (1720)	'some of my best linen'
Jubber v Jubber (1839)	'a handsome gratuity'
Re Kol b's WT [1961]	An instruction to purchase 'blue chip' investments

Trusts of part of property

This situation arises where there is an attempt to create a trust over part of a bulk of **tangible property**, for example the furniture in a home or a warehouse filled with desktop computers. Where there is a trust of *part of a bulk of tangible property*, the trust property will only be certain if it has been separated from the rest.

RE LONDON WINE CO **[1986] PCC 121**

LWC stored cases of wine in various warehouses. When wine was purchased by customers, they received a certificate of title which indicated that the wine would be held on trust for them until dispatched. When LWC went into liquidation, the question arose whether the wine was held on trust for the customers or was to be considered part of LWC's general assets available to creditors. It was held that there was no trust as the wine ordered by customers had not been separated from the general stock and therefore the subject matter of each trust could not be identified.

Note: under **s 20A Sale of Goods Act 1979**, purchasers of an unsegregated part of a larger bulk of property will be considered tenants in common of the whole property as soon as they have paid. This has the effect of protecting their purchases from creditors in the event of liquidation or receivership.

However, where there is a trust of part of some **intangible property**, such as shares, there is no need to identify the specific shares to be held on trust.

HUNTER V MOSS **[1994] 1 WLR 452**

Moss owned 950 shares in a company and was found to have declared himself trustee of 50 of those shares for Hunter. However, Moss sold all his shares and kept the proceeds for himself. When Hunter sought a share of the proceeds, Moss argued that the trust was void because he had not separated or identified the specific shares to be held on trust for Hunter.

Dillon LJ distinguished ***Re London Wine Co*** on the basis that, unlike cases of wine or other tangible property, these shares were indistinguishable from one another. Therefore, no segregation was required as holding any 50 of the 950 shares on trust would achieve the same thing.

REVISION TIP

Remember that this case applies to trusts of a part of a *homogeneous* larger whole. When approaching a problem question, pay close attention to the facts. If, for example, the question relates to a portion of shares where the shares are of different types or relate to shares in different companies, the rule in ***Hunter v Moss*** will not apply and the trust will be void if there is no further identification of the relevant property (***Re Harvard Securities Ltd (in liquidation)*** [1998]).

LOOKING FOR EXTRA MARKS?

Despite the fact that ***Hunter v Moss*** (1994) was followed in ***Re Harvard Securities Ltd (in liquidation)*** [1998], and more recently in respect of complex financial securities in ***Pearson v Lehman Brothers Finance SA*** [2010], there have been many criticisms of the law in this area. Hayton, in (1994) 110 LQR 335, raises a number of significant criticisms of which you should be aware:

- Is Dillon LJ's argument that there is no difference between a testator giving 50 shares to a legatee in his will and a settlor declaring himself trustee of 50 of his shares correct?
- Difficult questions may arise if that the 'trustee' sells part of his holding—for example, has he sold his own shares or the beneficiary's, or, if the transaction is taxable, who is liable—the seller or the beneficiary? Consider this argument in light of Worthington's argument in 'Sorting Out Ownership Interests in a Bulk: Gifts, Sales and Trusts' [1999] JBL 1, that such issues could be resolved through the rules of tracing (see chapter 12).
- Is the broad distinction in the cases between trusts of parts of unascertained bulks of tangible and intangible property convincing?

The beneficial interests under the trust must be certain

The beneficial interests under the trust must also be clear. Two cases illustrate the problems that may arise in this context.

BOYCE V BOYCE **(1849) 16 SIM 476**

A testator established a trust of four houses for his daughters, Maria and Charlotte. Maria was to choose which house she wanted, and the other houses would be held on trust for Charlotte. However, Maria died before making her choice. The trust failed as it was no longer possible to say which houses would be held on trust for Charlotte.

The property had been clearly identified but the beneficial interest had not. The trust would have succeeded if the trustees had been given the power to choose the house, but in the absence of this power, neither the trustees nor the court could determine the beneficial interest.

In the following case, the question was whether the instructions given to the trustees were certain enough to allow them to carry out the terms of the trust.

RE GOLAY'S WT **[1965] 2 ALL ER 660**

A trust was set up whereby the beneficiary was to 'receive a reasonable income' from the testator's properties. The court held that this was a valid trust as the phrase 'reasonable income' allowed the trustees (and the court, if need be) to make an *objective* assessment of what that might be, based on the beneficiary's circumstances. Therefore, the trust was sufficiently certain because, while the income might vary over the years, the trustees would always have an objective yardstick by which to act. On the other hand, the trust would have failed if the properties were to be sold in order to provide a reasonable one-off sum of money for the beneficiary. This is because the trustees would have no way of determining what a 'reasonable' payment would amount to. Arguably, the wording of the trust suggests that the beneficiary would not receive all the money, but then what portion of the proceeds would be reasonable?

Note: the legal issues surrounding the certainty of beneficial interests will not apply in respect of discretionary trusts. This is because the class to benefit merely holds a *spes* (hope) of benefiting; the extent to which they can benefit, if at all, is at the absolute discretion of the trustees.

A link between certainty of intention and certainty of subject matter

If there is a lack of certainty as to the subject matter of the trust, this will cast doubt on whether the settlor truly intended to create a trust (***Mussoorie Bank Ltd v Raynor*** (1882)).

The effect of lack of certainty of subject matter

If there is a lack of certainty as to the subject matter the trust fails, and the property will return to the settlor or estate on resulting trust.

Certainty of objects (beneficiaries)

Certainty of objects relates to the question of who the beneficiaries of a trust are. Every trust—with the exception of charitable trusts—must satisfy the certainty of objects requirement. The certainty of objects test is different for fixed trusts and discretionary trusts.

- *Fixed trust*—the beneficial interests are fixed, for example a trust to benefit Razia and Shahana in equal shares.
- *Discretionary trust*—this is a type of trust in which the trustees are given the power to appoint people as beneficiaries of the trust. Members of the class of potential beneficiaries do not hold any beneficial interest until trustees exercise their discretion to appoint in the beneficiaries' favour. The amount the beneficiaries receive is at the discretion of the trustees.

Fixed trusts

In order to satisfy the certainty of objects requirement, a full list of the beneficiaries must be able to be created (***IRC v Broadway Cottages Trust*** [1955]), ie all the beneficiaries must be able to be identified. (See chapter 11 for a discussion of the trustees' options if the whereabouts or continued existence of a beneficiary cannot be ascertained.) In ***OT Computers Ltd (In Administration) v First National Tricity Finance Ltd & Others*** [2003], an attempt to set up a trust to protect monies owed to 'urgent suppliers' of a struggling company failed because the meaning to be given to the adjective 'urgent' was not made clear, making it impossible to draw up a full list of beneficiaries.

Discretionary trusts

A different approach was taken in respect of discretionary trusts in the key decision of ***McPhail v Doulton***:

MCPHAIL V DOULTON (RE BADEN'S TRUSTS (NO 1)) **[1971] AC 424**

The settlor set up a fund for the benefit of employees of Matthew Hall & Co Ltd and their relatives and dependants at the 'absolute discretion' of the trustees. The House of Lords had to decide: (i) whether this was a trust or a power; and (ii) the appropriate test for the certainty of objects requirement. While all the judges agreed that this was a discretionary trust rather than a power, they were split regarding the appropriate test. On a three to two majority, Lord Wilberforce, who delivered the leading judgment of the majority, held as follows:

1. The complete list approach adopted in ***IRC v Broadway Cottages*** [1955] was overruled in respect of discretionary trusts.
2. The test for certainty of objects in discretionary trusts is the same as the test for fiduciary powers in ***Re Gulbenkian's Settlement*** [1970], namely *whether it could be said with certainty that any given individual is or is not a member of the class.*

Applying the test in *McPhail v Doulton: Re Baden's Trusts (No 2)*

Having decided on the test for certainty of objects for discretionary trusts, the case was returned to the court of first instance for the test to be applied. Despite the court deciding that it satisfied the new test, the **executors** of Baden's will relentlessly contested its validity, and the case came before the Court of Appeal for the second time.

RE BADEN'S TRUSTS (NO 2) **[1973] CH 9**

The trust set up by Baden was to benefit 'employees of Matthew Hall & Co Ltd and their relatives and dependants'. The issue in this appeal was whether the groups 'relatives' and 'dependants' satisfied the new test set out in ***McPhail v Doulton***—ie could it be said with certainty that any given individual was or was not a member of these classes?

The Court of Appeal held that *only if a class of beneficiaries is conceptually certain* will it be possible to satisfy the test of whether it can be said with certainty that any given individual is or is not a member of the class.

What is conceptual certainty?

Conceptual certainty has been described as 'linguistic or semantic certainty'—in other words, a class of beneficiaries will be conceptually certain when the description enables the group to be defined clearly. Consider the following examples:

EXAMPLE 1

1. A discretionary trust of £100,000 for members of the British Army who served in the Gulf War.
2. A discretionary trust of £50,000 for morally upstanding residents of Gloucester.

The first trust can be said to be conceptually certain as the group to benefit can be clearly understood. However, it is unlikely that the second trust would be valid as it is extremely difficult to define what exactly would be meant by 'morally upstanding'. For example, X may attend church regularly but may also cheat at poker. Y might give regularly to charity but cheat on their husband. If Z is in favour of same-sex marriage, does this mean they are morally upstanding or not? Where would the line be drawn?

Gifts subject to a condition precedent

Gifts subject to a condition precedent do not require the same degree of conceptual certainty as discretionary trusts.

TERMINOLOGY TIP

A gift made subject to a condition precedent is one to which the donee will not be entitled unless he or she satisfies the condition, for example '£10,000 to each of my children who graduate from university'.

***RE BARLOW'S WT* [1979] 1 WLR 278**

A testatrix provided that a number of her paintings could be sold at a reduced price to 'any members of my family and any friends of mine'. The gift in question here was the difference in price between the market value of the paintings and their reduced price. The central issue was whether the condition precedent—ie that they be family members or friends—rendered the gift void for uncertainty. The court upheld the gift. Whereas the objects of a discretionary trust must be conceptually certain, a condition precedent will be valid if *at least one person can be said to satisfy the condition*.

In a gift to a class, as the objects are only entitled to a *share* of the property, it is vital to be able to say whether any given individual is or is not a member of the class. However, in this case, the 'family and friends' were each given an *individual opportunity* to purchase the paintings. Therefore, a greater degree of uncertainty as to who satisfied this condition did not affect the opportunity they received.

REVISION TIP

While a gift to 'friends' may be valid as a gift subject to a condition precedent, a discretionary trust for 'friends' will be void for uncertainty, as it is impossible to define friends so that it could be said that *any* individual *is or is not* within the class.

Distinguishing conceptual uncertainty from evidential uncertainty

It is important to distinguish 'conceptual uncertainty' from 'evidential uncertainty'. Conceptual certainty relates to the certainty of the *class*; evidential certainty relates to the issue of whether or not an *individual* can be found or proven to be a member of the class. If a class is conceptually uncertain, the trust will be void, but evidential uncertainty will not defeat a trust.

Having discussed the meaning of conceptual certainty in general terms, it is important to return to ***Re Baden's Trusts (No 2)***. The Court of Appeal was asked if the groups 'dependants' and 'relatives' were conceptually certain. All the judges agreed that the group 'dependants' was conceptually certain. However, while they also agreed that the group 'relatives' was conceptually certain, the three judges each reached this conclusion by different reasoning!

Sachs LJ: the liberal approach

Sachs LJ started by defining 'relatives' to mean 'descendants of a common ancestor'. He argued that this was conceptually certain as its meaning was clearly understandable. He then stated that trustees have a fiduciary obligation to survey the range of possible beneficiaries. This involves the trustees gaining a sense of the general width of the class—it does not require an exhaustive list. Beyond that survey, anyone who can prove that they are a member of the class can be included.

Sachs LJ's approach clearly separates the question of evidential uncertainty by stressing that an exhaustive list is not required. Moreover, in response to the problem that a potentially limitless number of people can be included within the definition 'descendants of a common ancestor', he makes three points:

1. The trustees should exercise their discretion in a sensible way, thus making it more likely that they would choose close relatives in the general course of events.
2. Proof of one's relationship to another soon becomes very difficult, providing a natural limit on who could establish their membership of the class.

3. Most importantly, these issues are evidential and the fact that it will not always be possible to prove that any given individual is not a member of the class will not render the trust void.

This approach is arguably the purest interpretation of conceptual certainty. The only drawback is that Sachs LJ's reasoning provides no simple way for the trustees to work out whether the class to benefit under the trust is conceptually certain. Simple common sense may be a dangerous path for trustees, who could be liable if they distribute the money wrongly.

Megaw LJ: the middle ground

Megaw LJ also defined 'relatives' as 'descendants of a common ancestor'. However, he argued that a class would be conceptually certain if it could be said with certainty that *a substantial number of objects fell within the class*, even if there were a substantial number of others that could not definitely be said to be within or without the class.

- Megaw LJ's approach offers trustees more guidance in that the conceptual certainty of the group can be tested by seeking a substantial number of individuals who definitely come within the class.
- However, what exactly is meant by 'a substantial number'? Megaw LJ suggests that this is a question of common sense, but wary trustees will still find themselves questioning whether they have done enough, especially should the situation arise where there is definitely a substantial number of individuals and the trustees *cannot* say with clarity that they are within the class.
- Despite it being said that evidential certainty will not defeat a discretionary trust, Megaw LJ's approach rests on being able to provide *evidence* that a sufficient number come within the class.

Stamp LJ: the strict approach

Stamp LJ takes a literal approach to the test set out in ***McPhail v Doulton*** that to be conceptually certain it must be possible to say of *any given individual* that they are or *are not* within the class. On this basis, Stamp LJ rejected the idea that 'descendants of a common ancestor' could be conceptually certain and argued that the discretionary trust could only be valid if 'relatives' was defined as **next-of-kin**.

- Stamp LJ's reasoning seems determined to undermine the liberal implications of the decision in ***McPhail v Doulton***. Applying his approach, there would be no real difference between the new test adopted in ***McPhail v Doulton*** and the previous complete list approach of ***IRC v Broadway Cottages Trust*** [1955] as every individual's membership of the class would have to be capable of being established.

- It is questionable whether this approach would be followed in the future, particularly as Lord Wilberforce's full expression of the test states that a trust 'does not fail simply because it is impossible to ascertain every member of the class'.

LOOKING FOR EXTRA MARKS?

The issue of certainty of objects for discretionary trusts is complex. If you want to do well in this area, there is no substitute for reading ***McPhail v Doulton*** and ***Re Baden's Trusts (No 2)*** and taking your own detailed notes. You should particularly focus on how well the Court of Appeal in ***Re Baden's Trusts (No 2)*** uses 'conceptual certainty' in its judgments. Once you have done this, you can deepen your understanding of some of the problems in this area by reading Emery's discussion of this issue at (1982) 98 LQR 551.

Can conceptual uncertainty be cured?

There is some debate over whether conceptual uncertainty can be cured by reference to the decision or opinion of the trustees or a third party.

RE TUCK'S ST **[1978] CH 49**

A trust was established to benefit future baronets on the condition that they were of the Jewish faith and married to a wife of 'Jewish blood', as determined by the Chief Rabbi. The court upheld the trust: any conceptual uncertainty regarding the conditions was cured by the power given to the Chief Rabbi.

While Denning LJ simply argued that reference to the trustees' or a third party's opinion may cure conceptual uncertainty, Eveleigh LJ's reasoning rested on the narrower ground that there was no conceptual uncertainty because the settlor was 'in effect saying that his definition of "Jewish faith" is *the same as the Chief Rabbi's definition*' (emphasis added) (a conceptually certain class).

Note: ***Re Tuck's ST*** addresses the validity of *conditions precedent*. It remains unclear whether:

1. the same approach would be adopted in respect of a *discretionary trust* with conceptually uncertain objects; and
2. whether the courts would adopt the broad approach of Denning LJ or the more restrictive approach of Eveleigh LJ.

Both approaches remain problematic. Whereas Denning LJ's approach would ensure the validity of many more discretionary trusts, it would also seem to empower individuals named by the settlor to cure conceptual uncertainty in circumstances where the court would otherwise declare the trust void. On the other hand, Eveleigh LJ's approach maintains the need for conceptual certainty but rests on a very fine factual distinction that many settlors will not appreciate (see Webb and Akkouh, *Trusts Law*, 5th edn (2017), 3.17). Compare the following examples.

EXAMPLE 2

1. Bradley leaves £10,000 in his will to be held on discretionary trust for 'the men and women who have given me pleasure over my long and happy life'. He adds, 'in the event of any doubt, my wife can choose who qualifies'.
2. Bradley leaves £10,000 in his will to be held on discretionary trust for 'those men and women whom my wife considers have given me pleasure over my long and happy life'.

In (1), the group is conceptually uncertain. Giving someone the ability to decide who comes within the class will not cure this uncertainty as there is no objective way to determine what Bradley meant.

However, in (2) there is no conceptual uncertainty as the class in question is not 'those who have given me pleasure' but 'those whom *my wife considers have given me pleasure*'. As membership is to be decided by Bradley's wife, there is no difficulty in understanding how the class is to be determined.

Administrative unworkability

A trust may be void if the class to benefit is *so wide* that the trust would be administratively unworkable, for instance Lord Wilberforce's example of a trust for all the residents of Greater London in ***McPhail v Doulton***.

In ***R v District Auditor, ex parte West Yorkshire Metropolitan County Council*** (1986), a trust 'for the benefit of any or all or some of the inhabitants of the County of West Yorkshire' (some 2.5 million potential beneficiaries) was held to be void for administrative unworkability.

Note: administrative unworkability will also render a fiduciary power void because the fiduciary obligations of the holder require that the power is capable of being exercised in a responsible manner and that the selection of one person over another can be meaningfully justified. However, administrative unworkability will not affect the validity of a mere power (ie a power given to a non-fiduciary) (***Re Hay's Settlement Trusts*** [1982]).

The effect of lack of certainty of objects

A trust which lacks certainty of objects will be void and return on resulting trust to the settlor or his or her estate.

Comparing discretionary trusts and fiduciary powers

As you have seen, following ***McPhail v Doulton***, the test for certainty of objects for discretionary trusts and fiduciary powers is now the same. However, it is important to remember that there are still important differences.

The duties under the discretionary trust/fiduciary power

Discretionary trusts

McPhail v Doulton establishes that trustees have the following duties:

- to survey the field to identify the width of the class; and
- to distribute the income from the trust.

Note: watch out for *non-exhaustive discretionary trusts* which expressly allow the trustees to accumulate the income. In such trusts, the trustees may delay distributing for some time but must still ultimately distribute at some point.

Fiduciary powers

The donee of a fiduciary power is *not* under a duty to distribute the property. However, under ***Re Hay's ST*** fiduciaries have the following duties:

- to consider periodically whether to exercise the power;
- to consider the range of possible objects (beneficiaries); and
- to consider the appropriateness of appointments made—ie they cannot pick at random or without reason.

REVISION TIP

If an arrangement refers to a 'gift over in default of appointment' or a direction that remaining money is to return to the settlor's estate, this will be a fiduciary power, as the wording demonstrates that there is not a duty to distribute.

EXAMPLE 3

- Discretionary trust: 'I leave £100,000 to my wife to be held on trust at her absolute and unfettered discretion for the employees of Brillington Engineering Co Ltd.'
- Fiduciary power: 'To my trustees I leave £50,000 to share amongst those of my relatives who are most in need. In the event that all the money is not used up, any remainder will pass to my gardener, Ted.'

As there is a duty to distribute in a discretionary trust, there are no directions about what should be done with any remaining money. Compare this with the fiduciary power, where a beneficiary in default of appointment is indicated.

The rights of members of the class

Discretionary trusts

Members of the class are not beneficiaries until they are appointed to the trust—until that time they merely hold a *spes* (hope) of benefiting. This means that members of the class may challenge the decisions of the trustees but they *cannot* claim that they are entitled to be appointed, as this is at the absolute discretion of the trustees.

Decisions may be challenged on the basis that the trustees have:

- appointed outside the class;
- failed to consider their reasons for appointment; or
- acted in bad faith in making an appointment (eg appointing only to close friends within the class).

Note: if all the beneficiaries are *sui juris*, they may act together to wind up the trust under the rule in ***Saunders v Vautier*** (1841), as they own the entire beneficial interest (see chapter 10).

Fiduciary powers

As with discretionary trusts, members of a class under a fiduciary power cannot claim to be entitled to be appointed. However, decisions may be challenged on the basis that the fiduciaries have:

- appointed outside the class;
- failed to carry out their fiduciary obligations under ***Re Hay's ST***.

Unlike discretionary trusts, the court will not intervene to compel the fiduciaries to exercise their power. Furthermore, the objects of a fiduciary power cannot take advantage of the rule in ***Saunders v Vautier*** (1841) as the beneficial interest lies with the person entitled to the gift over in default of appointment.

KEY CASES

CASES	FACTS	PRINCIPLE
Hunter v Moss [1994] 1 WLR 452	An attempt to create a trust of 50 of the 950 shares owned by the trustee was upheld.	Trusts of part of an unascertained bulk of intangible property do not require segregation or specific identification to satisfy the certainty of subject matter requirement.
Knight v Knight (1840) 3 Beav 148	Concerned a will which included the statement 'I trust to the liberality of my successors to reward any others of my old servants and tenants according to their deserts'. The successor took the deceased's property absolutely.	Originating case for the three certainties requirement of intention, subject matter, and objects.
Lambe v Eames (1871) 6 Ch App 597	Concerned money left to a wife 'to be at her disposal in any way she may think best, for the benefit of herself and her family'. The wife took the property as a gift.	Emphasizes the difference between imperative words (which suggest that a trust is intended) and precatory words (which suggest a mere moral obligation).

CASES	FACTS	PRINCIPLE
McPhail v Doulton [1971] AC 424	Concerned the validity of a discretionary trust established for employees, relatives, and dependants.	The certainty of objects requirement for discretionary trusts is whether it can be said with certainty that any given individual is or is not a member of the class.
Palmer v Simmonds (1854) 2 Drew 221	A gift of the 'bulk' of the testatrix's estate failed.	The vagueness of the wording meant that there was no certainty of subject matter.
Re Baden's Trusts (No 2) [1973] Ch 9	Concerned whether the groups 'relatives' and 'dependants' satisfied the certainty of objects test for discretionary trusts.	In order to satisfy the test set out in ***McPhail v Doulton***, the groups to benefit must be conceptually certain. 'Conceptual certainty' refers to whether the group can be meaningfully *defined* (as opposed to meaning that all the beneficiaries can be *identified*).
Re London Wine Co [1986] PCC 121	An attempt to create a trust of part of an unascertained bulk of tangible property (cases of wine) failed.	Trusts of part of an unascertained bulk of tangible property must be segregated or specifically identified to satisfy the certainty of subject matter requirement.

KEY DEBATES

Topic	How defensible is the current approach to trusts of part of an unascertained bulk of intangible property?
Academic/author	Hayton/Worthington
Viewpoint	The current approach in ***Hunter v Moss*** raises problems in respect of legal principles and remedies in the event of a breach of trust.
Source	Compare Hayton (1994) 110 LQR 335 and Worthington (1999) JBL 1.

Topic	How can the complicated decisions on certainty of objects be unravelled?
Academic/author	Emery
Viewpoint	The reasoning of the different judges in ***Re Baden's Trusts (No 2)*** demonstrates that there is still some confusion around the meaning of conceptual certainty and evidential certainty.
Source	Emery (1982) 98 LQR 551.

EXAM QUESTIONS

Problem question

Anna was the managing director of a multinational company. She died in 2012 and her will contains the following bequests:

1. £50,000 to my sister, Ruth, whom I trust will use the money to continue supporting her daughter, Joanna.
2. £150,000 to Alistair and Fraser, to be held on trust for any of my trusted work colleagues in any amount at their absolute and unfettered discretion.
3. My favourite jewels are to be held on trust for my beloved granddaughter, Lucy, until her twenty-first birthday.

Discuss the validity of these bequests.

Essay question

The current approach to certainty of objects in discretionary trusts creates more uncertainty than it resolves.
Discuss.

Online resources

For an outline answer to this essay question, as well as multiple choice questions and interactive key cases, please visit the online resources.

Concentrate Q&As

For more questions and answers on equity and trusts, see the *Concentrate Q&A: Equity & Trusts* by Rosalind Malcolm.

Go to the end of this book to view **sample pages**.

4 Constitution

KEY FACTS

- There are three ways to benefit another with property.
- There are legal rules for validly transferring an interest in property.
- When the legal rules fail, equity has developed methods to prevent the intention of the transferor being defeated.
- Key principles to be discussed are:
  - → The 'rule' in ***Strong v Bird*** [1874];
  - → *donatio mortis causa*;
  - → the 'every effort' principle;
  - → unconscionability;
  - → proprietary estoppel;
  - → covenants to settle.

Introduction

When a person transfers legal title to another, the legal title is said to **vest** in the other person. This chapter will consider the rules for the transfer of title (ownership) in property in relation to different types of property. The general principle is that unless the property has been transferred by the correct legal rules then the transfer fails—it is said to be **imperfect**. The equitable maxim that 'equity will not perfect an imperfect gift' would be the starting position for the courts. If the transferee has not given valuable consideration, that person is said to be a **volunteer**. Failing to validly 'vest' title in the volunteer means that the volunteer has no enforceable legal rights. This is reflected in the equitable maxim that 'equity will not assist a volunteer'.

TERMINOLOGY TIP

It is sometimes the language of equity that students struggle with, so at a *basic* level this may help.

When a person has property, he or she is said to be the 'absolute owner'. In a simple, but artificial way it can be said that he or she has the legal title and the beneficial (equitable) title. A person who gives a lifetime gift is referred to as the donor; a person creating a trust of the same property would be called a settlor. If the same transactions were being created by a will, the person would be called the testator (or a testatrix if female).

The person who receives the gift (which means a transfer without consideration) is a donee; a person receiving an interest under a trust is a beneficiary; and a person receiving property under a will is a legatee or devisee. For now, the person giving the property will be called the transferor; the person who is intended to get the property will be called the transferee.

The maxim 'Equity will not perfect an imperfect gift' refers to any transfer of legal title, including to a third party to hold on trust.

This chapter begins by briefly considering the legal rules in relation to validly transferring property to another person. It then deals with equitable rules that have developed to overcome the strict application of the legal rules of vesting.

Equity is a gloss on the common law and, as such, has implications beyond the creation of trusts. The rules for transfer of ownership as a gift overlap with the transfer of legal title to the trustee. This chapter is closely linked with chapter 5 on the formalities for creating a trust.

Benefiting another with property

Milroy v Lord (1862) identified three ways in which an absolute owner of property could benefit another with his or her property:

- an outright gift;
- a transfer of legal title to a third person to hold on trust for the benefit of another; or
- declaring that the absolute owner now holds that property on trust for another.

Figure 4.1 Three ways to benefit another with your property

1. Gift

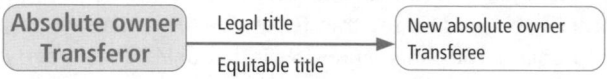

2. Transfer to third person to hold on trust

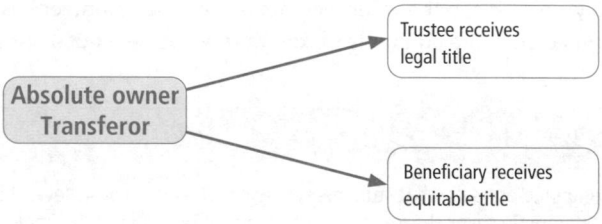

3. Absolute owner declares that he or she holds property on trust for another

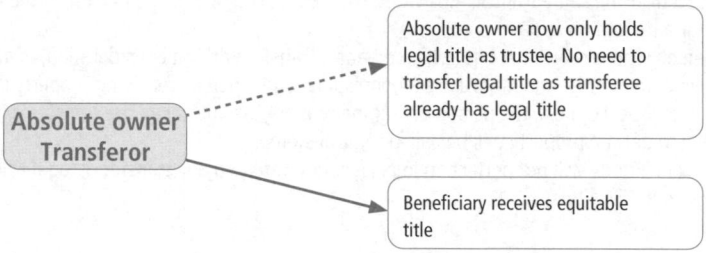

Figure 4.1 shows that it is artificial to talk of the absolute owner having legal and equitable title. The legal and equitable interests have not been separated. However, as with the previous Terminology tip, as a device for learning the principles, it may help to think of the interests in this way.

LOOKING FOR EXTRA MARKS?

A *common mistake* made by students when dealing with constitution issues is either to try to find a trust where the intention was to make a gift or to only consider who has the equitable interest when the transferor intended to create a third person as trustee. Chapter 5 considers the requirements for dealing with the beneficial ownership of property under a trust. These two topics are closely related but they have been separated out here to help you in your revision. *Keep distinct the legal requirements for constituting the transfer of an interest in property and the formalities for creating and dealing with a trust interest.*

A good plan of the answer usually remedies this, and an answer that has been planned really pays off.

REVISION TIP

In answering questions, the focus will be on how equity steps in to modify the legal rules. Do not wander into a long explanation of the legal rules. *Briefly* explain how the legal rule for transfer of title has failed, then explain the equitable rules which may apply.

When lawyers talk of a transfer it is said to be 'perfect' if all the legal requirements for a valid transfer have been complied with. If they have not, then the transfer is said to be 'imperfect'.

Different legal rules apply to different types of property. Remember that property includes *any* thing, tangible or intangible, that is capable of being owned. The following sections set out the rules for the valid transfer of the most common types of property transfer.

Land

A transfer in land or an interest in land is set out in **s 52 Law of Property Act 1925**.

- Transfer must be by deed (defined in **s 1 Law of Property (Miscellaneous Provisions) Act 1989**).
- Transfer is completed by registration at the Land Registry (**s 27 Land Registration Act 2002**).

See ***Richards v Delridge*** [1874].

Stocks and shares which regulate the ownership of companies

Private limited company:

- Memorandum of transfer.
- Registration of shares.
- **Stock Transfer Act 1963; Companies Act 1985**.
- Public limited company (plc):
- If there has been compliance with the electronic CREST system, then the correct instruction will be adequate.

See ***Milroy v Lord*** (1862).

Chose in action

This includes such things as cheques, debts, or rights under a contract.

- Compliance with **s 136 Law of Property Act 1925**, which requires endorsement.

See ***Jones v Lock*** (1865).

Chattels

This includes such things as paintings, jewellery, etc.

- By deed, ***Jaffa v Taylor Gallery Ltd*** (1990); or
- compliance with ***Re Cole*** [1964]:
  - delivery;
  - intention that legal ownership is transferred.

GLAISTER-CARLISLE V GLAISTER-CARLISLE **(1968)**
The owner of a miniature female white poodle was upset that his wife had allowed his poodle to mate with his wife's black poodle. He threw the white poodle at her and said, 'She is your responsibility now'. The court held that the language was too vague to transfer the legal title, despite the delivery.

The requirement for delivery can be actual delivery or constructive. This may include, for example, delivery of car keys, representing the delivery of the car itself. It may also be informing the intended donee where he or she can find the chattel: ***Thomas v Times Book Co*** [1966].

Money

A valid transfer of money merely requires delivery.

Transfer of an equitable interest

Another type of property that can be transferred is the ownership of a beneficial interest. The legal requirements to transfer this interest to another are set out in **s 53(1)(c) Law of Property Act 1925**. This applies to the beneficial interest in *any* type of property, *not* just interests in land. This type of transfer is dealt with in detail in chapter 5.

REVISION TIP

These clear legal rules, from either statute or common law, for the valid transfer of property rights provide the necessary certainty in dealing with property ownership. Learn the legal requirements for each type of property covered in this chapter. Explain this first in an exam before moving on to say that equity has developed means to overcome problems of imperfect title transfer.

Equitable principles which perfect a transfer

Where legal title has not vested correctly, equity has established exceptions to the legal rules outlined earlier. It is important to establish the legal rules *first*, then consider which—and there may be more than one—of the equitable rules applies to perfect title.

Legal title vests in another capacity (fortuitous vesting)

Where the legal owner promises to transfer property (or promises that he or she will not enforce the repayment of a debt) but fails to do this in his or her lifetime, the gift should fail. However, if the promised property vests in the potential transferee in another capacity, the courts have held that the transfer has been perfected: ***Strong v Bird*** [1874]. To be able to rely on the 'Rule in ***Strong v Bird***' the requirements are that:

- there is a clear intention to make an *inter vivos* gift to the **transferee**;
- there is a present intention to give: ***Re Freeland*** [1952];
- the intention continues unchanged until death: ***Re Gonin*** [1977]; and
- the intended transferee obtains legal ownership by appointment as executor or personal representative: ***Re James*** [1935].

REVISION TIP

When reading the exam question ensure that you note who the executors are. This is usually at the end of the question. Ensure that you read the whole question.

Intention

The intention must be a clear intention to give immediately and there has only been some practical barrier to the transfer. It must not be an intention to give in the future. The rule originated in the release from debts, but it has been extended:

- to chattels: ***Re Stewart*** [1908]; and
- to an intention to transfer legal title to hold as trustee: ***Re Ralli's WT*** [1964].

LOOKING FOR EXTRA MARKS?

It is not clear whether the decision in ***Re Ralli's WT*** is an extension of ***Strong v Bird*** or a different principle altogether.

Donatio mortis causa

Property transferred under a will must comply with the **Wills Act 1837. Section 9** requires that the will be in writing, signed by the testator, and witnessed by two people who are not beneficiaries. However, a deathbed bequest can supersede the will if it complies with the requirements of a *donatio mortis causa* (DMC) as set out in ***Cain v Moon*** [1896] and more recently reviewed by the Court of Appeal in ***King v Dubrey*** [2015], ie:

- if the bequest is made in contemplation of imminent death;
- if the bequest is made contingent (conditional) on death; and
- there is actual or constructive delivery of the property.

Contemplation of death

This is more than contemplation of death, which everyone must face. It can be in contemplation of hazardous undertakings, active service during war, or a dangerous trip. It will not matter that the death actually occurs by a different means; in ***Wilkes v Allington*** [1931] the donor had terminal cancer but actually died of pneumonia. This was still held to be valid. However, see recently in ***Keeling v Keeling*** [2017], when the alleged donor did not die from a heart attack, made a full recovery, and survived a further six months. It will not apply in the contemplation of suicide: ***Re Dudman*** [1925] but see the case of ***Mills v Shields*** [1948].

Contingent on death

If the transferor recovers, the intended gift fails. Therefore, the gift is revocable if death does not occur. It can also be expressly revoked by taking back **dominion** of the property.

Actual or constructive delivery

This means that the transferor hands 'dominion' to the transferee, by giving the transferee the means to control the property. This will be dependent on the nature of the property. Where the goods are tangible this may not be difficult, but where the property is intangible, such as money, there may be evidential problems. In the latter situation the courts will look for relevant evidence to indicate the transfer of dominion (see Table 4.1).

Table 4.1 Examples of constructive delivery

PROPERTY	CASE EXAMPLES OF CONSTRUCTIVE DELIVERY
Safety deposit box	***Re Lillingston*** [1952]: keys to a trunk, which held another key to another box, which held a further key. Interestingly, the subject matter of the DMC also included all the property in the first trunk
Car	***Woodard v Woodard*** [1995]: giving the keys to a car
Bank accounts	***Re Dillon*** [1890]: the relevant passbook will be adequate
Unregistered land	***Sen v Headley*** [1991]: the only keys to a safety box which contained the relevant title deeds
Registered land	Although the **Land Registration Act 2002** states that the land certificate is merely evidence of ownership, it may form sufficient evidence of delivery of 'dominion' (see Pearce and Stevens, *Land Law*, 3rd edn (2005), p 79)
Shares	***Staniland v Willott*** (1852) suggests that handing the executed share transfer form will suffice

Examples

Additionally, the property must be capable of forming the subject matter of a DMC. A cheque made by the transferor cannot be the subject matter of a DMC as a DMC is a mandate that ends on death: ***Re Beaumont*** [1902]. However, a cheque payable to the transferor can be: ***Re Mead*** (1880).

Every effort has been taken by the transferor

The property has failed to vest despite every effort of the transferor to perfect title in the transferee: ***Re Rose*** [1952]. The principle to be gained from this exception is that where power to complete the transfer is out of the hands of the transferor, equity will 'look upon as done that which ought to be done'. In ***Re Rose*** the forms for transfer of shares were completed and sent to the company. There was a three-month delay between sending the forms to the company and registration at the company of the transfer. The court held that transfer was effective when the transferor had done all that he could to complete the transfer. Effectively at this point the shares were held on constructive trust by the donor for the intended donee.

It seems from this case that the transferor must have 'gone beyond the point of no return'. In effect, the transferor has practically lost dominion of the property. Compare ***Re Rose*** with ***Re Fry*** [1946], where the transferor had completed forms to transfer title and sent the forms to be registered. The company needed the consent of the Treasury to make the registration. The transferor had completed all the forms to get this consent but had died before the consent was given. The court held that the transferor still held power of the shares and had not done all that was required to transfer them.

If a rule can be gleaned from the cases, it seems from ***Mascall v Mascall*** (1984) that the courts will perfect the transfer when the transferor can no longer change their mind and the property has been taken out of the control of the transferor.

Unconscionability

In ***Choithram International v Pagarani*** [2001], Lord Browne-Wilkinson said that while 'equity will not aid a volunteer, it will not strive officiously to defeat a gift'. In that case, Mr Pagarani died after orally declaring the transfer of his property to a trust foundation, of which he was one of the trustees. The Privy Council found that there was sufficient oral and written evidence of his intention to make an immediate unconditional gift to the foundation. As he already had legal title and was one of the trustees, the transfer could be perfected.

Lord Browne-Wilkinson considered that the situation fell between the typical ***Milroy v Lord*** criteria for transferring an interest to another in that it was not a gift and neither was it actually a transfer to a third party to hold on trust (see Figure 4.1) but was where the intended donor, who has legal title, intends that they and another person will hold the property of trust for a beneficiary. It can only have been an intention to transfer the property on trust. As the donor was one of the trustees, the courts of equity could require the executors to transfer the interest to the trust foundation.

However, this decision was used by Arden LJ in ***Pennington v Waine*** [2002] as a basis to extend the equitable jurisdiction of the principles set out in ***Re Rose*** considerably. The owner of shares wanted to transfer them to her nephew. The relevant forms were completed but not registered, being on file at her solicitors. Her nephew took on some responsibility for the running of the company, which the transfer gave him. All parties acted as if he had the shares. On her death, the court was asked to perfect the transfer.

It appears from the decision in ***Pennington v Waine*** that where:

- there has been a promise to transfer property to a transferee,
- the transferee has then acted, in relation to that property, as if it had been transferred to the transferee, and
- it is unconscionable to rely on the strict rule of law to deny the transferee the promised property, the courts will require that the property be validly transferred.

Arden LJ, in a comprehensive judgment, reviews the history of the law on perfecting legal title. She felt unconstrained by the decisions in ***Re Rose*** and relied on the comments of Lord Browne-Wilkinson as providing the authority to perfect the transfer where it would be unconscionable for the transferor to recall the gift; however, the decision is not without criticism. In ***Curtis v Pulbrook*** [2011], the High Court considered that the decision was actually one of detrimental reliance and came within the principles of proprietary estoppel (see 'Estoppel' below). Had this been the case there may have been less strident criticisms of the decision.

LOOKING FOR EXTRA MARKS?

A *common mistake* is for students to see the principle of ***Pennington v Waine*** as the remedy for all failure in vesting. On the facts of the case, there was a catalogue of relationships which Arden LJ felt created the relevant equity. Equity is not about doing what may appear morally right regardless of principle. Equity develops on clear principles and will, unless equity demands otherwise, 'follow the law'. After all, remember ***Jones v Lock*** (1865): the father had promised in front of witnesses that the cheque was for the child and yet the child was denied the property. It is suggested that this decision may be restricted on its facts but was recently applied in ***Khan v Mahmood*** [2021].

Estoppel

Estoppel is the equitable principle that enforces promises which are unsupported by valuable consideration. Proprietary estoppel, unlike promissory estoppel, can form the basis of a claim (***Pascoe v Turner*** [1979]), so it can act as a sword, not only a shield. The requirements are that:

- there is a clear promise, which can be by acquiescence: ***Ramsden v Dyson*** (1866);
- there is reliance; and
- it would be inequitable not to enforce the assurance.

Promise

The promise must be unequivocal, which means that the courts must be able to identify the property over which the equity arises. In ***Yeoman's Row v Cobbe*** [2008], the House of Lords held that in a commercial agreement a promise in a 'gentleman's agreement' meant that there was no property over which the estoppel could be raised. The situation may have been different if there had been an enforceable contract. However, shortly after, in a domestic situation in ***Thorner v Major*** [2009], the House, with Lord Scott sitting in both cases, reached a different conclusion. The agreement had been vague but clear enough on which to base reliance.

Reliance

The burden is on the claimant to prove a causal link between the assurance and the act in reliance. In ***Gillett v Holt*** [2001] the claimant had worked for the defendant since he was 16. The claimant had rejected opportunities to work elsewhere and better himself on assurances by the defendant that he would leave the farm to the claimant. Over 40 years later they fell out and the defendant made a new will leaving the farm to another person. It was held that the claimant had relied on the assurances.

However, in ***Coombes v Smith*** [1986] the claimant moved into a house owned by Smith when she became pregnant by him, leaving behind an unhappy marriage. The court held that both these acts were not in reliance of any assurance by Smith but were the actions of a woman in love with a man and unhappy in her marriage. This illustrates the need for reliance but has been criticized in its narrow view of Coombes' motives.

If a promise and reliance can be proven, then evidentially the courts can find the necessary basis on which to raise a remedy in equity. Reliance can be a variety of actions and it is for the court to apply the minimum equity to do justice. Table 4.2 shows some examples where the courts have found sufficient equity.

Table 4.2 Examples of reliance

DETRIMENT OR CHANGE OF POSITION	AUTHORITY
Improvements to land	***Pascoe v Turner*** [1979]—decorating and repairs ***Matharu v Matharu*** [1994]—installing new kitchen ***Gillett v Holt*** [2001]—making substantial improvements
Working for low pay	***Wayling v Jones*** [1995]—working in cafe for partner on promise of having property left by will ***Gillett v Holt*** [2001]—working for 40 years on low wages
Personal disadvantage	***Greasley v Cooke*** [1980]—caring for the family ***Re Basham*** [1986]—not buying own property, or leaving employment to live nearby ***Gillett v Holt*** [2001]—not taking employment elsewhere

Illustrative cases

Remedies on finding an estoppel will be the 'minimum equity to do justice'. This is an unclear situation, based on the extent of reliance, how much detriment has been suffered, etc. This can range from an absolute transfer to the promisee in ***Thorner v Major*** [2009], a licence to remain on the property in ***Greasley v Cooke*** [1980], or merely financial compensation in ***Jennings v Rice*** [2002].

LOOKING FOR EXTRA MARKS?

In addressing a possible estoppel argument, a link could be made between the unconscionability argument in ***Pennington v Waine*** and the comments of the High Court in ***Curtis v Pulbrook*** and the role of unconscionability in establishing an estoppel.

In another direction it would be worth reading the judgment of Lord Scott in ***Thorner v Major***, where he felt that the remedy would be better as a remedial constructive trust. In chapter 9 the issue of constructive trusts is discussed in more detail.

Covenants to settle

A covenant is a promise contained in a deed. Because the common law sees a deed as consideration this creates a contract at common law, without the need for further consideration. If there is no 'valuable consideration', equity does not see the promise as part of a contract; equity does not recognize the deed as consideration (see Table 4.3).

Table 4.3 Examples

FACTS	EQUITY	COMMON LAW
1. Anne enters into a deed with Dell to transfer her house to him to hold on trust for their children, Luke and Katie.	This is not a specifically enforceable contract as equity does not see a contract.	The common law may award damages, but what is Dell's loss? (see ***Hadley v Baxendale*** (1854) in contract law).
2. Anne enters into a contract for £20 to transfer her house to Dell to hold on trust for their children, Luke and Katie.	This is a valid contract; as the property is unique, an order for specific performance may be awarded.	This is a valid contract; as the property is unique, an order for specific performance may be awarded.
3. Anne promises her future husband, Dell, that she will transfer money to him to hold on trust for any children they may have. They marry and have two children, Luke and Katie.	This is a valid contract; as the property is unique, an order for specific performance may be awarded.	This is not a contract as there is no consideration given for the promise.

The consequences of this are that if there is a covenant to settle property, ie I enter into a covenant with a trustee to transfer property to them to hold on trust for my family, but I fail to make the promised transfer, the remedies available will depend on the presence of consideration.

A breach of contract can be remedied by specific performance (see chapter 13), ie if the property is unique (***Falke v Gray*** (1859)). The first requirement is that there must be a valid contract. Equity will not award specific performance when it does not recognize a contract. If there is a covenant to settle which is supported by a deed alone the contract cannot be specifically performed. If there is a contract supported by consideration which equity does recognize, then equity may allow an order for specific performance and order the constitution (transfer) of the promised property. This means that until the transfer is properly constituted the property is held on constructive trust by the promisor until validly transferred.

A further confusion is that equity does recognize marriage as consideration (see ***Pullan v Koe*** [1913]).

Complications

1. In equity, not only is Anne party to the contract in situation 3, but so are Luke and Katie. As such, in addition to Dell, Luke and Katie can also force Anne to make the transfer: ***Re Cook's ST*** [1965].
2. At common law, Dell cannot claim for specific performance or damages as he has had no loss, and neither can Luke or Katie because of the doctrine of privity. If they were party to the deed they could make a claim in their own right: ***Cannon v Hartley*** [1949]. Any claim in common law will, however, be limited to the common law remedy of damages and no specific performance is available.
3. **Section 1 Contract (Rights of Third Parties) Act 1999** provides that, at the time of contracting, those intended to benefit from the contract shall have the same rights of action as those party to the contract, regardless of consideration. They cannot be in a better position than the person who entered into the contract. The problem remains that if equity would not recognize the contract, as made by deed, then it will still not recognize it under the Act.
4. Can Dell sue on behalf of Luke and Katie? There have been moves in contract law to allow such recovery (***McAlpine v Panatown*** [2001]) but this goes against general contractual principle and the doctrine of privity. The House of Lords has stated that this is no longer needed since the passing of the **Contract (Rights of Third Parties) Act 1999**.
5. At common law you cannot make a contract for property which you do not own. However, equity has based its rules on the principle that 'equity looks upon as done that which ought to be done'. When the promisor acquires the promised property, it will immediately be held on trust for the promisee: ***Re Ellenborough*** [1903].
6. It could be argued that the promise to settle the property is the subject matter of the obligation, creating a trust of the promise; ***Fletcher v Fletcher*** (1844). This has been accepted in cases such as ***Don King v Warren*** [1998] but there is a general reluctance to undermine the doctrine of privity.

Conclusion

The law requires evidential certainty in relation to the transfer of ownership. Many of the rules set out in this chapter are there to satisfy this evidential burden. The first step in addressing this issue is to establish the legal rules in relation to all property. However, sometimes the legal rules have not been complied with and this failure will cause some injustice. The application of the legal rules in this situation can be particularly harsh. The intervention of equity to remedy the harshness of the legal rules is based on clear principles and clear criteria. It is sometimes assumed by students that equity is merely to achieve some general concept of 'justice'. This is too wide a view of the aims of equity and the principles on when equity will intervene with the legal rules are relatively certain. In an answer plan, you should be able to identify the legal rules and any (there may be more than one) equitable interventions.

KEY CASES

CASE	FACTS	PRINCIPLE
Cain v Moon [1896] 2 QB 283	The daughter gave her mother a deposit note worth £50. Contradictory evidence suggested that it had been a gift for the mother's care for the daughter during an illness. But later the daughter said: 'Have you got the deposit note safe? Never part with it. The bank-note is for you if I die.'	For a valid DMC there should be three elements—a transfer: 1. in contemplation of imminent death; 2. conditional on death; 3. on delivery.
Choithram International v Pagarani [2001] 1 WLR 1	Mr Pagarani set up a trust foundation, of which he was one of the trustees. He made an oral declaration that he intended the bulk of his remaining wealth to go to the trust foundation. There was both oral and written evidence of the intention to transfer the property to the trust foundation companies. Mr Pagarani died before title was transferred to the trust foundation. He was one of the trustees of the foundation.	The Privy Council said that as Mr Pagarani intended to make an immediate unconditional gift to the foundation and was one of the trustees of the foundation, he had legal title in the property, and that although the court will not perfect an imperfect gift, neither will it 'strive officiously' to deny the intention of the transferor. The legal title in the property would be transferred to the trust foundation (see 'Key debates' in the following section).
Gillett v Holt [2001] 1 Ch 210	The claimant had worked for the defendant since he was 16. The claimant had rejected opportunities to work elsewhere and better himself on assurances from the defendant that he would leave the farm to the claimant. Over 40 years later they fell out and the defendant made a new will leaving the farm to another person.	Where there was a clear, unequivocal promise, express or by acquiescence, made by the transferor, and this was followed by reliance by the transferee, which meant it was inequitable to allow the transferor to go back on the promise, the court would carry out the minimum equity to do justice. The facts had created an estoppel for the claimant, which in proprietary estoppel can found a cause of action (ie used as a sword).

CASE	FACTS	PRINCIPLE
Jones v Lock (1865) 1 Ch App 25	A father wanted to transfer the interest in a cheque, which was made out to him, to his infant son. He had made an oral declaration to that effect but had failed to endorse the cheque.	The transfer as a gift had failed as it required endorsement and the court would not create a trust out of an imperfect gift.
Milroy v Lord (1862) 2 DE G F & J 264	An attempt was made to transfer property to be held on trust. Although the transferor had made the transfer by deed and delivered it to the respondent, the failure of the transfer to be registered in the bank's books meant that the transfer was imperfect.	Where the transfer had failed because the transferor had failed to do all he could to perfect title, the courts would not complete the transferor's actions.
Pennington v Waine [2002] 1 WLR 2075	The owner of shares wanted to transfer them to her nephew. The relevant forms were completed but not registered, being on file at her solicitors. Her nephew took on some responsibility for the running of the company, which the transfer gave him. All parties acted as if he had the shares. On her death the court was asked to perfect the transfer.	Based on principles of unconscionability, the court would perfect the transfer to the nephew (see 'Key debates' in the following section).
Re Cole [1964] Ch 175	A husband took his wife through the home and said 'Look, it is all yours'. On his bankruptcy she claimed legal ownership of the furniture.	A transfer of chattels not by deed requires a delivery of the chattel with unequivocal words of transfer to be valid
Re Fry [1946] Ch 312	The transferor wanted to transfer shares but to do this he needed permission from the Treasury. He had not obtained this.	The transferor had not done all that was required of him to make good the transfer. Equity would not perfect the transaction.
Re Gonin [1977] 2 All ER 720	A mother had promised her daughter that she would have her house. But the mother believed that she would not be able to leave the house to the daughter, as her daughter was illegitimate. She then wrote a cheque to her daughter.	The writing of the cheque was evidence that the intention did not remain unchanged until death.
Re Ralli's WT [1964] Ch 288	A testator promised to establish a trust, which he never did. On death the promisee was appointed executor.	The trust was constituted. However, this decision is doubtful as an extension to ***Strong v Bird*** [1874] as there was no failed attempt.
Re Rose [1952] 1 All ER 1217	Rose transferred shares to his wife and trustees on 30 March. To complete the transfer, it had to be registered with the company. The transfer was registered on 30 June.	Where the transferor has done all in his power to make the transfer, and the only fault is a third-party inaction, over which the transferor has no control, equity will perfect the transfer.
Richards v Delridge (1874) LR 1 HL Eq 11	A grandfather wanted his leasehold interest in land to be held for the benefit of his grandson. He assigned the lease to the boy's mother but did not make the transfer by deed as required under **s 52 Law of Property Act 1925**.	Failure to complete the necessary legal requirements will mean the transfer fails.

CASE	FACTS	PRINCIPLE
Sen v Headley [1991] 2 All ER 636	The transferor was terminally ill with cancer; he told the transferee, with whom he had had a long-term close relationship, that he wanted her to have his house, saying, 'You have the keys. They are in your bag. The deeds are in the steel box'.	Confirming that land could be the subject of a DMC, the Court of Appeal confirmed the decision in ***Cain v Moon*** [1896] that a valid DMC required transfers made: 1. in contemplation of death; 2. conditional on death; 3. with actual or some indicia of the transferor giving 'dominion' (control) of the property to the transferee (sometimes called symbolic delivery).
Strong v Bird (1874) LR 18 Eq 315	A promise to forgo the payment of a debt was unenforceable at law for want of consideration. The promisee was appointed as the executor of the will of the promisor.	Where there has been a failure of the legal requirements of a valid transfer, but the transferee is appointed as executor or administrator of the transferor's estate, equity will perfect if there has been a continuing intention to give during the transferor's lifetime.
Thorner v Major [2009] UKHL 18	A young farmer, David, worked for an elderly relative, Peter, for many years on a farm. There were several comments by Peter that David would inherit the farm. The statements were vague and imprecise. Peter was a 'man of few words' and little formal education. Peter died intestate and David claimed that the estate was estopped from denying him an interest in the farm.	Although the extent of the farm was imprecise, the property itself (the farm) was clear. Although the evidence was imprecise as to the assurance, it was clear on the first-instance evidence that David and Peter had proceeded on the understanding that David would inherit the farm. The estate was estopped from denying this. Per Lord Scott, the decision is better decided as one of remedial constructive trust rather than estoppel as the property was of a future interest under a will rather than a present property.
Yeoman's Row Management Ltd v Cobbe [2008] UKHL 55	A property owner entered into a 'gentleman's agreement' to sell property to Cobbe when he had obtained planning permission, sharing the proceeds by an agreement they would draw up legally at a later date. After expending a great deal of money on the planning application, the property owner refused to complete the agreement. Cobbe claimed that the property owner was estopped from doing this.	There was no clear property over which the estoppel could be raised. The agreement was not a valid contract, which could form the basis of an estoppel. Both were commercially experienced people who took the risks in the 'gentleman's agreement'.

KEY DEBATES

Topic	Unconscionability
Viewpoint	The decisions in ***Choithram*** and ***Pennington v Waine*** are problematic. While the decision in ***Choithram*** may be based on a valid development of equity acting on the conscience of the parties and on the particular facts justified, it is suggested that the decision in ***Pennington v Waine*** has strayed too far. There is a lack of guidance on what makes a transaction unconscionable from Arden LJ and it has left the principle of ***Re Rose*** uncertain.
Source	Pearce and Barr, *Pearce and Stevens' Trusts and Equitable Obligations*, 7th edn (2018), comments at pp 101–5 on the decision, offering a good, concise criticism.

Topic	Proprietary estoppel
Academic/author	Robertson
Viewpoint	A review of the reliance issues in finding an adequate remedy in estoppel cases.
Source	Robertson [2008] Conv 295.

EXAM QUESTIONS

Problem question

Charles says to his brother James, 'You can have my shares in DDD Ltd.' Before Charles has time to transfer title in the shares to James he dies and James has been appointed as executor of Charles's will.

Sumita has been run over by a car and is seriously ill. She has been told that she will die soon. Her friend Ellie comes to visit her and Sumita says, 'I think I am going to die, I want you to have my car. Here are the keys and registration documents'. Sumita then dies.

Advise James and Ellie on who owns the property.

Essay question

The decision in ***Pennington v Waine*** has introduced a much-needed degree of flexibility in the strict rules on transfer of legal interests. Giving effect to the intention of the settlor should be the primary concern of the courts.

Discuss.

Online resources

For an outline answer to this essay question, as well as multiple choice questions, bonus material and interactive key cases, please visit the online resources.

Concentrate Q&As

For more questions and answers on equity and trusts, see the *Concentrate Q&A: Equity & Trusts* by Rosalind Malcolm.

Go to the end of this book to view **sample pages**.

5 Formalities

KEY FACTS

- There are rules in relation to the creation of an express trust over property.
- A trust can be created *inter vivos* (during the settlor's life) or by will.
- There are different rules in relation to trusts over an interest in land and property other than land.
- It is important to remember that when creating an express trust, the settlor must satisfy the formalities required for both the transfer of the legal interest in property (chapter 4) and the creation of the trust itself.
- There are different rules for the creation of an express trust and the transfer of the legal interest in property.
- There are formalities in transferring an equitable interest in *any* property.

REVISION TIP

This is a complex area of law and commonly examined. Ensure that you understand the content of chapter 4, which deals with how the ownership of property is transferred (constitution). This chapter will deal with how a trust is created in property, and how to transfer an equitable interest.

Introduction

This chapter discusses the formalities necessary to create a testamentary trust (made by a will) and an *inter vivos* trust and the formalities regulating the transfer of an existing equitable interest. There are different formalities in relation to the *creation* of trust dependent on the type of property subject to it. The main formalities considered in this chapter are set out in **s 53 Law of Property Act 1925 (LPA),** which is discussed in detail in the section 'Creation of an *inter vivos* trust of an interest in land'. There are three types of transactions relevant to this chapter:

- trusts of property other than land, including trusts of personal property;
- trusts of land or an interest in land; and
- dispositions of an equitable interest.

The need for formalities

One of the purposes of formalities is to create certainty of transactions and prevent fraud. It needs to be clear from the outset who has the benefit of an equitable interest. The certainty created by the formalities has advantages for several parties.

For the trustee

A trustee will need to be certain who the beneficiaries are; the trustees have duties and powers in relation to the trust property. If these powers and duties are performed incorrectly, the trustee may be held personally liable for any breaches.

For the beneficiary

Additionally, the beneficiary must be certain as to his or her actual interest in property. This will prevent fraud by the trustee. The clearer the allocation of property rights the easier for the trustee, the beneficiary, and ultimately the court to allocate the correct interest to the parties.

For the courts

In certain circumstances, the courts may need to intervene with the trust, such as in its variation or exercise of powers. The court will need to ensure it acts correctly in relation to competing interests.

For Revenue & Customs

A further purpose of the formalities is to be clear who has the benefit of property for the purposes of tax. The trustee will hold the legal title and would appear to be the person who should pay tax on any income the trust produces. Revenue & Customs will seek to recover tax due, which is why so many cases involve the HM Revenue & Customs Commission (HMRC, formerly the IRC).

Testamentary trusts

Many trusts are created by will. A requirement of all wills is that they must comply with the requirements of the **Wills Act 1837** to be valid. **Section 9** states that the trust must be:

- in writing;
- signed by the testator, or someone acting at the testator's direction in his or her presence; and
- in the presence of two witnesses who sign and attest the will in the testator's presence.

The reasons for these requirements are evidential and to prevent fraud or coercion. All testamentary documents must comply, as must any amendments made by **codicil**. These requirements will satisfy any need for the evidence of transfer of equitable interests or the creation of trusts. The main purpose of **s 53(1)(b) LPA** is evidential and the **Wills Act 1837** requirements satisfy this.

Creation of an *inter vivos* trust in property other than land

The creation of trusts of an interest in property other than land requires no formalities, other than the three certainties (see chapter 3). This will apply to such property as shares, money, paintings, etc. The most important thing that must be established is the certainty of intention to create a trust. Remember that this is a question of fact which must be established on a case-by-case basis. The certainty of intention can be demonstrated by words, written statements, or conduct: ***Paul v Constance*** [1977]. In establishing certainty of intention, the court will take the whole situation into account.

However, where the courts fail to find the sufficient certainty required for trusts (see chapter 3) they will not impose a trust to achieve justice: ***Jones v Locke*** (1865). This is a clear example of the maxims that 'equity will not perfect an imperfect gift' and 'equity will not assist a volunteer'.

Remember that creating a trust is a 'cruel kindness' as it creates such onerous obligations for the trustee. The courts are happy to create a trust on informal statements, but these must be clear that this is the true intention of the settlor.

Creation of an *inter vivos* trust of an interest in land

An express trust of an interest in land can be declared orally or in writing, but until it is in writing it is unenforceable. The statutory requirements for creating such a trust in land or interest in land are set out in **s 53(1)(b) LPA**:

> A declaration of trusts respecting land, or any interest therein must be **manifested** and proved by some writing signed by some person who is able to declare such trust or by his will.

So, two formalities must be satisfied (see ***Ong v Ping*** [2017]):

- there must be evidence of the trust in writing; and
- the evidence must have been signed by the settlor.

Interests affected

This rule applies to freehold, leasehold, and equitable interests in land (see the section 'Dealing with existing equitable interests').

Note: **s 53(1)(b) LPA** deals only with the *creation* of a trust over an interest in land. It does *not* deal with the transfer of legal title in land, nor does it deal with the creation of a trust in anything but an interest in land.

Evidenced in writing

While a valid trust will come into existence from the moment it is declared, until the requirements of **s 53(1)(b) LPA** are satisfied the trust will not be enforceable. It is valid at the *moment* it is declared with sufficient certainty, which can have important tax implications for the settlor and the beneficial claimant. It also means that should the trustee exercise his or her powers under the trust he or she will not be in breach. Although the trust is valid, it is unenforceable; the beneficiary cannot enforce the trust, for example by using his or her powers to vary a trust. In this situation there is a gap between validity and enforceability. The evidence, when it is written, must contain all the relevant terms of the trust, that is, the three certainties.

The writing required by **s 53(1)(b) LPA** does *not* need to be in the form of a *deed*. Written evidence signed by the settlor will suffice. This can be a letter or other informal document. Written and signed evidence of the trust can be provided at a later date: ***Gardener v Rowe*** (1828).

Signed by the settlor

Unlike **s 53(1)(c) LPA** (see the section 'Direct trustee to hold the beneficial interest for another'), the written evidence must be signed by the settlor; it cannot be signed by an agent. This is a matter of construction of **s 53(1)(b) LPA** read with **s 53(1)(c) LPA**, which specifically states that an agent can sign the written evidence, whereas **s 53(1)(b) LPA** states that this must be a person 'who is able to declare such a trust or by his will'.

LOOKING FOR EXTRA MARKS?

Examiners may have the intention to create a trust communicated by email or perhaps text. This is to stimulate a discussion on the need to have the declaration signed. There is no need to conclude on this but make a reasonable argument *if* it would satisfy the requirement. Perhaps compare with the principle of e-conveyancing in land.

REVISION TIP

In dealing with an exam question in this area remember to keep the legal transactions, explained in chapter 4, separate from the equitable formalities. Figure 5.1 may help your understanding of this.

Figure 5.1 Creating a trust in land with another as trustee (see Figure 4.1 (2))

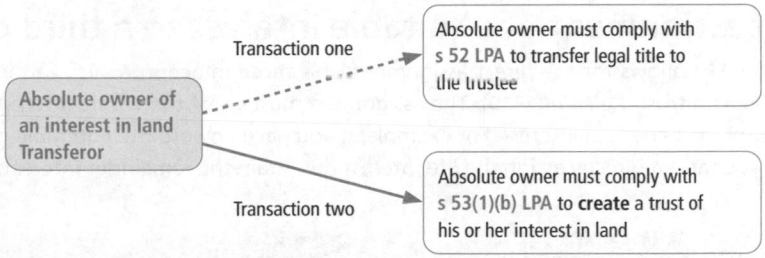

However, where a settlor declares him or herself trustee of an interest in land for a beneficiary, remember that the settlor will only have to declare the trust of land and complete the required formalities of **s 53(1)(b) LPA** as the settlor as trustee already has legal title to the land (see chapter 4 Figure 4.1 (3) on constitution to remind yourself of these issues).

Avoiding the formalities of s 53(1)(b) LPA

Formalities play an important role in tracking the correct ownership of property. For that reason, the courts are extremely reluctant to allow the required formalities to be avoided. However, the case of ***Rochefoucauld v Boustead*** [1897] provides an exception to the rule that writing formalities must be completed. If the settlor has transferred legal title to a trustee effectively, intending that it be held on trust, but has failed to evidence this in writing, the courts will usually not consider the trust to be enforceable.

If the result of this would be to allow the relevant statute to be used as an instrument of fraud, the court may accept oral evidence as proof of the transaction. 'Equity will not permit a statute to be used as an instrument of fraud' and it is commonly thought that an unenforceable trust is given validity by means of a constructive trust, imposed against the conscience of the person trying to misuse the relevant statutory provisions for their own fraudulent ends.

Dealing with existing equitable interests

The first point to remember is that an equitable property interest is property in the same way as land is. It is intangible, forming a **chose in action**, but nevertheless capable of being treated in the same manner as all property. It can be mortgaged, sold, and transferred. If you bear this in mind, you will be able to grasp this topic more easily.

Timpson's Executors v Yerbury [1936] identified four ways to benefit another person with a beneficial interest:

1. directly assign to a third party;
2. contract for valuable consideration to assign to another;
3. direct the trustees to hold for another;
4. declare that the interest is held by the beneficial owner on trust for another.

Direct assignment of equitable interest to a third party

Section 136 LPA allows for the direct assignment of a chose in action, which can include an interest under a trust: ***Re Pain*** [1919]. The assignment must be of the whole interest and not just a part of the beneficial interest. For example, if you have an absolute equitable interest in property you cannot directly assign the life interest but retain the **remainder interest**.

LOOKING FOR EXTRA MARKS?

The application of **s 136 LPA** to an interest under a trust has been doubted. See Snell's *Principles of Equity*, 32nd edn (2011). In developing an argument on this issue, read what is said on this matter. The formalities for a direct assignment are:

- the assignment must be in writing;
- it should be signed by the assignor; and
- express notice should be given to the trustee of the assignment.

If the formalities are not complied with, there may still be an assignment in equity which needs no particular formalities: ***William Brandt's Sons & Co v Dunlop Rubber Co*** [1905]. An assignment in equity requires:

- a clear intention to assign, manifested by words or conduct;
- a clear transfer of the interest from the assignor to the assignee; and

in addition, the interest transferred must be clearly identifiable.

There is no need to notify the trustee of the transfer. However, if notice is given to the trustee the assignee is protected from third-party claims and fraudulent receipt by the assignor: ***Kekewich v Manning*** (1851).

Contract for valuable consideration to assign to another

Where there has been a valid contract to **assign** an equitable interest, the contract may be capable of specific performance (see chapter 13 on equitable remedies). For such a transfer there must be a valid contract; note that, in equity, marriage will be valid consideration: ***Pullan v Koe*** (1913). Then it may be possible that such a disposition need not be in writing. The argument is based upon the application of **s 53(2) LPA**, which states that implied trusts do not need to comply with the requirements of **s 53(1) LPA**.

Implied trusts are considered in detail in chapter 9. One type of implied trust is a constructive trust. This is a trust that is 'constructed' around property when the courts believe that it would be unconscionable to deny an interest in property to a person who does not have legal title. In a contract, which is specifically enforceable—note that *not all* contracts are specifically enforceable—the parties' consciences are affected by the contract. 'Equity looks upon as done that which ought to be done' and the courts may force perfection of title.

LOOKING FOR EXTRA MARKS?

In ***Oughtred v IRC*** [1960], Upjohn J at first instance and Lord Radcliffe in the House of Lords considered that the benefit of the contract—a chose in action—was held by the legal owner on constructive trust for the benefit of the person who had provided valuable consideration. The Court of Appeal in ***Neville v Wilson*** [1997] endorsed this view. This is an area of academic debate as the House of Lords majority should be binding on the lower courts.

Direct trustee to hold the beneficial interest for another

The beneficial owner of property may direct the trustee to hold that beneficial interest for another person. The legal requirements to transfer a beneficial interest to another are set out in **s 53(1)(c) LPA**:

> a **disposition** of an equitable interest or trust subsisting at the time of the disposition must be in writing signed by the person disposing of the same or by his agent thereunto lawfully authorised in writing or by will.

This applies to *any* type of property held beneficially, *not* just interests in land.

LOOKING FOR EXTRA MARKS?

The definition of equitable interests within **LPA (s 205(1)(x))** defines these as in relation to existing 'in or over land' but this is not the result of its application in ***Grey v IRC***.

- The wording of the section refers to **subsisting** equitable interests at the time of the disposition. This means that it applies *not* to the creation of a trust but where one is in existence (subsisting) and a person wants to transfer that benefit to another.

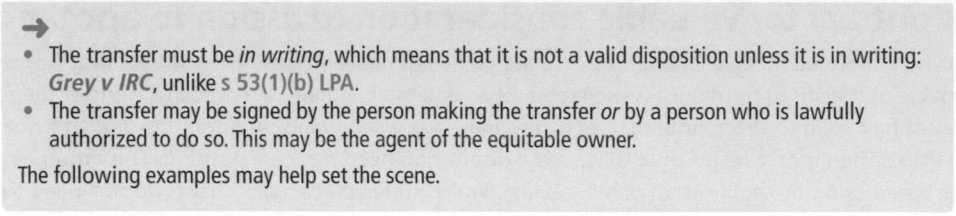

- The transfer must be *in writing*, which means that it is not a valid disposition unless it is in writing: ***Grey v IRC***, unlike **s 53(1)(b) LPA**.
- The transfer may be signed by the person making the transfer *or* by a person who is lawfully authorized to do so. This may be the agent of the equitable owner.

The following examples may help set the scene.

EXAMPLE 1

Johan declares that he will hold his shares in DDD Ltd on trust for his nephew Hendrick.

- There is no need to comply with **s 53(1)(c) LPA** as this is an original declaration of trust (see Figure 5.2).

Figure 5.2 Self-declaration of a trust

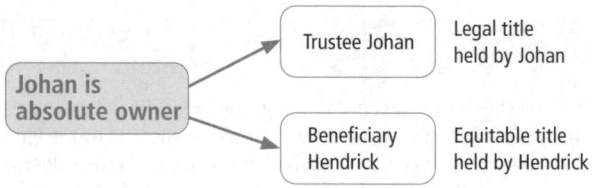

EXAMPLE 2

Hendrick, who now owns the beneficial interest in the shares, asks his trustee, Johan, to hold his beneficial interest in DDD Ltd for the benefit of his wife, Precious. He later writes a memorandum to confirm the transfer (see Figure 5.3).

- Hendrick must comply with **s 53(1)(c) LPA** as he only holds the beneficial interest, which is subsisting at the time he intends to give the interest away (a disposition) to Precious. The legal title remains with the trustee.
- The transfer is void until it is actually in writing. A claim that the writing is evidence of a previous oral disposition is invalid. As the transfer is void ab initio, you cannot have written evidence of a non-existent transfer. The transfer is said to be void for want of writing: ***Grey v IRC*** [1960].

Figure 5.3 Disposing of an existing equitable interest

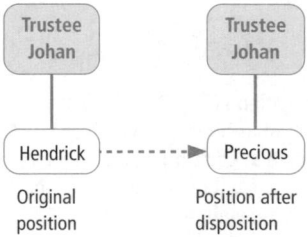

The *Vandervell* exception to s 53(1)(c) LPA

The requirements of **s 53(1)(c) LPA** are to ensure that the ownership of beneficial interest can be clearly identified by the trustee, beneficiary, the courts, and the Inland Revenue (now HMRC): ***Grey v IRC*** [1960]. Before going on to see how the ***Vandervell v IRC (No 1)*** [1967] exception operates, it is important to remember the following principle. A beneficiary who is absolutely entitled and competent can ask that the legal title to the trust property be transferred to him or her so that the beneficiary becomes the absolute owner; this is the rule from ***Saunders v Vautier*** (1841).

Figure 5.4 shows how the sequence of events would occur.

Figure 5.4 How the sequence of events may occur

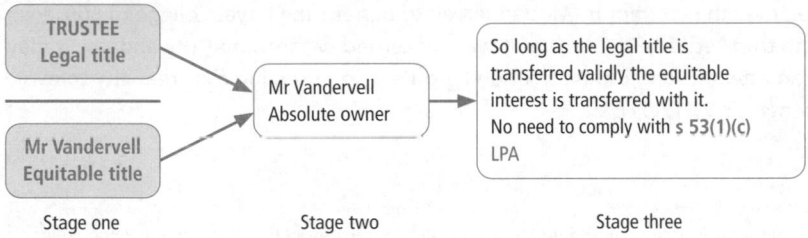

Once the title is held absolutely, at Stage two, the owner only has to comply with the legal requirements to transfer the legal title. Understanding this will make the principle in ***Vandervell v IRC (No 1)*** easier to understand.

Where a beneficial owner who is *absolutely* entitled and *competent* (*sui juris*) makes an *oral declaration* to the trustee that the trustee transfers *the legal title to a third party, intending that at the same time the beneficial title shall transfer to the same third party*, there is no need to comply with **s 53(1)(c) LPA**.

Looking at Figure 5.5 you can see that it simply removes the ***Saunders v Vautier*** (1841) step and can be justified on that basis.

Figure 5.5 The *Vandervell* exception

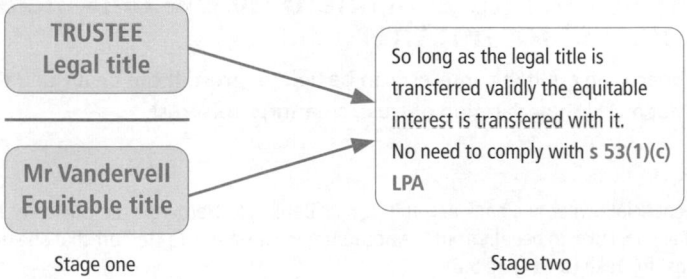

REVISION TIP

Examiners often use words that are ambiguous, such as 'give', 'transfer', 'convey'. This is because they want students to consider whether ***Vandervell*** applies.

Formalities are required to protect the trustee from any claim for breach of duty. This exception can be justified as the trustee, in transferring the legal title to another person, has no further obligations to the beneficiary.

Vandervell v IRC (No 2) [1974]

This case is complex and has been subject to academic criticism. There had been protracted litigation over the attempt by Mr Vandervell to benefit the Royal College of Surgeons and his children's trust settlement. Much of it was concerned with Stamp Duty and tax. It may appear that in an attempt to end this litigation Lord Denning used judicial creativity to avoid the requirements of **s 53(1)(c) LPA**.

VANDERVELL V IRC (NO 2) **[1974] CH 269**

On the advice of his accountant, when Mr Vandervell had transferred the shares to the Royal College of Surgeons an option to repurchase was granted to a trust company. At the time, Mr Vandervell had failed to specify the objects of the trust and therefore it was held on resulting trust for him.

The option was then exercised and declared to be held for the benefit of the children's settlement.

The Court of Appeal held that when the option was exercised the resulting trust of that property ceased to exist. Therefore, the property now held for the children was a new trust which required no formalities.

The Court of Appeal made a distinction between the option as one form of property which, when exercised, had ceased to exist. So, when the benefit created by exercising the option was declared to be held on trust for the children this was a completely *new* trust. It was not a 'disposition of a *subsisting* equitable interest'. It was in fact a declaration of trust in shares and required no formalities.

Declare that the interest is held by the beneficial owner on trust for another

As with all property, an equitable interest can be held on trust. It can be argued that this is not a disposition but merely a declaration of trust, creating a sub-trust.

EXAMPLE 3

Anne is the beneficial owner of a bank account at Bigs Banks plc. Herbert is the trustee of the account. Anne wants her son, Luke, to benefit from the account and she states to Herbert that she now holds the interest on trust for Luke (see Figure 5.6).

Figure 5.6 Declaring a sub-trust

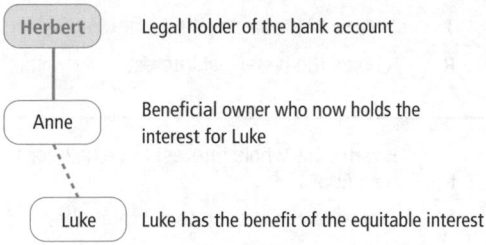

It is a question of whether the beneficial owner who declares a sub-trust is 'dispossessing' him or herself of an equitable interest. One argument is that the beneficial owner is not doing so as he or she is merely holding the interest on trust.

EXAMPLE 4A

Rishi is the beneficial owner under a bare trust of a house called 'Gills Farm' (see Figure 5.7).

Figure 5.7 Basic trust

T — Trustee holds the legal title for benefit of R

- - - -

R — R holds the beneficial interest

This is the starting position, with the trustee holding for Rishi. He wants to give this interest to his son, John. He writes to John telling him of his intention (see Figure 5.8).

Figure 5.8 Transfer of existing equitable interest

T — Trustee holds the legal title for benefit of J

- - - -

J — J now holds the beneficial interest

This would be the classic situation where Rishi is giving away (dispossessing himself of) his equitable interest and as such he must comply with **s 53(1)(c) LPA**. This is the normal trust position with which students are familiar but there are also situations where the beneficiary does not intend that the beneficial interest should be given to another but intends to hold this interest for the benefit of another person.

EXAMPLE 4B

Rishi is the beneficial owner under a bare trust of a house called 'Gills Farm'. He wants to hold this interest on trust for his son, John.

In this situation (see Figure 5.9) it appears that Rishi has not dispossessed himself of his interest; he has merely decided to hold this property on trust for another person. In this situation there is a

Figure 5.9 Declaring a sub-trust

Head Trust	T	Trustee holds the legal title for benefit of R
	R	R holds the beneficial interest

Sub-trust	R	R wants his whole interest to be held for the benefit of J
	J	J receives the exact interest that R had

sub-trust created. On a literal reading of the statute, as there is no 'disposition' then there should be no requirement that Rishi comply with **s 53(1)(c) LPA**. However, this seems contrary to the intention of the statute, which is to prevent fraud and allow the trustee to know to whom he or she owes an obligation. In fact, it appears that in creating the sub-trust Rishi *effectively* disposes of his interest as he can no longer exert any real control over the trust property other than to hold it for John in exactly the same way as the trustee held it for him. In fact, it is John who has the power to decide how the property should be treated.

Implications

If the property produces an income, then the trustee would have paid this money to the benefit of Rishi. Now the trustee would be required to pay the money to the benefit of John. He may do this by paying it to Rishi who then pays it to John, but this is merely a procedural step; it is John who is the real beneficiary of the trust (see Figure 5.10).

Figure 5.10 Possible implication

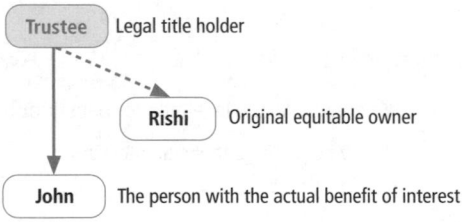

This situation illustrates the reason that formalities are required: if the trustee pays the money to Rishi when in reality the benefit belongs to John then the trustee may be in breach, risking the possibility that the trustee may be personally liable for any losses. Remember, one of the purposes of formalities is to enable the trustee to be sure to whom he or she owes a duty.

However, an alternative argument is that there is no need to comply with **s 53(1)(c) LPA** when the beneficial owner retains some control of the beneficial interest, such as declaring a discretionary trust of the beneficial interest. The reasoning by Chitty J in ***Grainge v Wilberforce*** (1889) and comments by Upjohn LJ in ***Grey v IRC*** [1958] would suggest that there is no need to comply with **s 53(1)(c)** as this is not a disposition of an equitable interest.

The distinction between these two situations was rejected by the Court of Appeal in ***Nelson v Greening & Sykes (Builders) Ltd*** [2007], where the difference between the effect in practice and the effect in law was made. So, it would seem that declarations of sub-trust are not dispositions of a beneficial interest within the meaning of **s 53(1)(c) LPA**.

LOOKING FOR EXTRA MARKS?

When dealing with a sub-trust it is important to identify what property is being held on trust because if the equitable interest is in land then, as it is the creation of a new (sub-)trust in land or an interest in land, it must also comply with the requirements of **s 53(1)(b) LPA**.

Conclusion

This chapter has considered the formalities which are required to create a trust in property—any property—including an equitable interest. Additionally, there are formalities for the transfer of beneficial interests. The purposes of these formalities are evidential. The requirements of a trust in land or an interest in land are particularly stringent, which reflects the importance the law places on land transactions. This chapter should be read with chapter 4 on constitution. Also, in relation to a trust of personalty, remember that there is a close link with the requirements of certainty of intention. Chapters 3, 4, and 5 must be read and understood in relation to each other (see Table 5.1).

Table 5.1 Summary of constitution and formalities

THREE WAYS TO BENEFIT ANOTHER		
Gift	Legal title to be transferred (constitution) Identify the legal rules for the relevant property	Equity may perfect this transfer by: • every effort principle • rule in ***Strong v Bird*** (1874) • *donatio mortis causa* • unconscionability/estoppel
	Equitable interest to be transferred **Section 53(1)(c) LPA** required with a direct assignment, contract, or gift	***Re Vandervell (No 1)*** [1967] may provide an exception Declare a sub-trust Constructive trust of a specifically enforceable contract
Declare self a trustee	Personalty—requires the three certainties Land requires the three certainties and fulfilment of **s 53(1)(b) LPA 25 ('The formalities')**	This may be remedied by ***Rochefoucauld v Boustead*** [1897]
Declare another person as trustee of your property	Must satisfy the constitution requirements and formalities	Covenants to settle

KEY CASES

CASE	FACTS	PRINCIPLE
Grey v IRC [1960] AC 1 HL	The transferor wanted to transfer the beneficial interest without attracting Stamp Duty. He made an oral declaration that the beneficial interest was to be held for his grandchildren. He claimed that the documents which stated this merely confirmed the transfer, which he made orally.	An attempt to make an oral disposition of a subsisting equitable interest is void for want of writing.
Jones v Locke (1865) LR 1 Ch App 25	A man returned home from a trip and, being chastised by his wife for bringing no gift for their new son, took a cheque from his pocket. The cheque was made out to the father and he said, 'Look here it is all for baby'. The father died before he could transfer legal title to the baby.	That this was not a valid declaration of trust as there was insufficient certainty of intention. Equity will not create a valid trust out of an imperfect gift.
Oughtred v IRC [1960] AC 206 HL	Mrs Oughtred had the life interest in shares, then to her son P. She was also the absolute beneficiary of shares. To avoid death duties P and Mrs Oughtred agreed to exchange their interests. This was later evidenced in writing.	The House of Lords by a three to two majority did not uphold this argument. Viscount Radcliffe for the minority held that the exchange happened orally, and there was no need for any written evidence. The interest was held on constructive trust and, under **s 53(2) LPA**, it was outside the scope of **s 53(1)**. The minority view has, however, found favour in the Court of Appeal in such cases as ***Neville v Wilson*** [1996].
Rochefoucauld v Boustead [1897] 1 Ch 196	The Comtesse de la Rochefoucauld owned land in Ceylon which she transferred to the defendant intending that he hold it on trust for her benefit. This intention was not evidenced in writing. He mortgaged the land and she sought a declaration that he held it on trust for her.	The Court of Appeal held that evidence other than writing could be admitted otherwise the instrument (at that time the **Statute of Frauds**) could be used as an instrument of fraud.
Vandervell v IRC [1967] 1 All ER 1	Mr Vandervell was the beneficiary under a bare trust of shares. He wanted to endow the Royal College of Surgeons with the shares. He directed that the shares be transferred to the Royal College of Surgeons. At the same time an option to purchase the shares was granted to a trust company. At the point of creation, the objects of the trust of the option were unspecified.	Where an equitable owner, absolutely entitled and capable of doing so, makes an oral declaration to the trustee to transfer legal title to a transferee, intending at the same time that the equitable title be transferred to the same transferee, there is no need to comply with **s 53(1)(c) LPA**.
		Failure to specify the objects of the trust of the option meant that the trust company held on resulting trust for Mr Vandervell.

CASE	FACTS	PRINCIPLE
Vandervell v IRC (No 2) [1974] 3 All ER 205	The option was held for Mr Vandervell on resulting trust. It was exercised in 1961 in favour of his children's settlement. Between 1961 and 1965 dividends were declared for the benefit of the children's trust. At Mr Vandervell's death in 1967 his executors claimed that the dividends should have been held on resulting trust for him and should not have been paid to the children's settlement.	The exercise of the option had ended the resulting trust of the option and a new trust had been created of the shares for the benefit of the children. A creation of a trust of shares required no formalities. Per Denning MR and Lawton LJ, in any event Mr Vandervell would have been estopped from denying the children's claim to the benefit because (i) their money had been used to exercise the option; (ii) Mr Vandervell had approved the paying of the dividends to the settlement.

KEY DEBATES

Topic	The decision in *Rochefoucauld v Boustead* [1897]
Academic/author	Pearce and Barr
Viewpoint	The authors refer to several views. The rule allows other evidence to be used despite the clear words of the statute. Would this still be valid in light of the updating of the principle in the **Law of Property Act in 1925**? Is it better to see this as a constructive trust rather than an exception to the principle of **s 53(1)(b)**?
Source	Pearce and Barr, *Pearce and Stevens' Trusts and Equitable Obligations*, 7th edn (2018), pp 123–4.

Topic	The decision in *Rochefoucauld v Boustead* [1897] The constructive trust created around a valid contract to assign a beneficial interest
Academic/author	Pearce and Barr
Viewpoint	The authors refer to several views. The majority of the House of Lords felt that a constructive trust did not arise, and the transaction was within **s 53(1)(c)** but only by three to two. A strong minority was followed by the Court of Appeal in ***Neville v Wilson*** [1997]. What should the court do in these situations?
Source	Pearce and Barr, *Pearce and Stevens' Trusts and Equitable Obligations*, 7th edn (2018), pp 130–3.

EXAM QUESTIONS

Problem question

Kirsty wins the lottery and feels very generous. On 1 March, Kirsty calls George to tell him that she intends to hold her leasehold over Blackacre on trust for him.

On 31 March, Kirsty writes to her friend, Hari. In the letter, Kirsty explains what she has done with Blackacre. The letter is signed.

She then writes to Sanjeev asking him to be the trustee of her freehold cottage, Whiteflower, for the benefit of her friend, Hester.

Kirsty is the absolute beneficial owner of shares in Telico Ltd She calls her trustee Jose and tells him to transfer the shares to Charlie.

Advise the parties as to the ownership of the property.

Essay question

The confusion created by the decision in ***Neville v Wilson*** [1997] is contrary to the clear requirements of **s 53(1) Law of Property Act**.

Discuss.

Online resources

For multiple choice questions and interactive key cases, as well as outline answers to this essay question, please visit the online resources.

Concentrate Q&As

For more questions and answers on equity and trusts, see the *Concentrate Q&A: Equity & Trusts* by Rosalind Malcolm.

Go to the end of this book to view **sample pages**.

Charitable trusts

6

KEY FACTS

- Charitable trusts differ from private trusts in a number of ways.
- A charitable trust must be:
  1. for a recognized charitable purpose;
  2. for the 'public benefit'; and
  3. for exclusively charitable purposes.
- The public benefit requirement raises different issues under each head of charity.
- The **Charities Act 2006** reformed the law in this area.
- Legislation related to charities and their regulation was consolidated by the **Charities Act 2011**.
- *Cy-près* is a power which allows failing charitable trusts to be applied to other related charities.

How is a charitable trust different from other types of trust?

The beneficiaries of the trust

In a private express trust, the beneficiaries hold the equitable interest in the property and can enforce the terms of the trusts against the trustees. Whereas a private trust will benefit certain *individuals*, a charitable trust is said to benefit the *public*, or some part of it. This is significant for two reasons:

- *Enforcement of the trust*: as there are no specific named beneficiaries in a charitable trust, who can enforce the terms of the trust? In general, if there is no one to enforce a trust, it will be void (see chapter 7). However, in the case of charitable trusts, this role is ultimately performed by the **Attorney-General**.
- *Certainty of objects*: generally, all trusts must satisfy the three certainties (see chapter 3). However, charitable trusts are exempt from the certainty of objects requirement: ***Morice v Bishop of*** Durham **(1805)**.

The advantages of charitable status

The work of charities is highly valued in our society and, as a result, charitable trusts are accorded a number of advantages:

- *Tax advantages*: charitable trusts are exempt from a number of taxes, including income tax, corporation tax, and capital gains tax. This enables charities to retain more of their assets.
- *The rule against perpetuities*: in contrast to other trusts, property can be dedicated indefinitely to a charitable purpose (contrast this with the rule against inalienability in relation to private purpose trusts in chapter 7). By allowing charitable trusts to exist indefinitely, they can develop greater expertise and resources.

The role of the Charity Commission

The legal rules in relation to charitable trusts have been developed over the years primarily through the courts. However, our understanding of what is 'charitable' is constantly evolving and the courts are ill-suited to keep pace with these changes. For many years, therefore, charitable trusts have been regulated by the **Charity Commission**.

The Charity Commission does not create new legal rules: its decisions remain subject to the final say of the courts. However, the role of the Commission has become increasingly significant:

- The Commission has over time recognized 'new' purposes which it considers analogous to existing legal principles. Many of these were given statutory recognition by the **Charities Act (CA) 2011**, for example the advancement of amateur sport.
- The Commission has a duty to provide guidance on the meaning of the public benefit requirement for charitable trusts (**s 17 CA 2011**) and trustees 'must have regard' to that advice (**s 17(5)**), meaning that the Commission's view of the law has taken on an increased importance. (See, eg, the challenge to the Charity Commission guidance on the public benefit requirement for private schools in ***Independent Schools Council and others v Charity Commission for England and Wales*** [2011].)
- The Commission has a number of objectives, including to ensure public confidence in, and the accountability of, the charitable sector (**s 14 CA 2011**). While the Commission has regulatory powers to instigate inquiries into the activities of charities (**s 46**) and powers to both suspend (**s 76**) and remove trustees (**s 79**), there has been ongoing criticism of its effectiveness. See, for example, the report by the National Audit Office, *The Regulatory Effectiveness of the Charity Commission* (2013).

REVISION TIP

Problems with the charitable sector are increasingly in the news (eg KidsCompany, Oxfam, and the WWF). You can use the Charity Commission website (http://www.gov.uk/government/organisations/charity-commission) to better understand the legal issues behind current events and bring a contemporary context to your understanding of this area.

What are the legal requirements of a valid charitable trust?

Figure 6.1 The requirements of a valid charitable trust

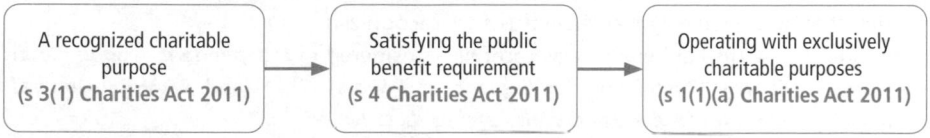

What are the recognized charitable purposes?

All charitable trusts must be for a recognized charitable purpose (see Figure 6.1). Charitable purposes were first defined in the Preamble to the **Statute of Charitable Uses 1601**. While this Act has long since been repealed, the Preamble was for many years retained as a foundation from which the definition of charitable purposes could be extended.

The Pemsel heads of charity

In ***Commissioners for Special Purposes of Income Tax v Pemsel*** [1891], four general heads of charity were identified: (i) the relief of poverty; (ii) the advancement of education; (iii) the advancement of religion; and (iv) other purposes beneficial to the community. The fourth category was designed to include analogous charitable purposes which did not fit easily into the other headings, for example:

SCOTTISH BURIAL REFORM AND CREMATION SOCIETY LTD V GLASGOW CORPN **[1968] AC 138**
A trust supporting the maintenance of crematoria was upheld as charitable under the fourth heading because the maintenance of crematoria was analogous to the 'repair of churches', which is expressly mentioned in the **1601 Preamble**.

Section 3 of the Charities Act 2011

The **Charities Act 2006** updated the ***Pemsel*** categories to reflect both advances in the law and current Charity Commission practice.

Legislation relating to charities and their administration was consolidated by the **Charities Act 2011** and the new heads of charity can now be found in **s 3 Charities Act 2011**. **Section 3(1)(a)–(c) CA 2011** preserve the first three ***Pemsel*** categories. The remaining categories **(d)–(m)** mainly comprise purposes previously recognized as 'other purposes beneficial to the community' and analogous purposes recognized over the years by the Charity Commission. These heads are discussed in detail in the following sections.

Note: all statutory references in this chapter are to the **Charities Act 2011**, unless specified otherwise.

The trust must be for the public benefit

The general rule is that the charitable trust must be of benefit to the public or to some section of the public: ***Re Scarisbrick*** [1951]. The public benefit requirement plays an important role in ensuring that only genuinely charitable trusts are recognized.

The public benefit requirement was carefully considered in ***Independent Schools Council and others v Charity Commission for England and Wales*** [2011] and ***Attorney-General v Charity Commission for England and Wales and others*** [2012]:

- Public benefit must be understood in two senses:
  - public benefit in the first sense: the *nature* of the purpose addressed by the charity must be a benefit to the community;
  - public benefit in the second sense: those to benefit from the charity's work must be sufficiently numerous to constitute a section of the public rather than a private class of individuals.

As an aspect of this understanding of public benefit, any institution which entirely excludes the poor from its activities will not be of public benefit in the second sense. For example, a cancer hospice for millionaires may be of public benefit in the first sense as it helps care for the ill, but it will not satisfy the public benefit requirement in its second sense as it excludes the poor from its activities.

- What constitutes public benefit will vary for each charitable purpose and will depend on the context of each case.

This point is important as it relates to changes to the public benefit requirement brought about by the **Charities Act 2011**. Prior to this reform, it was said that charities for the relief of poverty, advancement of education, and advancement of religion (the first three heads of charity identified in ***Pemsel*** [1891]) were 'presumed' to be of public benefit. However, **s 4(2) CA 2011** removes this presumption with the effect that all purposes must be capable of demonstrating that they are of public benefit.

LOOKING FOR EXTRA MARKS?

The effect of the **Charities Act 2011** on the public benefit requirement has been hotly debated, making it an interesting topic for analysis and critique. The judgments in ***Independent Schools Council and others v Charity Commission for England and Wales*** [2011] and ***Attorney-General v Charity Commission for England and Wales and others*** [2012] are lengthy but thorough in their analysis of the public benefit requirement, and there is much to be gained from reading these cases in full.

The trust must have exclusively charitable purposes

If a trust is to benefit from the advantages of charitable status, it must operate for exclusively charitable purposes.

The construction of the gift

The wording must make it clear that a gift or trust is made for charitable purposes (see Table 6.1).

Table 6.1 Examples of wording indicating that a trust is or is not for exclusively charitable purposes

CASE	WORDING	EXCLUSIVELY CHARITABLE?
Re Atkinson's Will Trust [1978]	A gift to 'worthy causes'	No: 'worthy causes' could not be said to be limited to exclusively charitable purposes
Re Best [1904]	A gift for 'charitable *and* benevolent' purposes	Yes: the word 'and' allows the court to interpret the second word as being included within the meaning of 'charitable'
Re Macduff [1896]	A gift for 'charitable *or* other' purposes	No: the use of 'or' implies that the other purposes will be something *other than* charitable

Ancillary non-charitable purposes

Section 1(1)(a) Charities Act 2011 defines a 'charity' as one which 'is established for charitable purposes *only*' (emphasis added). However, it will not be fatal if the trust also carries out *incidental* non-charitable purposes. Whether a non-charitable purpose is ancillary to the main purpose of the trust is a question of fact and a matter of degree, depending on the circumstances of each case: ***Attorney-General v Ross*** [1986]. A non-charitable purpose which is linked to the overall charitable aims of a trust will be more likely to be acceptable: ***Re Coxen*** [1948]. However, the more resources or time a charitable trust spends on non-charitable purposes, the less likely it will be held to be merely ancillary.

REVISION TIP

Examiners often include this issue in problem questions as it is a good way to test whether students are paying attention to the facts of the question. Remember to think about all three requirements when answering a question on charitable trusts.

The heads of charity under the Charities Act 2011

This section considers how the basic principles discussed earlier have been applied under the different heads of charity.

Section 3(1)(a): charities for the relief or prevention of poverty

Defining 'poverty'

Poverty is defined relatively and has a wider meaning than destitution—it includes those who might be said to 'go short': ***Re Coulthurst*** [1951]. It is important to analyse each situation carefully to determine whether the trust is truly aimed at the relief of poverty. Compare the following cases.

RE SANDERS **[1954] CH 265**

A gift to provide housing for the 'working classes' of Pembroke Dock was held not to be for the relief of poverty. Although the 'working classes' may have relatively low incomes, this did not mean that they could not afford housing. The use of the phrase 'working classes' did not sufficiently restrict the gift to a class of the poor.

RE NIYAZI'S WILL TRUSTS **[1973] 3 ALL ER 785**

A gift to build a working men's hostel in Cyprus was upheld as a trust for the relief of poverty. This case is different from ***Re Sanders*** because it involved building a hostel. The court believed that such temporary accommodation would only be used by those whose income meant that they could not afford more permanent housing, thus sufficiently restricting the gift to poor working men.

The prevention of poverty

Section 3(1)(a) Charities Act 2011 expanded the ***Pemsel*** definition to include the '*prevention* and relief of poverty'. This addition would include, for example, charities providing financial or debt management advice.

The public benefit requirement

The public benefit requirement for such charities is more relaxed than for the other heads. This is because of the value the courts have traditionally attached to the relief of poverty.

This viewpoint is confirmed in the following case:

ATTORNEY-GENERAL V CHARITY COMMISSION FOR ENGLAND AND WALES AND OTHERS **[2012] WTLR 977**

The Attorney-General asked the Upper Tribunal to provide guidance on whether the **Charities Act 2006** had impacted upon the public benefit requirement for charities which seek to relieve the poverty of a narrow class of potential objects, such as relatives or those employed by the same employer. The Upper Tribunal confirmed that the existing generous approach to public benefit in respect of this head of charity was correct. Such charities *need only satisfy the requirement of public benefit in its first sense*, ie that the purpose pursued by the organization is beneficial in nature to the community (see **paras 63–8**). As relieving poverty is clearly beneficial to the entire community, the public benefit requirement will still be satisfied even if the purpose might otherwise fail to satisfy public benefit *in the second sense* by being focused upon a narrow class of objects, such as relatives or those connected by a common employment relationship.

An example of one such charitable purpose can be seen in ***Re Scarisbrick*** [1951], in which a charity for 'needy relations' of the settlor's children was upheld.

DINGLE V TURNER **[1972] AC 601**

A charity to pay pensions to poor *employees* was upheld. The House of Lords emphasized the distinction between a charitable trust and a private trust. The key issue is the primary intention of the settlor. If the gift aims to relieve poverty among a particular *description* of poor people, it will be charitable. However, if it was merely a gift to particular poor people with the intention of relieving poverty, it will be a private trust.

However, this generous approach to public benefit has resulted in some dubious decisions.

RE SEGELMAN **[1996] CH 171**

A trust for 'poor and needy' relations was upheld as valid even though the class to benefit comprised only 26 people. The trust was upheld only because the trust also included the relatives' future children.

While the narrow class in ***Re Segelman*** [1996] has often been thought of as borderline, the reasoning in ***Attorney-General v Charity Commission for England and Wales and others*** [2012] confirms the continuing acceptability of such targeted purposes. It now seems clear that as long as a purpose to relieve poverty can be shown to benefit the community in the first sense, it will not matter if the class of potential objects is poor relatives or employees.

Exclusively charitable purposes

Charities that relieve poverty must still have exclusively charitable purposes. In ***Re Gwyon*** [1930], a trust to provide knickers for boys who lived in Fareham was held not to be charitable because it did not exclude boys who were not poor.

Section 3(1)(b): charities for the advancement of education

Defining 'education'

In ***IRC v McMullen*** [1981], Lord Hailsham defined education as 'the picture of a balanced and systematic process of instruction, training and practice containing . . . spiritual, moral, mental and physical elements'. It is clear that education can encompass schools, universities, and a wide variety of other purposes (see Table 6.2).

Research

Research can be a valid educational purpose. However, the research must be of benefit to the public in some way.

RE BESTERMAN'S WILL TRUSTS, 21 JANUARY 1980, UNREPORTED
Slade J argued that a trust for research will be charitable if: • the subject matter of the proposed research is a useful subject of study; and • it is contemplated that knowledge acquired as a result of the research will be disseminated to others.

Table 6.2 Case examples of educational charitable purposes

CASE	EDUCATIONAL PURPOSE
Re British School of Egyptology [1954]	Promoting the study of Egyptology
Re Lopes [1931]	London Zoo
Re Dupree [1945]	A chess tournament for young people
Incorporated Council for Law Reporting v Attorney-General [1972]	Production of the Law Reports
Re Hopkins [1965]	Research into the contested authorship of some of Shakespeare's plays
IRC v McMullen [1981]	The promotion of football for *young people* in schools and universities.

The court will also assess the merit of the research. For example, in ***Re Shaw's WT*** [1957], a trust to create a new 40-letter alphabet was rejected because it did not add anything useful to the sum of knowledge.

Note: research may also be a valid charitable purpose under **s 3(1)(d)**, and **s 3(1)(f) CA 2011** (discussed later).

The public benefit requirement

The case of ***Independent Schools Council and others v Charity Commission for England and Wales*** [2011] set out the two senses of public benefit that educational purposes must satisfy:

- Public benefit in the first sense: the *nature* of the purpose addressed by the charity must be a benefit to the community. It was observed that this will be readily satisfied as improving education is beneficial to the community as a whole, regardless of which group benefits. However, the clever example given of a school for pickpockets demonstrates how education may not always benefit the community!
- Public benefit in the second sense: those to benefit from the charity's work must be sufficiently numerous to constitute a section of the public or community rather than a private class of individuals.

Section of the community?

OPPENHEIM V TOBACCO SECURITIES TRUST CO **[1951] AC 297**

A trust to help pay for the education of the children of employees and ex-employees of British-American Tobacco was held *not* to be charitable. Even though the company employed more than 110,000 people, the majority of the House of Lords confirmed that there are two sections of the community which are not wide enough to satisfy the public benefit requirement:

- where membership is determined by a *personal nexus* with the donor—for example, family or other relations; and
- where membership is based on contract—for example, a contract of employment.

As this benefit was supplied by virtue of their employment, the trust did not benefit either the community or a section of it.

In ***Oppenheim***, Lord MacDermott delivered a strong dissent in which he argued that the majority's approach takes no account of how much public benefit will be generated by a trust. While a trust which could benefit thousands is rendered invalid because of the group's nexus with the settlor, a trust for the education of children living in a village of 100 would satisfy the public benefit requirement.

A 'section of the community' is often contrasted with a 'private class of fluctuating individuals'. The former implies an impersonal connection suggesting a benefit to the public, while the latter group of persons are personally connected, indicating a private benefit only. However, in ***Dingle v Turner*** [1972], Lord Cross (*obiter*) argued that while the employees of a small firm might rightly be identified as a private class of fluctuating individuals, it is difficult to say the same of a company employing thousands of workers, many of whom will be entirely unknown to one another.

The main thrust of these arguments is that the current approach is artificial and may exclude trusts which ought to be recognized as charitable. Lord Cross argued that while the number which would benefit was significant, ultimately the court should examine the purpose of the trust to assess whether, on its true construction, it is intended to advance education or whether it is a 'fringe benefit' that the taxpayer should not be expected to subsidize.

LOOKING FOR EXTRA MARKS?

While the majority approach in ***Oppenheim*** helps to distinguish charitable and private trusts, it remains open to criticism. Read the judgments in ***Oppenheim*** and Lord Cross's judgment in ***Dingle v Turner***. These will help you to assess the strengths and weaknesses of the majority approach in ***Oppenheim*** and demonstrate a more critical appreciation of the law.

Exclusively charitable purposes

Preferences

Despite the strong line taken in ***Oppenheim*** against personal connections, there is some authority that a preference for a private class may be allowed. It is not permitted to give an absolute priority to a private class (***Caffoor v Income Tax Commissioner*** [1961])—for example, 'claims by members of my family must be satisfied first'—as this puts the public in second place to a private class and therefore cannot be said to be charitable. However, a *preference* for a private class may be acceptable.

RE KOETTGEN **[1954] CH 252**

A trust for the education of British-born people with a preference for a private class (employees of a company and their families) succeeded. In this case, the testatrix stated that no more than 75 per cent of the trust income was to be applied in any given year to the private class. Upjohn J upheld this trust because it was open to everyone; it was only at the selection stage that the preference took effect. The fact that the trustees did not always apply the full 75 per cent to the private class was also significant.

This decision was criticized in ***IRC v Educational Grants Association Ltd*** [1967], where it was argued that a trust cannot be charitable merely because it is *potentially* for the public benefit. Instead, it can only be said to be charitable when it is operated for the public benefit. It could be argued that as long as a trust operates for primarily charitable purposes, an ancillary non-charitable purpose should be permissible. However, there are two objections to this argument:

- Ancillary non-charitable purposes are generally more acceptable where they help to further legitimate charitable purposes; allowing a preference for a private class can only be said to accomplish this if one argues that without allowing the preference, there would be no charitable trust in the first place. However, this argument makes charity hostage to a testator's more selfish impulses.

- Is a preference which allows up to *three-quarters* of its income to be used for the benefit of a private class truly an *ancillary* purpose, merely because the trustees had not used the preference to its full extent? A charitable trust should be defined by its operation for the public benefit and not merely its *potential* to do so.

Section 3(1)(c): charities for the advancement of religion

Defining 'religion'

Originally the courts were quicker to recognize different forms of Christianity as religions. However, the modern approach has been more open, and all the major world religions have now been recognized:

- The law adopts a *neutral stance* between different religions but assumes that some religion is better than none: ***Neville Estates v Madden*** [1962].

THORNTON V HOWE **(1862) 31 BEAV 14**

A gift to promote the religious beliefs of Joanna Southcote, who claimed that she would give birth to the new Messiah, was upheld as charitable—it did not matter if the court believed the religion to be foolish or even devoid of foundation. However, the court will not recognize a religion whose tenets are subversive of all morality.

- The court will not discriminate against religions with only a small number of followers: ***Funnell v Stewart*** [1996].

While these cases discuss what will *not* be taken into account when deciding what constitutes a religion, the question of what characterizes a religion has been less satisfactorily answered.

RE SOUTH PLACE ETHICAL SOCIETY **[1980] 1 WLR 1565**

The court had to decide whether an organization whose aims were the study and dissemination of ethical principles and the cultivation of a rational religious sentiment was charitable. Its members were agnostics—ie they neither affirmed nor denied the existence of a higher power.

Dillon J distinguished ethical and religious beliefs: the former concerned man's relationship to man while the latter concerned man's relationship to God. He commented (*obiter*) that religion involved two elements:

- faith in a god; and
- worship of that god.

While the court accepted that this was a charity for the advancement of *education*, it rejected the idea that it was a religion as it lacked these two elements.

The problem with this definition is that not all faiths, recognized as religions, meet these requirements. Some religions, such as Buddhism, are atheistic—ie they do not require belief in any higher being. Other religions may not involve any form of deity worship at all.

A statutory definition of 'religion'

However, this problem has been addressed by **s 3(2)(a) Charities Act 2011**, which provides: 'religion' includes—

(i) a religion which involves belief in more than one god, and

(ii) a religion which does not involve belief in a god.

This section confirms that both *polytheistic* religions—ie religions involving the worship of many gods, such as many forms of Hinduism—and *non-theistic* religions—ie those which do not believe in any deity, such as Buddhism—are included within the definition of religion. By dispensing with the need for a godlike figure, the range of beliefs which may qualify as religious is likely to be broadened. However, in order to be charitable, a 'religion' must still involve some form of worship.

The meaning of worship was considered, albeit in a different context, by the Supreme Court in ***R (on the application of Hodkin) v Registrar General of Births, Deaths and Marriages*** [2014]. In accepting that a church of the Church of Scientology was a place of religious worship in which marriage ceremonies could be performed, Lord Toulson argued that 'worship' must include religious rites and services broader than the more traditional theistic notions of worshipping a particular deity or god-like figure.

LOOKING FOR EXTRA MARKS?

It can be confusing to understand when a non-theistic order would be considered a religion. As the Charity Commission determines whether an organization can be registered as a charity for the advancement of religion, it often has to engage with this question and the current law. Read and contrast the Charity Commission decisions on why the Druid Network could be registered as a charity for the advancement of religion while the Temple of the Jedi Order could not.
See: http://www.gov.uk/government/publications/druid-network and http://www.gov.uk/government/publications/the-temple-of-the-jedi-order.

The public benefit requirement

The public benefit is satisfied if the public has access to the benefits of the religion.

GILMOUR V COATS [1949] AC 426
A trust for an order of cloistered nuns was held *not* to be charitable because the public had no access to the nuns and therefore could not be said to benefit. An argument that the public would benefit from the nuns' prayers on their behalf was rejected as too vague and intangible.

RE HETHERINGTON **[1990] CH 1**

A trust for the saying of masses for *family members* was held to have public benefit because they were performed in *public* and would have an 'edifying and improving effect' upon those in attendance.

Note: trusts for the performance of purely *private* masses or ceremonies will not be charitable. However, they may be valid as a private purpose trust: ***Re Caus*** [1934] (see chapter 7 for more detail).

LOOKING FOR EXTRA MARKS?

In January 2014, following a very public dispute, the Charity Commission finally agreed to register the Preston Down Trust (PDT) as a charity. The PDT represents a Plymouth Brethren Christian Church Meeting Hall in Devon. The Charity Commission had been concerned that the practices of the Plymouth Brethren did not satisfy the public benefit requirement, in particular because of the limited extent to which they engaged with wider society. However, after discussions with the Charity Commission, the PDT revised its trust deed in order to address those concerns and its new application was accepted. This decision illustrates the important role the Charity Commission plays in working with organizations to enable them to register as charities. However, the reasoning also questions the status of longstanding decisions, such as ***Thornton v Howe*** (1862), suggesting that the non-judgmental attitude to religions set out in that case was founded on the presumption of public benefit that has since been removed by **s 4(2) CA 2011**. As trustees are obliged to have regard to Charity Commission guidance, its view can have a significant impact on how the law develops. Reading the full decision will provide insight into how the Charity Commission applies the public benefit requirement, how it balances benefits and detriments in that process, and its own views on the impact of **s 4(2)**.

See www.gov.uk/government/publications/preston-down-trust.

Section 3(1)(d)–(m): the other heads of charity

This section will examine a sample of charitable purposes under **s 3(1)(d)–(m)** in order to highlight some of the interesting issues that can arise when considering whether a trust is charitable.

Note: each purpose under these heads must be of public benefit in its first sense. In addition, the test for public benefit in its second sense is that set out in ***Oppenheim***, ie the class of potential objects should not be restricted by family relationship or a common employer.

REVISION TIP

Examiners often come up with unusual purposes to test students' ability to identify which head of charity will be relevant. Read the Charity Commission Guidance on Charitable Purposes, which provides practical examples of the sorts of activities covered by each head (see http://www.gov.uk/government/publications/charitable-purposes/charitable-purposes).

Section 3(1)(d): the advancement of health or the saving of lives

A wide variety of purposes is included under this head, including hospitals, medical research, the provision of housing for medical staff, and the creation of cycle paths.

Private medical care

Charities are allowed to charge for their services. However, the charity should not be profit-making, ie any profits should be used to further the charity's purposes. Therefore, a trust to support a private hospital can be charitable.

RE RESCH **[1969] 1 AC 514**

A bequest to a private hospital was upheld as charitable. It was not fatal that the beneficiaries were not poor—even though it might be difficult for the poor to afford treatment, they were not excluded.

The public benefit requirement was satisfied as there was clearly a need for such facilities and medical treatment within the community. Lord Wilberforce also argued that the court could take into account indirect benefits. In this case, private medical care freed up hospital beds in the public sector.

LOOKING FOR EXTRA MARKS?

The continuing charitable status of private education and hospitals was hotly contested during the passage of the Charity Bill 2004 through Parliament. While the decisions of ***Independent Schools Council and others v Charity Commission for England and Wales*** [2011] and ***Attorney-General v Charity Commission for England and Wales and others*** [2012] confirm that the **Charities Act 2006** does not invalidate trusts for such organizations, private education, and hospitals raise significant questions about the acceptable levels of public benefit required for charitable status. A useful discussion of these issues can be found in Peter Luxton, 'Public Benefit and Charities: The Impact of the Charities Act 2006' in Dixon and Griffiths (eds), *Contemporary Perspectives on Property, Equity and Trust Law* (2007), p 181.

Section 3(1)(f): the advancement of the arts, culture, heritage, or science

Examples of purposes under this head include a trust to promote the performance of choral works (***Royal Choral Society v IRC*** [1943]), the preservation of sites of historical interest, and scientific research. Charitable purposes must have merit and the courts will often use expert evidence to help determine this. In ***Re Pinion*** [1965], a trust to preserve the settlor's collection of *objets d'art* was rejected on the basis that it was a 'mass of junk'! This purpose may be analysed as satisfying public benefit in its *second sense* (as it would be open to the public as a whole) but failing to satisfy public benefit in its *first sense* (as the court doubted that the collection would benefit the community).

Section 3(1)(g): the advancement of amateur sport

This head of charity gives statutory recognition to the decisions of the Charity Commission, which, for some time, had permitted such charities on the basis of the physical and mental benefits to the community:

- This head relates to *amateur* sports; the support of professional sports is not charitable.
- Sport is defined widely to include both physical activities (eg netball) or those involving mental exertion (eg chess): **s 3(2)(d)**.
- Such trusts do not have to address some lack among the intended beneficiaries (contrast recreational charities under **s 5 CA 2011**, discussed later).

Section 3(1)(h): the promotion of human rights, conflict resolution or reconciliation, or the promotion of religious or racial harmony, or equality and diversity

While the wording clearly indicates the types of purposes intended here, it is important that you understand the law's approach to 'political trusts'—a political trust cannot be a valid charitable trust: ***McGovern v Attorney-General*** [1982]. Note: this restriction applies to *all* heads of charity. There are two reasons for this:

- It is difficult for the courts to ascertain whether a political objective will be for the public benefit.
- As the ultimate administrator of trusts, it would be inappropriate for the courts or the Attorney-General to advocate political changes which may conflict with government policy.

Defining 'political purposes'

McGovern v Attorney-General [1982] sets out a non-exhaustive list of political purposes:

- purposes supporting the interests of a particular political party (eg ***Re Hopkinson*** [1949]);
- purposes which seek to change the law of this or foreign countries (eg ***National Anti-Vivisection Society v IRC*** [1948]) (cf ***Human Dignity Trust v Charity Commission for England and Wales*** [2014] which held that the financial support of litigation that asked whether legislation offended against recognized human rights was not political as it did not seek change, only clarification of the status of particular laws);
- purposes which seek to change government policy or the decisions of governmental authorities, in the United Kingdom or elsewhere.

Compare the following cases:

SOUTHWOOD V ATTORNEY-GENERAL [2000] WL 877698
PRODEM, an organization which aimed to educate the public on the evils of war and advocated disarmament, was held not to be charitable. While the court did not object to the promotion of peace as an object, PRODEM was denied charitable status because its central purpose was not to encourage discussion of how peace might be achieved, but to act directly to bring about a specific change in government policy.

ATTORNEY-GENERAL V ROSS [1986] 1 WLR 252
It was held that the funds of a student union were held on charitable trust. The payment of money to the NUS, a non-charitable organization, was merely ancillary to the acceptable aim of representing the student body.

The Charity Commission provides further guidance on the extent to which charities can engage in political activities in 'CC9: Campaigning and Political Activities by Charities' (see https://www.gov.uk/government/publications/speaking-out-guidance-on-campaigning-and-political-activity-by-charities-cc9) (see Figure 6.2):

- A trust with directly political purposes cannot be charitable.
- However, a trust which engages in political activities as a way of furthering its charitable purposes is more likely to be acceptable.

Figure 6.2 Acceptable political activities

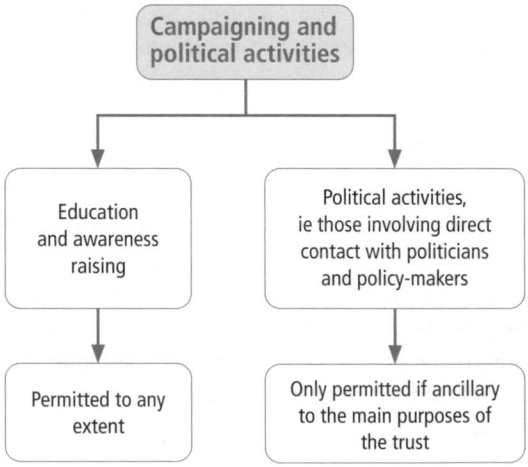

Section 3(1)(i): the advancement of environmental protection or improvement

This heading includes purposes such as the promotion of recycling, conservation efforts, or the preservation of land of particular scientific interest. Supporting expert evidence may be required to help decide whether such trusts are in the public benefit; for example, in deciding whether a trust to preserve badger habitats is charitable, the public benefit in preservation will have to be weighed against the argument that badgers are responsible for spreading disease to livestock.

Section 3(1)(j): the relief of those in need by reason of youth, age, ill-health, disability, financial hardship, or other disadvantage

Examples of valid purposes under this head include charities providing meals on wheels for the elderly, and homeless shelters.

- The trust must address a need of the identified beneficiaries and not just provide a benefit: ***Joseph Rowntree Memorial Trust Housing Association Ltd v Attorney-General*** [1983].
- Providing for non-essential or luxury items is not permitted: ***Re Cole*** [1958].

Example 1

Compare the following two purposes:

1. £100,000 to improve the range of books in Braille for the blind.
2. £100,000 to provide housing for the blind.

The first purpose would be valid as it addresses a need of the blind. The second purpose would be unlikely to be valid as housing does not address a need of this group *as blind people*. If the second purpose provided the money to help provide housing specially adapted for the blind, this *would* have addressed a need. However, the blind cannot be said to *need* the provision of housing *because* they are blind.

Section 3(1)(k): the advancement of animal welfare

Animal welfare charities provide a good example of *indirect* public benefit. ***Re Wedgewood*** [1915] emphasized their value in *enhancing public morality and making us better people*. There is some authority which supports the idea that the public must have access to charities for animal welfare: ***Re Grove-Grady*** [1929]. However, it is arguable that the public can benefit by more restricted access, remote viewing, educational facilities, or contribution to science.

REVISION TIP

It is important to remember that charities under this head are for the welfare of animals or certain types of animals *generally*. If you are presented with a scenario involving a gift for the welfare of *specific* animals, such as the settlor's pet cat, this will not be charitable, but may be a private purpose trust, subject to the usual perpetuity rules—see chapter 7.

Section 3(1)(m) includes 'any other purposes . . . '

Section 3(1)(m):

- acts as a residual head of charity and contains purposes which do not fit neatly into the other heads and charitable purposes under **s 5 (s 3(1)(m)(i))**; and
- performs the same role as the fourth head of ***Pemsel***—'other purposes beneficial to the community'—by allowing new purposes to be developed by way of analogy with other existing or new purposes (**s 3(1)(m)(ii)–(iii)**).

Section 5: recreational and similar trusts

Section 5 CA 2011 incorporates the provisions of the **Recreational Charities Act 1958**. This Act had been passed in order to preserve the charitable status of a number of bodies long-recognized as charitable, such as the Women's Institute and village halls, following the House of Lords' decision in ***IRC v Baddeley*** [1955] that recreational purposes were not charitable.

Section 5 sets out the conditions under which bodies that provide or support the provision of recreational or leisure activities may be considered charitable (see Figure 6.3).

Cy-près

Cy-près literally means 'near there'. It is a doctrine which deals with the situation where a charitable gift cannot be applied to the purposes intended by the settlor. It works by allowing the purposes of the gift to be *varied* so that the property can be applied to a related charitable purpose. In effect, *cy-près* saves the gift from failing and returning on resulting trust to the testator's estate or being given to the Crown.

Section 62 CA 2011 lists the circumstances in which *cy-près* can be used. These include situations where it is impossible, impracticable, illegal, or inefficient to carry out the purposes of the trust.

Figure 6.3 The operation of s 5 Charities Act 2011 (recreational charities)

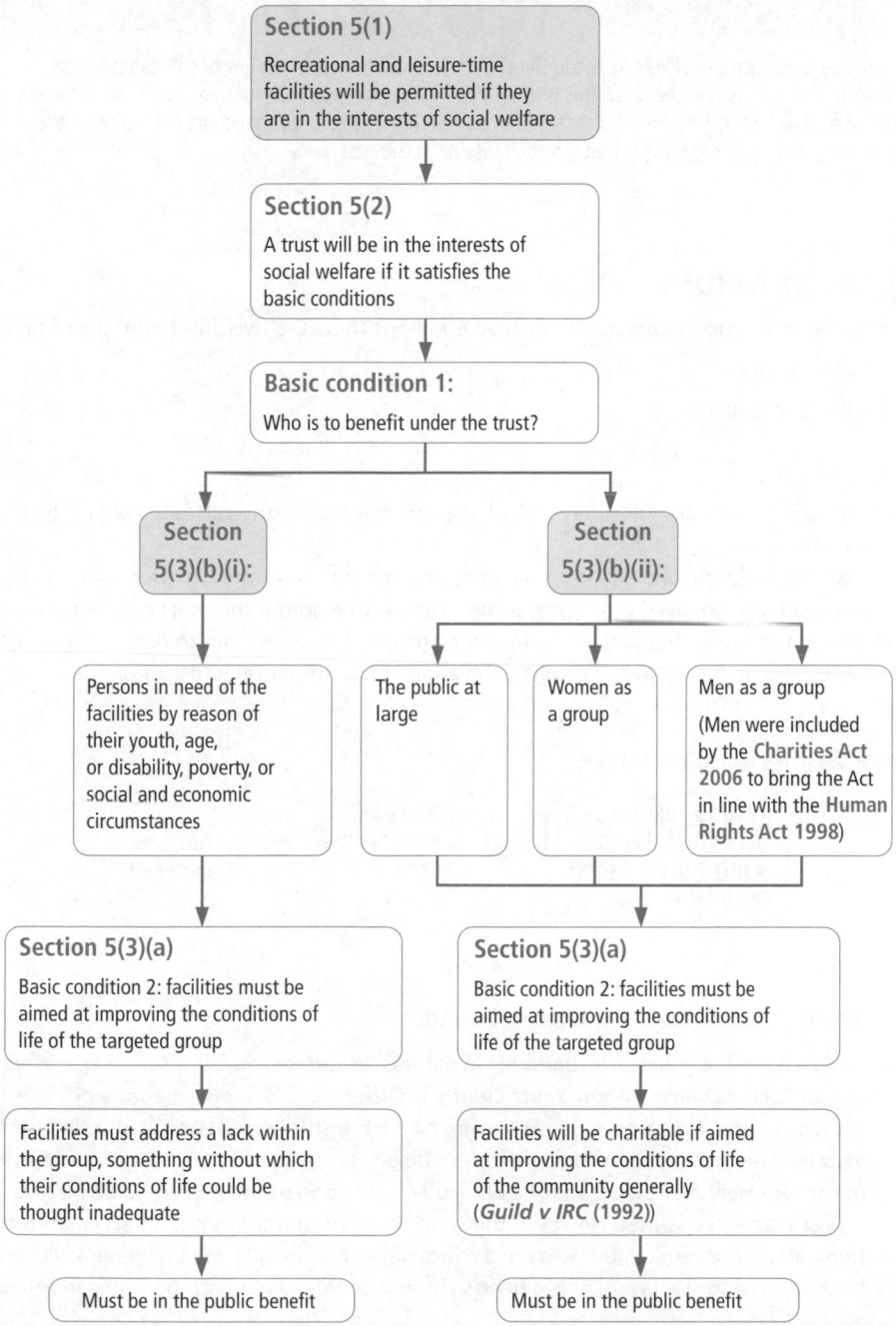

REVISION TIP

In an exam, you are most likely to encounter *cy-près* in a context where it has become impossible to carry out the purposes of the trust. This is usually quite easy to spot: look for facts mentioning the closure of a charity or its facilities. But remember, *cy-près* can only be used in respect of charitable trusts. It cannot be used to 'save' a gift that is not charitable in the first place.

Types of failure

Cy-près can intervene when a charitable trust is failing. There are two different types of failure:

- initial failure;
- subsequent failure.

Initial failure

Initial failure occurs when the purposes of the gift fail *before* the gift has taken effect (see Figure 6.4).

In cases of initial failure, the gift will lapse and return on resulting trust to the testator's estate unless it can be saved by *cy-près*. *Cy-près* can only be used if the court can find a general charitable intention on the part of the testator. The court, in effect, has to determine whether the testator would have wished the gift to be applied to another related purpose.

Figure 6.4 An initial failure timeline

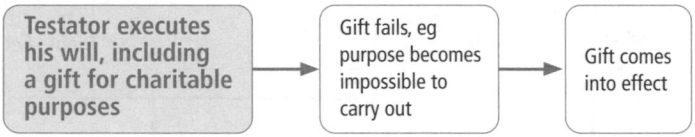

Factors indicating a general charitable intention

- Where the rest of the will is charitable in nature: ***Re Satterthwaite's WT*** [1966]. In ***Knipe v British Racing Drivers' Motor Sport Charity & Others*** [2020], a testamentary gift was left for the 'Cancer Research Fund'. However, no such institution existed at the time of the testator's death. The court concluded that the gift was intended for the general purpose of cancer research rather than for a particular institution so the monies could be given to cancer research charities. However, the court also noted that even if a particular institution had been intended, this was not a critical aspect of the gift and the generally charitable nature of the will would have been sufficient to infer a general charitable intention.

- Where the charity to benefit never existed: if a gift is left to a charity which, in fact, *never existed*, the court will construe the testator's intention as generally charitable: ***Re Harwood*** [1936].
- Where the gift is to an **unincorporated association**: unincorporated associations do not have legal personality and consequently cannot own property in their own right (see chapter 7). Therefore, if a charitable gift is made to an unincorporated association which has been dissolved, the courts are more likely to construe the gift as being for the *charitable purposes* of the association and apply the money *cy-près* to another body carrying out these purposes: ***Re Finger's WT*** [1972].

Factors indicating no general charitable intention

- Where the terms of the gift are precise or specific: the more specific the terms of a testator's gift, the less likely it can be said to demonstrate a general charitable intention: ***Re Rymer*** [1895].

EXAMPLE 2

£100,000 to help patients of the Cranford Physical Spinal Injuries Centre purchase equipment that can assist in their continued recovery.

Should the Centre cease to exist prior to the testator's death, cy-près would not be used in this case. The terms of this gift are very specific—as there are no longer any patients, the gift will lapse. A general gift to help the Centre would have allowed the court to consider whether there were other factors demonstrating a general charitable intention.

- Where the gift is to a corporation: in contrast to gifts to unincorporated associations, corporations have legal personality. This suggests that the gift is to a specific body to carry out charitable purposes, rather than a general gift for charitable purposes: Re Finger's WT [1972].

A number of these considerations are illustrated in this recent decision:

ATTORNEY-GENERAL V ZEDRA FIDUCIARY SERVICES (UK) LTD **[2020] EWHC 2988**

In 1928, an anonymous donation of £500,000 was made to establish a 'National Fund' to discharge the National Debt (then, £7.6 billion). By 2020, the Fund had increased in value to £512.2 million but the National Debt had also increased to £2,004 billion.

When the identity of the donor was discovered, his descendants argued that the money should pass to them by way of resulting trust as the purpose of the gift was impossible to achieve and, because it had always been impossible to achieve, that this was a case of initial failure with no evidence of a general charitable intention that would enable the money to be applied *cy-près*.

The court held that this was not a case of initial failure. When the Fund was established, it had been a possibility that the National Debt could have been discharged and our knowledge of current conditions could not be applied in hindsight to conclude that this purpose had been impossible from the start. Therefore, this was an example of subsequent failure (see below), where the purpose had become impossible *after* the gift had come into effect.

Finally, the court argued *obiter* that, even though it was unnecessary in the circumstances, a general charitable intention could be inferred. Adopting the approach taken in ***Re Woodhams*** [1981], the court considered whether any proposed modification of the gift's purpose would frustrate the intentions of the testator. As the donor had compared the Fund to gifts made for the betterment of the nation, such as gifts of historical buildings or art, it was clear that his intention was to benefit the nation generally, as opposed to the specific purpose of discharging the National Debt.

Removing restrictions on the purposes of a charitable gift

Sometimes the recipient of a charitable gift will be unwilling to accept the gift because of the testator's restrictions upon its use. In these circumstances, the court may construe the gift as being for general charitable purposes and remove the restrictions.

RE LYSAGHT **[1966] CH 191**

The Royal College of Surgeons threatened to disclaim a gift to provide medical scholarships because it excluded women, Jews, and Roman Catholics. The court held that there was a general charitable intention to further medical education and applied the money *cy-près* to the Royal College without the settlor's restrictions.

Subsequent failure

Subsequent failure occurs when there is a failure in carrying out the purposes of the gift *after* the gift has taken effect (see Figure 6.5).

In cases of subsequent failure, *cy-près* operates *automatically*. In effect, as the gift has already been dedicated to charitable purposes, the court can vary the purposes and apply the money to another related charity. To identify cases of subsequent failure, you must be able to identify *when* the charitable gift takes effect:

- A charitable gift takes effect at the time of the death of the testator, ie when the will comes into effect.
- It does not matter if the will has not yet been administered: ***Re Slevin*** [1891].

It also does not matter if the gift is a remainder interest which only takes effect after the death of a life tenant: ***Re Wright*** [1954].

Figure 6.5 A subsequent failure timeline

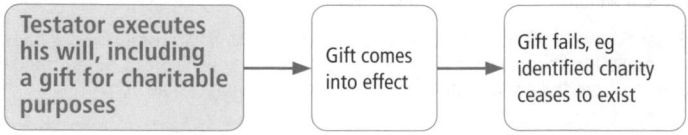

KEY CASES

CASES	FACTS	PRINCIPLE
Attorney- General v Charity Commission for England and Wales and others [2012] WTLR 977	Concerned a reference from the Attorney-General seeking clarification on the validity of charities that sought to relieve the poverty of a narrow class of potential objects, such as relatives or employees.	The **Charities Act 2006** does not affect the charitable status of trusts for the relief of poor relatives or employees. Public benefit has two senses (the first concerning the beneficial nature of activities and the second regarding who is to benefit), but charities for the relief of poverty only have to be of public benefit in the first sense.
Dingle v Turner [1972] AC 601	Upheld a gift to provide pensions for poor ex-employees.	Trusts for poor employees are charitable. Lord Cross's dissent critiques the ***Oppenheim*** approach to public benefit as artificial.
Gilmour v Coats [1949] AC 426	Trust for the benefit of cloistered nuns not for the public benefit.	Charities for the advancement of religion require the public to be able to access the religion.
Independent Schools Council v Charity Commission [2011] All ER (D) 198 (Oct)	The ISC successfully challenged Commission guidance on the public benefit requirement for private schools.	The Commission had misinterpreted the existing law: as long as there is some level of financial support possible for poor students, the public benefit requirement should be evaluated on a case-by-case basis, taking into account both direct and indirect benefits.
McGovern v Attorney-General [1982] Ch 321	Concerned the validity of Amnesty International as a charitable organization.	Political purposes are not allowed in charitable trusts but engaging in political activities to further a charitable purpose may be acceptable as ancillary non-charitable purposes.
Oppenheim v Tobacco Securities Trust Co [1951] AC 297	A trust for the education of employees of British-American Tobacco held not to be charitable.	Apart from charities for the relief of poverty, a charitable trust will not be for the public benefit if it only benefits relatives or employees.
Re Scarisbrick [1951] Ch 622	A trust for poor relations upheld as charitable.	Public benefit means for the benefit of the community or some section of it.
Re South Place Ethical Society [1980] 1 WLR 1565	An Ethical Society was held not to be a charity for the advancement of religion.	'Religion' involves faith in a god and worship of a god (see also **s 3(2)(a) CA 2011**).

KEY DEBATES

Topic	How are charitable trusts different from other types of trust?
Academic/author	Warburton
Viewpoint	The distinctive treatment of charitable trusts requires them to be treated separately from the main body of rules on trusts.
Source	Warburton, 'Charitable Trusts—Unique?' (1999) Conveyancer 20.

Topic	What is the effect of the Charities Act 2006 (now consolidated in the Charities Act 2011) on the public benefit requirement?
Academic/author	Charity Commission
Viewpoint	Section 17 Charities Act 2011 charges the Charity Commission with issuing guidance on the public benefit requirement in order to improve the accountability and good working practices of the charitable sector. In light of the decisions in ***Independent Schools Council and others v Charity Commission for England and Wales*** [2011] and ***Attorney-General v Charity Commission for England and Wales and others*** [2012], the Charity Commission describes how it has revised its initial guidance to reflect these decisions and provides a clear and helpful analysis of the issues raised.
Source	Public Benefit: The Public Benefit Requirement (PB1) (2013) (www.gov.uk/government/publications/public-benefit-the-public-benefit-requirement-pb1) and Legal Analysis: Public Benefit (2013) (www.gov.uk/government/publications/legal-analysis-public-benefit)

Topic	The Charity Commission's modern approach to decision-making
Academic/author	Luxton and Evans
Viewpoint	Using two recent decisions by the Charity Commission on the advancement of religion, the authors analyse its approach and argue that the Charity Commission needs to justify its decision-making more clearly within the framework of existing legal principles.
Source	Luxton and Evans, 'Cogent and Cohesive? Two Recent Charity Commission Decisions on the Advancement of Religion' (2011) 75 Conveyancer and Property Lawyer 144.

Topic	How satisfactory is the law's approach to charities with political purposes?
Academic/author	Santow
Viewpoint	Even with the further guidance issued by the Charity Commission, the current approach to political purposes is uncertain and may restrict the ability of charities to contribute fully to the development of democratic society.
Source	Santow, 'Charity in its Political Voice: A Tinkling Cymbal or a Sounding Brass?' in M Freeman (ed), *Current Legal Problems* (1999) p 255.

EXAM QUESTIONS

Problem question

Oliver James executes his will in 2005, which contains the following provisions:

1. £1,000,000 to build a Recreation Centre for the elderly in Lincoln;
2. £100,000 to Broadfield University to provide scholarships to law students, in the hope that they will challenge the increasing attacks by successive governments on our civil liberties;
3. £500,000 to further the good work of the Mountcastle Cancer Hospice.

Oliver dies in 2008. In December 2007, the Mountcastle Cancer Hospice closes. Discuss the validity of these trusts.

Essay question

Critically discuss the impact of the **Charities Act 2011** on the public benefit requirement.

Online resources

For an outline answer to this essay question, as well as multiple choice questions and interactive key cases, please visit the online resources.

Concentrate Q&As

For more questions and answers on equity and trusts, see the *Concentrate Q&A: Equity & Trusts* by Rosalind Malcolm.

Go to the end of this book to view **sample pages**.

7 Non-charitable purpose trusts

KEY FACTS

- Trusts generally need a human beneficiary.
- There are limited exceptions to the beneficiary principle.
- Transfers to unincorporated associations appear to have extended the exceptions.
- Gifts with a particular purpose have been held valid in commercial situations.
- Valid purpose trusts must comply with the rules on **perpetuity**.

Introduction

Trusts that do not have a human beneficiary are generally void: ***Re Astors ST*** [1952]. The beneficiary principle requires a valid trust to have human beneficiaries: ***Morice v Bishop of Durham*** (1804). (See chapter 3 to review the requirement of certainty of objects which is not limited to the certainty of beneficiary.) Charitable trusts are the largest exception to the 'beneficiary principle'. However, there are further 'anomalous' exceptions to this rule:

- monuments: the erection and upkeep of monuments and graves;
- animals: the upkeep of individual animals;
- masses: the saying of private masses (religious service in church).

REVISION TIP

There is a correlation between these categories and charitable trusts and some exams may ask you to consider why a particular trust may fail as a charitable trust but succeed as a non-charitable purpose trust. Although both do not need to satisfy the beneficiary principle their objects (objectives) must still be sufficiently certain, either as clearly charitable or within a recognized purpose.

They are 'gifts of imperfect obligation' because the trustee does not have to carry out the obligations and there are no human beneficiaries to enforce it. Because they do not satisfy the beneficiary principle, and have no human beneficiary, the courts have taken a strict approach to the categories of purpose trusts. These 'troublesome, anomalous and aberrant' exceptions have developed historically, and they should not be extended: ***Re Endacott*** [1960]. Despite this strict approach it will be seen later that the categories seem to have been extended.

Requirements of a non-charitable purpose trust

There are general barriers to the enforcement of purpose trusts which will limit their application. They must satisfy these hurdles in addition to falling clearly within the accepted 'anomalous exceptions'.

Perpetuity rules

Any purpose trust which is held to be valid must comply with the rules of perpetuity:

1. *The rule on remoteness of vesting*: the property must come into the ownership of a person within the relevant period. This rule is not applicable to the recognized purpose trusts.

2. *The rule against Inalienability*: a settlor cannot rule from the grave, tying up his property once he has died. To prevent this, a non-charitable purpose trust cannot continue forever, unlike a charitable trust. The applicable rule is the common law period of a *human* life in being plus 21 years. The **Perpetuities and Accumulations Acts of 1964 and 2009 (s 18)** *do not* apply to this rule.

The perpetuity period does not have to be legally defined, but it must be clear that it is within that period. In ***Re Hooper*** [1932] the period was limited by the words 'so long as the trustees can legally do so'. This was held to be a valid declaration of the perpetuity period.

LOOKING FOR EXTRA MARKS?

Look at the Law Commission website for some background and articles by Charles Harpum, who was instrumental in devising reform in this area.

The anomalous exceptions

Monuments

A trust for the upkeep of an individual monument or grave which is not part of the fabric of a church is not charitable. This is because an individual monument or grave has no public benefit whereas improving the fabric, or body, of a church will benefit those who use the church (see chapter 6).

The bequest itself must be sufficiently certain in its purpose. In ***Re Endacott*** [1960] a residual gift to provide 'a useful memorial to myself' was invalid as it was too broad. It was unclear what was meant by 'useful memorial'.

The relevant perpetuity period of inalienability was an issue in ***Musset v Bingle*** [1876], where a bequest to erect a monument to the testator's first husband was valid but a second bequest for its upkeep was void. It did not fail for perpetuity in relation to the erection of the monument as it was assumed that the monument would be erected within the period. However, as no period was stipulated for the upkeep of the monument this part of the trust failed.

Animals

A trust for the upkeep of *particular* animals can only be enforceable as a non-charitable purpose trust; it must be limited to the relevant perpetuity period (inalienability). In ***Re Dean*** (1899) a trust for the upkeep of horses and hounds was held to be valid.

LOOKING FOR EXTRA MARKS?

In ***Re Dean*** the period was for 50 years 'if they live that long' and was held to be valid. Presumably, this was because the animals were unlikely to live that long, but perpetuity was not addressed in the case.

It is clear from ***Re Kelly*** [1932] that the 'life in being' required by the perpetuity period must be a human life. The anomaly between these two decisions may be worthy of note.

Masses

The saying of masses (church services) in public will be charitable, even if the object of the masses is dedicated to a private individual: ***Re Hetherington*** [1990]. The saying of masses in private or cloistered orders can be an anomalous exception, limited to the relevant perpetuity period, inalienability: ***Gilmour v Coates*** [1949].

Miscellaneous

This category was limited to the promotion of fox-hunting: ***Re Thompson*** [1934]. With the ban on fox hunting this is unlikely to be upheld as valid today.

Unincorporated associations

The courts were reluctant to allow trusts to operate outside the accepted 'gifts of imperfect obligation': ***Re Endacott***. However, the courts have been asked to consider how gifts to a group of people should be interpreted. The policy underlying the anomalous exceptions is to encourage community benevolence. If a gift to a small community club is not charitable it may fail, defeating the intention of the donor and the policy of community benevolence. These small groups often take the form of unincorporated associations.

An unincorporated association is formed when two or more people come together for a common purpose, such as a gardening club. They will be bound by rules: ***Conservative and Unionist Central Office v Burrell*** [1982]. These groups can be organized local political groups or informal book clubs.

Unincorporated associations have no legal personality, existing in their own right, and therefore cannot own property. There are four accepted ways that the gift of property to an unincorporated association can be interpreted according to ***Re Recher's WT*** [1972]:

- an outright gift to the members to hold as joint tenants or tenants in common;
- a trust for the association's purpose;
- a trust for the members and future members of the association;
- an outright gift to the members as joint tenants subject to their contractual obligations.

An outright gift

This interpretation states that each member of the association takes the property as an outright gift. They can hold this either as **joint tenants** or as **tenants in common**. This interpretation is possible depending on the nature of the property, but in ***Re Grant's WT*** [1980] Vinelott J thought that this interpretation would be uncommon without clear evidence of the settlor's intention.

Finding the settlor's intention

The nature of the property and how the property is transferred to the members will be relevant in finding the relevant intention. If they are joint tenants, then each member of the joint tenancy holds the entire interest among themselves. Should one of the joint tenants sever his or her interest that joint tenant can take his or her share of the property as an absolute gift. So, the property must be capable of being severed.

If the gift is given as tenants in common, each member takes his or her share as an absolute gift immediately: ***Cocks v Manners*** (1871). If there is an ambiguity in the gift the courts will look at the nature of the property to infer an intention.

EXAMPLE 1

A gift of £300 to a gardening club with 30 members. It is perfectly possible that each member could take £10 each. So, they can be tenants in common or joint tenants—the property is capable of **severance**.

EXAMPLE 2

A gift of an acre of land to a gardening club with 30 members. It is possible but unlikely that the donor/settlor intended that each member take 1/30 of the acre for his or her own use. It is unlikely that the property was intended as an outright gift and this interpretation would fail.

REVISION TIP

Note that this is not a trust at all but a gift to the members. Ensure that you understand the difference between a joint tenant and a tenant in common. All property can be held as either a joint tenant or a tenant in common; a common mistake is for students to think that these terms only apply to land, or worse that they only apply to leasehold interests.

A trust for the purpose of the association

This would fail as a purpose trust as it is neither charitable nor within the anomalous exceptions. The courts have tried to make the distinction between the interpretation of the bequest as a gift to the members and for a purpose. If the members can do what they want with the property and it can be held individually it is likely to be construed as a gift. If the members cannot do what they want with the property it is likely to be a trust for a purpose and void: ***Leahy v Attorney-General for New South Wales*** [1959].

A trust for the members and future members

This is a possible interpretation in which the current members will hold the property on trust for themselves and for future members subject to the trust complying with the rules of perpetuity. The relevant rule on perpetuity here will be the remoteness of vesting which is subject to the relevant **Perpetuity and Accumulations Act**. This interpretation was recognized in ***Leahy v Attorney-General for New South Wales*** [1959].

REVISION TIP

This is not an anomalous exception as it is a trust for the members, who are human beneficiaries. It may be difficult to ascertain the beneficiaries as the membership will fluctuate to a great extent over this period, which suggests that this would be a discretionary trust. What would happen to members who left the club? Would **s 53(1)(c) Law of Property Act 1925** apply when members leave and others remain? How would the shares be allocated between members who have just joined and those who are members for the whole perpetuity period? In a problem question, do not dwell on these issues, but a brief explanation of how the difficulty usually prevents this interpretation may be useful. An essay may focus on the problems with this analysis.

A gift for the members subject to their contractual obligations

The contractual analysis is the most popular interpretation. It is seen as a gift to the current members who beneficially own the property; it is an 'accretion to funds': ***Re Grant's WT*** [1980]. This means that it is merely a direct contribution to the club funds. How they distribute their interests in the property is regulated by their internal, contractual rules. This will solve the problem of what will happen when a member leaves as his or her contract will stipulate the distribution of assets on dissolution of the association or if a member leaves the organization.

Making the 'contractual analysis' work

The association must be in control of its own finances: ***Re Grant's WT***. The association must have within its contractual agreement, which regulates the running of the club, rules on how the finances of the association are held. It must not be subject to control from another organization or superior body.

RE GRANT'S WT **[1980] 1 WLR 360**

The gift was to a local Labour Party committee. The rules of the party meant that the local party was not in control of its own internal rules, or able to decide what happened to funds should it cease to exist. The court held that the gift could not be a gift to the members subject to their rules as they were not in control of their own finances.

Advantages of this analysis

The contractual analysis is the most popular interpretation for the courts as it raises no problems with perpetuities. This is because the property vests immediately in the members and as it is not a purpose trust the rule on inalienability does not apply.

However, this interpretation will not aid a settlor who wants to ensure that the 'purpose' of the settlement is carried out. As the members are in charge of their own financial arrangements, if they agree to use the gift for a different purpose or divide the property up and take absolutely, the settlor cannot prevent this. The 'purpose' is merely the motive for the settlement.

An alternative approach

This last interpretation seems to satisfy the ownership issue, but it may defeat the intention of the settlor. As the members obtain the property as a gift then, subject to the rules of the association, they can deal with the property as they wish. It seems that the categories have been extended by the decision in ***Re Denley's Trust Deed*** [1969]. Although this case did not refer to an unincorporated association it could be applied to such a gift.

The problem with the gift was that the 'purpose' of use as a sports ground could not be achieved with any of the ***Re Recher's WT*** [1972] interpretations. If the contractual analysis was applied then the members of the club could defeat the purpose, and the members would need to be identified.

Having established that the purpose was sufficiently clear Goff J considered whether it failed the beneficiary principle. He found that there was no problem with the beneficiary principle requirement. He considered that the purpose of the beneficiary principle, requiring a human beneficiary, was to prevent possible fraud by the trustee. In the present case there were identifiable persons who would enforce the trust—the members of the sports club. This being the case there should, in principle, be no bar to enforcement of this type of trust. It was assumed that the members of the club would act as 'watchdogs' of the purpose.

TERMINOLOGY TIP

Do not refer to the identifiable persons in a ***Denley*** trust as identifiable beneficiaries as they do not have any beneficial interest. It seems that they merely have a right to enforce the obligation. This will help in explaining the interests.

LOOKING FOR EXTRA MARKS?

How to identify the individuals for the ***Denley*** trust is a matter of debate. It has been suggested that the given postulant test, ***McPhail v Doulton*** [1971], used for discretionary trusts should be applied but this is not a settled principle. Another interesting debate is that the decisions in ***Re Denley*** and ***McPhail v Doulton*** have loosened the need for the trust property to be owned and that the beneficiary merely has the role of enforcer, requiring the *locus standi* to bring an action rather than the ability to be able to own the trust property, and arguably unable to utilize the rule in ***Saunders v Vautier*** (1841).

This type of trust must be limited to the perpetuity period in relation to inalienability. ***Re Denley*** was not concerned with an unincorporated association; indeed, in ***Re Grant's WT*** it was said that ***Re Denley*** was in fact a discretionary trust with an identifiable class of beneficiaries who could be identified by the ***McPhail v Doulton*** test for certainty. The principle from ***Re Denley*** was applied to unincorporated associations in ***Re Lipinski's WT*** [1976].

RE LIPINSKI'S WT [1976] CH 235
Property was left by the testator to construct and improve buildings for the use as a sports and social club for Jewish children, said to be in memory of his late wife. The court held the trust to be valid.

Oliver J said that the 'purpose' of celebrating his late wife was merely a motive for the settlement. He referred to this as being 'an accretion' to funds, referring to the contractual analysis of interpreting the gift. This was because Oliver J felt that the individuals could, if they wished, use the settlement for any purpose they chose, subject to the social club rules (see Table 7.1 for a comparison of the two approaches).

Table 7.1 Comparing the two approaches

RE RECHER'S WT	RE DENLEY
Gift to the individual members	Trust for a clear purpose
Held by the club subject to its rules of allocation of rights	Benefits an identifiable class of persons which will satisfy the beneficiary principle issues
Association must be in control of its own funds and assets should they dissolve: ***Re Grant's WT***	Must be limited to the perpetuity period (rule against inalienability—life in being plus 21 years)
Club can do as it wants with the gift	Assumed the association will carry out the purpose

LOOKING FOR EXTRA MARKS?

The decision in ***Re Lipinski*** is a confusing mix of analyses. One view of the decision in ***Re Denley*** is that the purpose with 'ascertainable individuals' to act as watchdogs is the preferable interpretation where the settlor wants to ensure that the 'purpose' is carried out. Goff J seemed to assume that the 'ascertainable individuals' would carry out the purpose but without stating what would make them do this. However, ***Re Lipinski's*** interpretation *would* suggest that Goff's assumption of enforcement would not necessarily apply.

Additionally, ***Re Lipinski*** mixes ideas of gifts and trusts. ***Denley*** trusts must comply with the rule on perpetuities but a gift does not have to. It is better to keep these two views separate. The better interpretation is the contractual analysis: ***Artistic Upholstery Ltd v Art Forma Ltd*** [1999]. In an essay, be prepared to comment critically on ***Re Lipinski***.

Dissolution of unincorporated associations

How the association holds funds will have important implications for the allocation of property when the association dissolves. If the contractual analysis is applied, the contract between current members will regulate the distribution of the property: ***Re Bucks Constabulary Widows' and Orphans' Fund Friendly Society (No 2)*** [1979]. It was considered in ***Re Bucks*** that if only one member were left, due to death or people leaving, the property would be *bona vacantia* and go to the Crown. This approach was rejected in ***Hanchett-Stamford v Attorney-General*** [2008].

LOOKING FOR EXTRA MARKS?

The decision in ***Re West Sussex Constabulary's Widows, Children and Benevolent Fund (1930) Trusts*** [1971] made the distinction in the way money was given to the association. Donations to collection tins, money paid for raffles, etc was held *bona vacantia*, but larger donations and legacies would return to the donors on resulting trusts (see chapter 9).

Conclusion

Purpose trusts fall into charitable and non-charitable categories and are closely linked in some courses. As a trust may be valid as a charity, explain why it may succeed or fail, and then consider whether it falls into one of the anomalous exceptions. A more complex issue arises with a 'gift' to an unincorporated association. The four interpretations should be explained with the extended ***Denley*** construction.

KEY CASES

CASE	FACTS	PRINCIPLE
Leahy v Attorney- General for New South Wales [1959] AC 457	Land and furniture was left for the benefit of nuns of the Catholic church.	The gift was to a group of people for a purpose that would fail.
Re Denley's Trust Deed [1969] 1 Ch 373	Land was left to be used as a sports ground for employees of a company and any other persons the trustees may have allowed to use the grounds.	The land was held for ascertainable individuals who would supervise the trust. It was not a purpose trust and was not contrary to the beneficiary principle as the individuals would ensure no fraud.
Re Grant's WT [1980] 1 WLR 360	Money was left for the use of a local political party.	The money left to the unincorporated association could not be held on the contractual analysis as the local club was not in control of its own finances but regulated by the national party.
Re Recher's WT [1972] Ch 526	The testatrix left property to the Anti-Vivisection Society.	The gift was not a purpose trust but an accretion to the funds of the association for the members, subject to their contract, to do with as they wished. There was no problem with inalienability as the members could, if they wished, wind up the association and take their property. Note: the gift failed on another point as it had ceased to exist by the time the testatrix died.

KEY DEBATES

Topic	*Re Denley* trust
Academic/ author	Rickett
Viewpoint	In the *Denley* trust the beneficial interest is held in suspense, enforceable by the settlor and the beneficiary.
Source	Rickett (1991) 107 LQR 70. As a starting point for the discussion see Pearce and Barr, *Pearce & Stevens' Law of Trusts and Equitable Obligations*, 7th edn (2018), pp 288–94.

EXAM QUESTIONS

Problem question

Advise on the validity of a bequest, in Johan's will, to the Shannon Gardening Club of £10,000. Johan's will requires the money to be used to purchase a piece of land to be used as an allotment for local children.

Essay question

Explain how the courts have interpreted a gift to an unincorporated association and outline the problems associated with them.

Online resources

For an outline answer to this essay question, as well as multiple choice questions, bonus material and interactive key cases, please visit the online resources.

Concentrate Q&As

For more questions and answers on equity and trusts, see the *Concentrate Q&A: Equity & Trusts* by Rosalind Malcolm.

Go to the end of this book to view **sample pages**.

8 Secret trusts

KEY FACTS

- Secret trusts are testamentary trusts which operate outside the requirements of the **Wills Act 1837**.
- Secret trusts can be either fully secret or half secret.
- All secret trusts have requirements as to communication, acceptance, and reliance.
- There are time differences in the need for communication for the two types of trust.
- Secret trusts of land can operate but it is unclear if these are express or constructive.
- There are theoretical problems in justifying the operation of trusts which are unresolved.

Introduction

Wills are public documents, which enables effective taxation and fraud on potential legatees. However, some testators wish to be more discreet in who they leave property to; historically, illegitimate children are given as a reason. Additionally, early statutes (since repealed) prevented bequests to women or leaving land on trust to a charity, so a secret trust was a vehicle to avoid this: ***Katherine, Duchess of Suffolk v Herenden*** (1560). These historical justifications are arguably less relevant now. Secret trusts are a method used to avoid this publicity.

The secret trust also continues to be of use to indecisive testators who can defer the final decision about who is to benefit without having to rewrite their existing will.

Section 9 Wills Act 1837 imposes the requirements for the creation of a valid will:

- the will must be in writing;
- it must be signed by the testator; and
- it must be witnessed by two persons.

The requirements imposed by this Act are designed to ensure that a will contains a clear, complete, and formalized record of how a testator's estate should be distributed. Therefore, if the statute were to be strictly applied, secret trusts could not be enforced.

Justifications for secret trusts

Fraud theory

In ***Katherine, Duchess of Suffolk v Herenden*** (1560), the court held that Herenden was bound by his promise to take ownership of the estate for the Duchess of Suffolk. To enforce the statute strictly would have allowed Herenden to avoid the obligations of his promise: 'Equity will not allow a statute to be an instrument of fraud.'

In the case of ***McCormick v Grogan*** (1869), Lord Hatherley LC confirmed that secret trusts are imposed to prevent, in this case, a secret trustee from defrauding a testator, who only left property to the secret trustee in reliance on his promise to carry out the testator's wishes.

Who is defrauded?

- The testator? It would be difficult to prove that the testator is defrauded since he or she is dead. The *intention* of the testator is defeated, but since this was an attempt to avoid the requirements of the **Wills Act 1837**, perhaps the testator should not be protected.
- The secret beneficiaries? If the secret beneficiary is denied his or her benefit, this is only because the testator failed to comply with the formalities required by the **Wills Act 1837**. Again, the argument can be seen as circular as there are no beneficiaries if there is no valid trust.

Who commits the fraud?

- The secret trustee by denying the existence of the trust?
- The testator, who left property in a way that contravenes the policy of the **Wills Act 1837**?
- The secret beneficiary is only entitled to assert his or her claim over the property insofar as it is acceptable for the testator to avoid the legal requirements set out in the **Wills Act 1837**.

LOOKING FOR EXTRA MARKS?

Read the judgments in ***Blackwell v Blackwell*** [1925] for the different views taken by the judges in approaching the fraud theory. In essence, if the fraud theory applies then really the secret trust is a form of constructive trust. See the online resources for further commentary.

Dehors the will

The alternative justification for the enforcement of secret trusts avoids the problem of the **Wills Act 1837**. It can be argued that the trust is declared *inter vivos* (in the testator's lifetime and not through the will) and the will merely constitutes the transfer. If this were the case, the trust would arise ***dehors*** (outside) the will and therefore would not be contrary to the **Wills Act 1837**.

While this argument may appear attractive initially, there are a number of significant problems which flow from this approach. As soon as the trust is created, the *beneficial interest* in the property would be transferred to the secret beneficiary. As such, the testator would no longer be able to change his or her mind, or that part of the will which relates to the property to be held on trust. This goes against the principle that wills are ambulatory (meaning that they can be revoked or amended up until the testator's death).

The testator would no longer be able to do anything with the property as he or she no longer owns the beneficial interest. It is extremely unlikely that this would have been the testator's intention as the whole idea is that the property is the testator's until he or she dies! If the '*dehors* the will' theory was correct, then, in effect, creating a secret trust would be like locking property in a safe to which only the beneficiary has the key.

LOOKING FOR EXTRA MARKS?

There are problems with this analysis. One is that it appears to allow a trust of future property, or expectancy. This means that at the time the trust is declared, there is no way of knowing whether the property will still be part of the testator's estate when he or she dies. Such trusts of future property are generally considered to be impossible: ***Re Ellenborough*** [1903]. Second, if the trust is *inter* →

➜ *vivos* then a secret trust of land would require compliance with **s 53(1)(b) Law of Property Act 1925 (LPA)**. However, this generally has not occurred. One way to explain this is to make the link between the fraud theory and '*dehors* the will', ie that when the secret trustee/testator agrees to create the trust his or her conscience is affected by the agreement, creating a constructive trust of the land; this links with the fraud theory. In this case, **s 53(2) LPA** states that **s 53(1)(b) LPA** will not apply. See the discussion of such a principle (although not in relation to secret trusts) in ***Ottaway v Norman*** [1972].

Neither justification for secret trusts is entirely satisfactory. Contrary to the **Wills Act**, equity has sought to enforce secret trusts in order to give effect to the testator's final intentions. This may be taken to reflect the original purpose of equity—to do justice where a strict application of the legal rules would lead to an unfair result.

While the debate over how secret trusts may be justified persists, the courts have continued to enforce such trusts, and despite arguments that they are no longer required, surveys of lawyers have proved that they are alive and well.

Categories of secret trusts

There are two types of secret trust: *fully secret trusts* and *half secret trusts*. A fully secret trust will appear to be a gift on the face of the will. The testator will appear to have left the property as an outright gift: for example, 'To Bijal I leave my house'.

In a half secret trust the will contains reference to the existence of a trust, but the beneficiaries and the terms of the trust remain secret.

The case of ***Ottaway v Norman*** [1972] clearly sets out that to establish a valid secret trust there must be:

- an intention to create a trust;
- communication of that intention; and
- acceptance of the trust obligation.

In ***Blackwell v Blackwell*** [1929], the House of Lords held that a half secret trust must satisfy the same basic requirements as a fully secret trust. An interesting recent decision on this is ***Rawstron (Executors of the Estate of Lucien Freud) v Freud*** [2014], although note there are some differences, discussed in 'Standard of proof' at p .

Intention

In ***Kasperbauer v Griffith*** (2000), Peter Gibson LJ clarified that in order to create a valid secret trust, a testator must have intended to create a trust, complying with all of the three certainties (see chapter 3). In ***Marley v Rawlings*** [2014], it was stated that a will should be interpreted in the same way as a contract, looking at the natural meaning of the relevant words and the overall purpose of the will in fulfilling the intention of the testator.

Communication

What must be communicated?

The case of ***Re Boyes*** (1884) establishes that the testator must communicate to the trustee *both* his intention to establish the secret trust and the terms on which that property is to be held. If the trustee only knows of the testator's intention to create a secret trust but not its terms, the trust will fail. However, it is possible for the details to be contained in a sealed document, only to be opened after the testator's death ***Re Keen*** [1937], Lord Wright comparing this to a ship sailing under sealed orders (constructive delivery). In this situation the secret trustee should know that the sealed document contains the details required for a valid trust. This is a logical result because a trustee must know what he or she is meant to do with the property received (see chapter 3 and the three certainties). The intention and terms of a trust may be communicated either orally or in writing by the testator or their agent: ***Moss v Cooper*** (1861).

Fully secret trusts

When must this communication take place?

Fully secret trusts can be communicated at any time before the death of the testator, when the will comes into effect. In ***Wallgrave v Tebbs*** (1855) the secret trustees only found the request to use it for charitable purposes in the testator's papers after his death. The failure to inform them of the trust before the will came into effect meant that they took as a gift.

Who must be told of the trust?

In a fully secret trust, if communication is not made to all of the intended secret trustees, the question of whether they will *all* be bound depends on two things:

- *how* the trustees were intended to hold the property; and
- the *timing* of the communication.

You will know that *all* property can be held as either joint tenants or tenants in common. In ***Re Stead*** [1900] the testator only informed one secret trustee, Mrs Witham, of her intention before the will was executed. Farwell J held that only Mrs Witham was bound by the trust; Mrs Andrew (the other intended secret trustee) took free of the obligation.

This case establishes a complicated set of rules for deciding when communication to only some of the trustees will bind the others. It is pointless to try to justify this set of rules as even the trial judge was not entirely convinced that they made sense!

REVISION TIP

Warning: it is a common mistake for students to confuse the ordinary use of the term 'tenancy' as referring to the occupation of land with the legal use of this term, which includes the ability to hold any type of property, from a bank account to a palace, in a form of co-ownership. Do not fall into this trap! Look for words such as 'to hold in equal parts', which may mean that the tenants are tenants in common, as these are words which indicate that separate interests are being created.

To try to make this clearer, have a look at Figure 8.1.

Figure 8.1 Communication

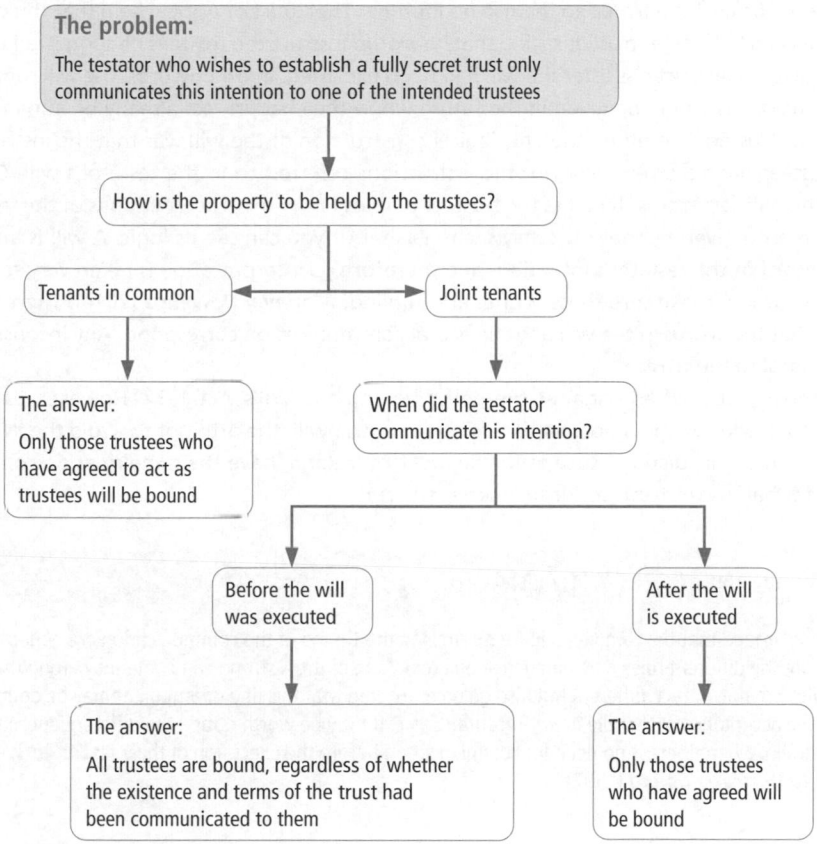

Half secret trusts

The major difference between fully secret and half secret trusts relates to *when* the communication must take place. In a half secret trust, communication should take place before or at the time that the will is **executed** (when the formalities of **s 9 Wills Act 1837** are met). The basis of this rule was *obiter* comments by Lord Sumner in ***Blackwell v Blackwell*** [1929], which were later applied in the cases of ***Re Keen*** [1937] and ***Re Bateman's WT*** [1970].

The communication must be consistent with the will

In ***Re Keen*** [1937], before the execution of his will the testator had given one of his trustees instructions contained in a sealed envelope to be opened on his death. However, after he died the relevant bequest in his will stated that the property was left to the trustees for purposes that *would be communicated* to them in his lifetime. The Court of Appeal held that this did not create a valid half secret trust as saying that he *would* instruct the trustees he suggested that he would give his instructions *after* the will had been executed. In other words, the will suggested that instructions would be given in the future when they had in fact already been handed to the secret trustee. Therefore, the only logical construction of the will was that the instructions the trustees had received were *not* the instructions referred to in the testator's will. On this basis, the half secret trust failed as the trustees did not know the true intentions of the testator.

The reason given by the court may seem harsh, but you can see its logic. A will is a formal legal record of the testator's intentions and therefore its interpretation is taken very seriously by the courts to make sure those wishes are fulfilled; ***Marley v Rawlings*** [2014]. Therefore, it is vital that the words in the will and the actual communication correspond. Any inconsistency will be fatal to the trust.

All secret trusts offend against the policy behind the **Wills Act 1837**. However, as a half secret trust, with unknown object, is referred to in the will, the attempt to avoid the **Wills Act** is clear. (Other jurisdictions, such as the Republic of Ireland, have the same rules on communication for half secret trusts as for fully secret trusts.)

LOOKING FOR EXTRA MARKS?

It can be argued that the comments in ***Re Keen*** as to the timing of the communication are *obiter* and therefore the different rules on communication are not absolute. A strong candidate may argue that the rules are not, in fact, different but also go on to explain that this line of argument may be doubtful since the acceptance of the rule in ***Re Bateman's WT***. It may be worth noting the different approaches in Australia, where there is no need for communication before the execution of the will: ***Ledgerwood v Perpetual Trustee Co Ltd*** (1997).

REVISION TIP

Remember to check for consistency between the will and the actual instructions.

Who must be told of the trust?

All trustees of a half secret trust should be told of the testator's intentions. What will happen if communication only takes place to one of the trustees? Unlike a fully secret trust, half secret trustees *cannot* claim the property as their own. This is because the will makes it clear that the property is not intended as an outright gift but is to be held on trust. Instead, the property will be held on resulting trust back to the estate.

REVISION TIP

This is one of the areas where there are different rules. A *fully* secret trust must be communicated before death, while for half secret trusts it is debatable if the communication needs to be before the execution of the will.

Acceptance

The final requirement for the creation of a valid secret trust is that the trustee must accept the terms of the trust. The case of ***Ottaway v Norman*** [1972] states that this can be either:

- expressly; or
- by **acquiescence** (silence).

MOSS V COOPER **(1861) 4 LT 790**

The secret trustee who had been informed of the testator's intentions told the other two intended trustees; one expressly accepted but the other remained silent. The court held that having learned of the trust, his silence amounted to acceptance. The key point here is that he knew of the trust but failed to object.

What happens to property in the event that a secret trust cannot be established?

The decision in ***Rawstron v Freud*** [2014] has discussed the differences between fully and half secret trusts and the consequences of the failure of each, the issue of communication being central.

Fully secret trust

If the three requirements of intention, communication, and acceptance are not satisfied, the fully secret trust will fail. However, what will happen to the property?

There are two possibilities:

1. If the person who was intended to be a secret trustee had no knowledge of the trust, that person will be able to take the property for him or herself; ***Wallgrave v Tebbs*** (1855).
2. If the person knew that property was being left to him or her to hold on trust but had no idea what the purpose of that trust was to be, that person cannot keep the property for him or herself. Instead, the legatee will hold the property on trust back to the estate. There are two reasons for this:
   - Because the testator has failed to communicate the three certainties required for all trusts, hence the secret trust will fail and therefore the legatee is not bound to pass the property on to the person the testator wanted to benefit.

- Because the legatee also knew that the testator never intended the legatee to have that property for him or herself, the legatee's conscience is affected and he or she cannot keep the property for him or herself. As it has not been proven that the property must be passed to the intended beneficiary of the secret trust, it must go back to the testator's estate. It is said that this is held on resulting trust but as it seems to be based on the conscience of the trustee it is arguably constructive.

RE BOYES (1884) 26 CH D 531
The testator left the residue of his estate to his solicitor, who had been told that he was to hold it on trust and that he would be informed of the terms of that trust by letter. However, the solicitor did not learn of the terms of the trust until after the testator's death. Despite the solicitor's willingness to carry out the terms of the trust, it was held that he held the property on resulting trust for the estate.

Half secret trust

Unlike a fully secret trust it is clear in a half secret trust that there was an intention to create a trust, so the secret trustee cannot claim the property as a gift. The trust will fail, and the property will be held for the testator's estate.

Proving the existence of a secret trust

The burden of proof

The burden of proof lies on the person trying to establish that the trust exists. Remember, in this respect the same rules apply to fully secret and half secret trusts.

Standard of proof

Although originally the standard of proof was very high (that required to rectify a written instrument: ***Ottaway v Norman*** [1972]), over the years, it has become less stringent. ***Re Snowden*** [1979] states that the standard of proof required is the 'ordinary civil standard of proof'. Table 8.1 recaps the general rules applicable to the creation of fully secret and half secret trusts.

Table 8.1 Summary

	FULLY SECRET TRUST	HALF SECRET TRUST
Appearance	Appears as gift on the face of the will	Appears as trust on the face of the will (purpose and beneficiaries unknown)
Intention	Must intend to create a trust and satisfy the three certainties (***Kasperbauer v Griffith*** [2000])	Must intend to create a trust and satisfy the three certainties (***Kasperbauer v Griffith*** [2000])

Table 8.1 *Continued*

	FULLY SECRET TRUST	HALF SECRET TRUST
Communication	What? Existence of the trust and its terms (***Wallgrave v Tebbs*** (1855)) How? Orally or in writing • Terms of the trust can be in a sealed envelope if the trustee knows it contains the existence and terms of the secret trust (***Re Keen*** [1937]) When? Before death of testator (***Wallgrave v Tebbs*** (1855)) If communication not to all trustees? • Tenants in common: only those who accept the trust are bound Joint tenants: (a)If communication before the will executed, all bound (b)If communication after the will is executed, only those who accept are bound (***Re Stead*** [1900])	What? Existence of the trust and its terms (***Blackwell v Blackwell*** [1929]) How? Orally or in writing • Terms of the trust can be in a sealed envelope if the trustee knows it contains the terms (***Re Keen*** [1937]) as long as the letter is given before the will is executed • Communication must be consistent with the will—not a future communication (***Re Bateman's WT*** [1970]) • Sealed instructions must be delivered before the will is executed. When? Before or at the time of the execution of the will (***Blackwell v Blackwell*** [1929]) If communication not to all trustees? • Trustees cannot claim property as their own • If will allows communication to some trustees, all bound if communication before will is executed If will says all trustees know, if this is not the case, the entire trust fails (***Re Keen*** [1937])
Acceptance	Express or inferred by acquiescence (***Moss v Cooper*** (1861))	Express or inferred by acquiescence (***Moss v Cooper*** (1861))
Failure	• If trustee has no knowledge of trust, he takes beneficially If the trustee knows a trust was intended but not its terms, trustee holds on resulting trust (***Re Boyes*** (1884))	• Trustee cannot claim property as his own—holds on resulting trust

Developing understanding

These issues have been kept separate to help you focus on the core requirements for secret trusts before considering some of the more unusual questions that arise in this area.

Can the secret trustee change his mind?

During the lifetime of the testator this causes no problems; the secret trustee merely informs the testator, who can simply amend the will. However, there may be problems if the secret trustee has a change of mind after the death of the testator or on finding that he or she will not or cannot perform the instructions contained in a sealed envelope. A valid trust has been created and as the trustee knows there is no intention of an outright gift, he or she cannot claim it. There are two contrary views on the result:

- ***Re Maddock*** [1902] suggests *obiter* that the trust will fail (to be held on resulting trust to the estate).
- In ***Blackwell v Blackwell*** [1929] *obiter* comments by Lords Buckmaster and Warrington suggest that as equity will not allow a trust to fail for want of a trustee, the courts can appoint a replacement—willing—trustee.

The possibility of the trustee claiming the property as a gift increases in fully secret trusts, but the principle should still apply.

Can the testator change the terms of the secret trust?

This issue was considered in the context of a half secret trust in the case of ***Re Colin Cooper*** [1939]. The testator left £5,000 on a half secret trust, the purposes of which had been communicated to trustees before his will was executed. The testator later added a codicil to his will which increased the amount to £10,000. However, he failed to communicate this to the secret trustees before his death. The Court of Appeal held that only the original £5,000 was subject to the obligations of the trust. The remainder was held on resulting trust to the estate.

As this was a half secret trust, the trustees could not claim the additional amount as their own property. It is unclear if the same reasoning would apply to a fully secret trust. As the trustees know that the property is subject to a trust, ***Re Boyes*** (1884) would presumably apply; additional property would be held on resulting trust for the estate.

If the amount to be held on secret trust was reduced, Sir Wilfred Greene MR argued, *obiter*, that the greater sum would be considered to cover any lesser sum that was substituted.

Problems caused by the 'dehors the will' explanation of secret trusts

As the trust is created outside the will there are several consequences.

- A witness to a will can benefit from a secret trust:

RE YOUNG **[1951] CH 344**
Mr Young left his estate to his wife; before his death he told her that their chauffeur should receive £2,000. This established a fully secret trust, with his wife as the secret trustee. However, the chauffeur was a witness to the will and **s 15 Wills Act 1837** prohibits witnesses from benefiting from a will. Therefore, if the benefit passed by the will it would be void. The court held that the trust was established when the terms were communicated to Mrs Young.

- A beneficiary of a secret trust who dies before the testator may still benefit from the trust:

RE GARDNER (NO 2) **[1923] 2 CH 230**

A testatrix left all her property to her husband for life, the remainder to be split by way of a fully secret trust among her nephew and nieces. One of the nieces died *two years before* the testatrix. **Section 25 Wills Act 1837** establishes the doctrine of lapse; if a beneficiary under a will dies before the testatrix, the bequest fails and lapses back into the residue of the estate. If the niece took under the Act, her share would lapse. However, Romer J held that the secret trust took effect *dehors* the will and had come into existence as soon as the husband had accepted. Therefore, the trust took effect free of the **Wills Act** and the deceased niece's estate was held to be entitled to her share.

If this decision is correct, a testator would not be able to change his or her will. This is because when the secret trustee accepted the trust, an *inter vivos* trust would be established over all her property. This is contrary to the ambulatory nature of a will and therefore can be changed or revoked at any time until the testatrix's death.

LOOKING FOR EXTRA MARKS?

Re Gardner [1923] illustrates all the problems with the '*dehors* the will' theory and is arguably incorrect. While it remains an authority, the weight of academic opinion suggests that it should not be followed. See 'Key debates' at the end of the chapter.

Can there be a secret trust of land?

Section 53(1)(b) LPA requires an enforceable declaration of a trust of land to be manifested or evidenced in writing. As the communication of the terms of a secret trust or half secret trust may be made orally, this merely indicates the trust's existence. Thus, it appears not to comply with **s 53(1)(b) LPA**. There are conflicting views to this problem:

- ***Re Baillie*** (1886): a half secret trust of land was held to fail because it was not evidenced in writing.
- ***Ottaway v Norman*** [1972]: the oral communication of a fully secret trust of a bungalow was accepted (although the formalities question was not explicitly raised).

This has led a number of commentators to speculate on whether secret trusts are express trusts or constructive trusts. It is arguable that secret trusts of land are acceptable on the basis of the rule in ***Rochefoucauld v Boustead*** [1897], which states that legal formalities will not be insisted on if they are being used to perpetrate a fraud (equity will not allow a statute to be an instrument of fraud). In other words, a legatee who is using the requirement of **s 53(1)(b) LPA** to make the trust fail so that he or she can claim the property for him or herself will not be allowed to succeed.

Conclusion

Secret trusts are characterized by conceptual uncertainty and inconsistency and are therefore a topic ripe for examination. The development of secret trusts aims to give effect to the final intentions of the testator. (See the online resources for a discussion of mutual wills, which is a further issue with testamentary dispositions.) The development of secret trusts echoes, perhaps, the decision in ***Choithram v Pagarani*** [2001], in which Lord Browne-Wilkinson stated that equity will not 'strive officiously to defeat the intention of the testator'. While the origins of secret trusts lie many years in the past, they still appear to be in use, reflecting their continuing usefulness in today's society.

KEY CASES

CASE	FACTS	PRINCIPLE
Blackwell v Blackwell [1929] AC 318	The testator gave legacies to five people to apply the income 'for the purposes indicated by me to them'. Instructions to the trustees were made orally, to benefit the testator's mistress and their illegitimate son.	The House of Lords established the validity of a half secret trust, satisfying the same basic requirements as a fully secret trust. Additionally, *obiter*, that should the secret trustee refuse to carry out the trust, this would not defeat the trust and a willing replacement would be appointed.
McCormick v Grogan (1869) LR 4 HL 82	The testator left property to Grogan and as he lay dying instructed Grogan that there was a letter instructing Grogan as to what to do with the property after the testator's death. The terms of the instructions were not obligatory: 'I do not wish you to act strictly on the foregoing instructions, but leave it entirely to your own good judgement to do as you think I would, if living, and as the parties are deserving.' Grogan complied with some of the wishes but not all.	• The wording of the letter was properly constructed as imposing merely a moral obligation upon Grogan. This was not sufficient to create a secret trust and therefore the claimant's action failed. • Secret trusts are imposed to prevent a secret trustee from defrauding a testator, who only left property to the secret trustee in reliance on his promise to carry out the testator's wishes.
Moss v Cooper (1861) 4 LT 790	The testator left property to three secret trustees: G, S, and O. The will and details of trust were drawn up by one of the secret trustees, who then communicated the details of the trust to the other two secret trustees, who neither expressly rejected nor accepted. S did accept eventually but O remained silent on the issue.	• It will be sufficient if the intention and terms of a secret trust are communicated to the trustees by an agent of the testator. • Silence can also amount to acceptance; knowing of the trust, he failed to object.

CASE	FACTS	PRINCIPLE
Ottaway v Norman [1972] 2 WLR 50	The testator left property to his housekeeper on the understanding that on her death she would leave the property to O. She died and left the property to N.	• Sets out the requirements for a valid secret trust. • Land can be the subject matter of a secret trust.
Re Keen [1937] Ch 236	The testator had given one of his trustees instructions contained in a sealed envelope to be opened on his death. He did this before his will was executed. However, after he died the relevant bequest in his will stated that the property was left to the trustees for purposes that *would be communicated* to them in his lifetime.	• Details of the secret trust could be in a closed envelope if, before the testator's death, the trustee knew of the testator's intention to create a trust and where he could find the terms of this trust (constructive communication). • The will must be consistent with the communication. The testator had already informed the trustees of his wishes, while the will referred to future communication.

KEY DEBATES

Topic	Fraud as a justification
Academic/author	Critchley
Viewpoint	That the argument for *dehors* is implausible and that fraud is the justification.
Source	Critchley, 'Instruments of Fraud, Testamentary Dispositions and the Doctrine of Secret Trusts' (1999) 115 LQR 631.

Topic	Secret trusts as *dehors* the will
Academic/author	Kincaid
Viewpoint	The relationship between the will and the secret trust and the justifications evaluated.
Source	Kincaid, 'The Tangled Web: The Relationship Between the Secret Trust and the Will' [2000] Conv 420.
Academic/author	Pawlowski and Brown

Topic	Secret trusts operate outside the will
Viewpoint	That the secret trust is an express trust which is created outside the will and may be justified on the basis of estoppel.
Source	Pawlowski and Brown, 'Constituting a Secret Trust by Estoppel' [2004] Conv 388.

EXAM QUESTIONS

Problem question

Jasper recently died; his will makes the following bequests:

- To Kamjit and Hamid I leave my home, Bushmills.
- To Jessica I leave my shares in Badgers Bridges Ltd to be held on trust, on terms of which they are aware.

The will is dated 12 December 2003. The same day, Jasper called Jessica and asked her to be his secret trustee. He also told her that the details of the trust were locked in his safe. Jessica accepted. Two days before his death Jasper met Kamjit and said that he had left his home to Kamjit, but it was to be for the benefit of their love child, Hector. Kamjit broke down and cried and said nothing.

Advise Jessica, Hamid, and Kamjit.

Essay question

The fraud theory cannot justify a secret trust as it is in itself a fraud on the requirements of the **Wills Act 1837**.

Discuss.

Online resources

For an outline answer to this essay question, as well as multiple choice questions, bonus material and interactive key cases, please visit the online resources.

Concentrate Q&As

For more questions and answers on equity and trusts, see the *Concentrate Q&A: Equity & Trusts* by Rosalind Malcolm.

Go to the end of this book to view **sample pages**.

Implied trusts

9

KEY FACTS

- Implied trusts can be either resulting or constructive.
- There are no formalities for the creation of implied trusts.
- The law has developed methods of identifying the creation of implied trusts.
- Implied trusts are particularly important in relation to the family home.

Introduction

The flexibility of equity to adapt to the changing demands of society and commercial needs is seen nowhere more clearly than in the use and development of implied trusts. This chapter will deal with the central issues of implied trusts and identify where they link to other areas of study. It is important to see trusts as a whole, rather than separate and discrete areas.

An important area for implied trusts is in relation to allocating rights in a family home. Lord Hope in ***Stack v Dowden*** [2007 noted that this area was of interest not just to the parties but to society in general. The cases reflect changing social attitudes to family roles and are a topic ripe for examination. The law in relation to implied trusts in this area has been dealt with in a separate section to help understand how the law on implied trusts applies.

Implied trusts

REVISION TIP

Be aware that implied trusts are a huge subject which can be examined in a variety of areas—as a remedy for breach of trust, enforcing property rights, failure of trusts, and protecting business interests. Different courses will place different emphasis on this area of law, so it is important to take the lead from your own course as to detail and depth. It is impossible in a revision guide to deal with all the complexities of this area.

Chapter 2 briefly considered implied trusts—resulting, constructive, and statutory. This chapter looks in a little more depth at resulting and constructive trusts. Implied trusts arise without the express declaration of trust by the settlor. This chapter considers how these trusts are identified by the courts. Resulting trusts fall into two categories: automatic or presumed. Constructive trusts are more difficult to define as the scope of their application seems to have been 'left deliberately vague' so that the courts can develop them as needed.

Resulting trusts

Resulting trusts are said to operate independently of the intention of the party, but this is not an absolute. The 'settlor' may not intend to create a trust but may still intend to benefit another person with the property. The courts look at the intention to benefit another person rather than the intention to create a trust: ***Twinsectra v Yardley*** [2002].

Automatic resulting trust

As stated in ***Twinsectra v Yardley*** [2002], the automatic resulting trust arises *despite* the intentions of the parties. They arise in the following situations:

1. uncertainty of objects;
2. failure of a contingency;

3. failure to dispose of whole beneficial interest;
4. surplus of funds after a valid purpose trust has completed its purpose;
5. money given for a stated purpose which can no longer be carried out.

Uncertainty of objects

Chapter 3 noted that failure to specify the beneficiaries of a trust means that the trust fails. Equity **abhors a vacuum** and the beneficial interest must be owned by someone and should not exist in suspension. So, the property is said to be held on resulting trust for the settlor: ***Vandervell v IRC*** [1967]. Additionally, poor drafting may result in failure (***Re Diplock*** [1948]) where a purported charitable trust is actually construed as a purpose which does not fall within one of the accepted **anomalous exceptions** (see chapter 7), in which case the property will result back to the settlor or his estate.

Failure of a contingency

Some interests are contingent (conditional); for example, a trust for Iain, should he reach the age of 25. If he fails to reach that age, then the conditions of the settlement have not been fulfilled. A person with a contingent interest has no vested interest in the property; if he or she cannot or does not meet the contingency then the trustee must hold the property for someone. As with the previous situation, this problem is resolved by an automatic resulting trust for the settlor: ***Re Ames Settlement*** [1946].

TERMINOLOGY TIP

A vested interest is a *present* right to property. It is owned by the person who has that interest. But a contingent interest is conditional, and the person has no property until the contingency is met.

Failure to dispose of whole beneficial interest

A failure to specify who owns the whole beneficial interest will mean that it is held for the settlor: ***Re West*** [1900]. For example, Anne leaves her shares to Iain for his lifetime; the trustee is clear that it is for Iain while he lives but who gets the property when Iain dies? The property will result back to Anne's estate.

Surplus of funds after a valid purpose trust has completed its purpose

A valid purpose trust, either charitable or an anomalous exception, may complete the purpose and have money left over. In this situation, the question arises as to what to do with the trust property and/or any donations.

Purpose trust with human objects

Where the purpose is not charitable and there are human objects of the trust, the question arises as to what to do with the donations (see chapter 7). There are two views on this situation:

- Where there is a pure purpose which is valid and complete, or there is money left at the end of the perpetuity period with no gift over, the money is returned to the donors/settlors: ***Re the Trust of the Abbott Fund*** [1900].
- The money is given to the objects of the trust as an outright gift. The purported purpose is seen as no more than a motive for the donation: ***Re Osaba*** [1978].

Purpose trust with no human objects

If the purpose has no human beneficiaries but is one of the anomalous exceptions, the property will result back to the estate of the settlor after the completion of the task or the end of the perpetuity period. Different rules will apply to charitable trusts (see chapter 6).

Unincorporated associations

A trust for an unincorporated association can be seen as a purpose trust (see chapter 7). When the association ceases to exist, there are two main interpretations of how to deal with the property held by the association:

- The property held by the association is held on resulting trust by the association for the individual members and will be divided between them in proportion to their contributions: ***Re Printers and Transferrers' Amalgamated Trades Protection Society*** [1899]. The problem with this interpretation is that the members and contributors may not be identifiable. So, this analysis can only work where the contributors are ascertainable.
- The property held by the association is held for the members of the association according to the contractual obligations in the association rules: ***Re Bucks Constabulary Widows' and Orphans' Fund Friendly Society (No 2)*** [1979]. The advantage of this is the ascertainability of the people entitled to the funds (see chapter 7 for further comments on this matter).

LOOKING FOR EXTRA MARKS?

An interesting view was taken by Goff J in ***Re West Sussex Constabulary's Widows, Children and Benevolent Fund (1930) Trusts*** [1971]. He differentiated between contributions made by members and funds raised by donations and fundraising raffles. It was suggested that those who donate to street collections have no intention of retaining an interest.

Money given for a stated purpose which can no longer be carried out

When money is paid to a person on the understanding that it will be used for a certain purpose then, if that purpose cannot be carried out, then the money will be held on resulting trust for the donor: ***Barclays Bank v Quistclose*** [1970]. This has been the subject of much academic discussion as Lord Wilberforce, expressing the view of the court, ruled that the money was transferred on trust for the payment of shareholder dividends (the primary trust). When the primary trust was not exercised, a secondary trust arose (the resulting trust) to return the money to the lender.

There are problems with this analysis; it seems illogical to have two trusts over the same property at the same time, at odds with the requirements of certainty (see chapter 3). Also, if there was a primary trust who were the objects? Not the shareholders, otherwise they should have had property in the money and it should have been paid to them on liquidation. It would also not explain how a *Quistclose Trust* can arise when the purpose of the loan is to buy machinery, as this would mean that the 'primary' trust would fail as a purpose trust (see chapter 7).

In ***Twinsectra v Yardley*** [2002], Lord Millett has interpreted this situation as a voluntary transfer, creating a trust with a power (see chapter 2) to apply for a specific purpose. This interpretation may be a method to allow the successful enforcement of the purpose as there are no restrictions on a power being for a purpose, whilst enabling the lender to have a proprietary claim over the loaned money. It will, however, require careful drafting to enable the courts to establish that the money was lent on trust (certainty of intention from words creating an express trust?) with the power to use for the stated purpose, buying machinery: ***Re EVTR*** [1987] or repaying loans: ***Twinsectra v Yardley***. If the power is exercised then the lender just becomes a creditor for the loan; if the power is not exercised then the money is held for the lender.

The focus for the courts is in finding the necessary intention when lending the money to the recipient. While holding in a separate account is good evidence, it is not essential: ***Re EVTR Ltd***. The courts will also look at the agreement between the parties to ascertain the intention. In ***Twinsectra v Yardley***, Lord Millett said that as the agreement indicated that the money was not at the free disposal of the recipient it was held on resulting trust for the settlor if not used for the specified purpose.

LOOKING FOR EXTRA MARKS?

Read the commentaries on ***Quistclose*** and ***Twinsectra***; consider whether the analysis of the primary and secondary trust has any validity. A focus for essays may be in identifying the nature of the trust; the language of the judges appears to reference constructive, while also calling them resulting trusts. There is much to commend them as express trusts with a power.

Also consider that the trust analysis protects the lender in a commercial context on insolvency but disadvantages other creditors. The use of a ***Quistclose*** trust seems to give a preference to certain creditors, which is contrary to the provisions in the **Insolvency Act 1986**. The litigation in relation to the collapse of Farepak is worth reading to gain an understanding in this area. (See the online resources for further discussion.)

Presumed resulting trusts

There are a number of situations in which the conduct of the parties will create a presumption that a resulting trust was intended. These are:

1. the voluntary conveyance of property to another;
2. the purchase of property in the name of another.

Remember that presumptions are only a starting point for the court and can be rebutted by evidence which indicates a different intention.

LOOKING FOR EXTRA MARKS?

There has been much academic debate, particularly between Professor Swadling and Professor Chambers, about the nature of the intention required to form this presumption. This can form the basis of an essay question: is it the intention to retain a beneficial interest or the absence of an intention to pass the beneficial interest (Lord Millett in ***Air Jamaica v Charlton*** [1999])? See the 'Key debates' section at the end of the chapter.

Voluntary conveyance

A voluntary conveyance refers to a transfer of property where the recipient does not provide **valuable consideration**. The maxim that 'equity presumes a bargain and never a gift' holds that a party would never give away property. In this situation, the presumption (the starting evidential point for the court) is that the property is held by the recipient of the legal title (presuming that the legal formalities for transfer are perfect—see chapter 5) for the benefit of the transferor.

Where the property transferred is real property (land) it is not subject to the requirements of writing: **s 53(2) LPA**. Here the presumption of resulting trust is undermined by **s 60(3) LPA**. This states that:

> in a voluntary conveyance, a resulting trust for the grantor shall not be implied, merely by reason that the property is not expressed to be for the use or benefit of the grantee.

It has been suggested that the effect of this section is that a resulting trust will no longer be presumed where the property conveyed is land. In ***Lohia v Lohia*** [2001] it was said that 'on a plain reading' of the section the presumption of resulting trust was abolished. However, other cases maintain that as a matter of basic equitable principle **s 60(3) LPA** does not prevent a resulting trust being presumed: see ***Hodgson v Marks*** [1971]. The position is, as Lord Browne-Wilkinson said in ***Tinsley v Milligan*** [1994], 'arguable'.

Purchase in the name of another

When one person provides either part or all of the money required to buy property but is not identified as the legal owner of that property, equity will again assume 'a bargain' and not a gift. In contrast to the voluntary conveyance of property considered earlier, this presumption applies regardless of whether the purchased property is **personalty** or **realty**, therefore **s 60(3) LPA** does *not* apply here.

Where two or more parties contribute towards the purchase they will hold the property in proportion to the contribution they made to the purchase price. The contribution must be prior to or at the time of purchase: ***Cowcher v Cowcher*** [1972].

Rebutting the presumption of resulting trust

As with all presumptions in law, it is for the party who is not relying on the presumption to rebut it.

The presumption of advancement

In certain relationships the presumption of a resulting trust is reversed by the presumption of advancement. Where the presumption arises, on a voluntary transfer or purchase in the name of another, the burden of rebuttal will be on the person claiming that there was *no advancement* (gift): ***McGrath v Wallis*** [1995] (see Table 9.1).

Table 9.1 Summary of the burden of proof

PRESUMPTION RAISED	WHERE THE BURDEN OF PROOF LIES
Resulting trust	On the recipient (donee)
Advancement	On the giver (donor)

Situations where the presumption of advancement applies are as follows:

1. Husband to wife—although in ***Pettitt v Pettitt*** [1970] Lord Diplock expressed a judicial reluctance to apply 'inferences of fact . . . [from the] intention . . . of spouses belonging to the propertied classes of a different social era'. Note that the presumption does not apply:
   - wife to husband: ***Abrahams v Trustees of the Property of Abrahams*** [1999]; and
   - man to mistress, no matter how dependent: ***Gavin-Mack v Gavin-Mack*** (1993).
2. Father to legitimate child: ***Shepherd v Cartwright*** [1955]. This presumption has been weakened in the modern financial climate: ***McGrath v Wallis*** [1995]. The presumption does not automatically apply between mother and child: ***Ward v Snelling*** (1994). However, it would be easier for the child to rebut the presumption of resulting trust because of the relationship of love and affection between the parties: ***Bennet v Bennet*** (1879).
3. Where a person is *in loco parentis* to a person to whom he or she acts as a father, the same presumption of advancement set out previously will apply: ***Re Paradise Motor Co*** [1968]. *Obiter* comments by Lindsay J in ***Re Cameron*** [1999] suggest that both parents are assumed to be *in loco parentis* unless the contrary is proved. In ***Silverwood v Silverwood*** (1997) the Court of Appeal assumed that the presumption of advancement would apply between mother and son.

Other relationships in which this presumption has been recognized include:

- father and illegitimate child: ***Beckford v Beckford*** (1774);
- stepfather and stepson: ***Re Paradise Motor Co*** [1968];
- grandfather and grandchild: ***Ebrand v Dancer*** (1680).

This presumption was to be removed by **s 199 Equality Act 2010** as it is outdated in current social situations, but as yet this section remains unenacted.

The transfer was merely a loan

Evidence can be provided that the grantor intended his or her contribution only as a loan and there was no intention of gaining an interest in the property, but merely a contractual right: ***Clark v Mandoj*** [1998].

The transfer was intended as a gift

Evidence, express or by conduct, which is sufficiently certain as to create the intention to give as a gift will rebut the presumption of a resulting trust: ***Fowkes v Pascoe*** (1875).

What evidence can be relied upon to rebut these presumptions?

Timing of evidence

Statements made before or at the time of transfer or purchase: acts or statements made before or at the time of transfer can be relied upon by *both parties* in addressing whether a presumption of resulting trust or advancement is to be rebutted. Statements made after transfer or purchase *cannot* be relied upon by the *maker* of those statements: ***Shepherd v Cartwright*** [1955].

LOOKING FOR EXTRA MARKS?

Shepherd v Cartwright [1955] suggests that acts or declarations which occur '*so immediately* after [the purchase] as to constitute part of the transaction are admissible' (emphasis added). It will be a question of fact whether later statements made after the transfer are part of the transaction. This may be a point of discussion in an exam.

Nature of evidence

Evidence of illegal purpose: the law in this area has recently been reviewed by the Supreme Court in ***Patel v Mirza*** [2016]. Although this was not a case related to trusts but to restitution, the principles apply equally to trusts law. Before this case, the situation had been the 'reliance' model from the decision in ***Tinsley v Milligan*** [1994]. In this situation, the person claiming a resulting trust merely had to point to the (primary) fact of a contribution to purchase and had no need to rely on evidence of the intention behind the primary fact. To rebut the presumption of resulting trust, the legal owner (Tinsley) had to rely on the introduction of evidence of their intention behind the primary fact, of carrying out a (joint) illegal purpose. By a majority, the House of Lords held that this evidence was inadmissible, rejecting the Court of Appeal 'public conscience' approach. Lord Goff had taken a broader approach, that as both were involved with the illegality then the court of equity should follow the law.

In ***Patel v Mirza*** by a majority decision, the Supreme Court has introduced a multifactorial approach to introducing the evidence of an illegal purpose. Lord Toulson stated that policy and proportionality should be considered, which may include:

- why the activity was made illegal;
- the centrality of the activity to the claim and its seriousness;
- what would be the policy consequences of denying the claim;
- whether denying the claim would be disproportionate to one party, considering such factors as the nature of the conduct of each party. (Did one party take a greater role in the actions?)

This introduces a more flexible and perhaps fairer method by which the illegal intention of the parties can be used to rebut the presumed intention of the parties.

LOOKING FOR EXTRA MARKS?

The decision in ***Tinsley v Milligan*** led to difficult decisions such as ***Tribe v Tribe*** [1996], when a father was allowed to introduce evidence of an illegal purpose, because that purpose was never carried through to completion. It was unclear from the decision in ***Tribe v Tribe*** how far the illegal purpose had to progress before it can be said to be capable of withdrawal. It is uncertain whether the majority decision in ***Patel v Mirza*** has improved the test; indeed, Lord Sumption in the minority, defended the reliance test, but it does remove the problems that arose from the different burden of proof in a presumed resulting trust and the presumption of advancement. So perhaps the law will be more flexible in the light of ***Patel v Mirza***, but is this flexibility desirable?

Constructive trusts

Unlike resulting trusts, the categories of constructive trusts are not clearly defined. They have been left 'perhaps deliberately vague' (per Edmund-Davies LJ in ***Carl Zeiss Stiftung v Herbert Smith*** [1969]). They have been used as a residuary category of trusts which are imposed by the courts when 'justice . . . may require'.

It can be simply stated that the courts 'construct' a trust around the conscience of the legal owner. The institutional constructive trust is then imposed when the relevant facts are found and 'arises by operation of law as from the date of the circumstances which give rise to it: the function of the court is merely to declare that such trust has arisen in the past', per Lord Browne-Wilkinson, ***Westdeutsche Landesbank Girozentrale v Islington LBC*** [1996].

LOOKING FOR EXTRA MARKS?

Remedial constructive trusts have been used in other jurisdictions such as Australia and New Zealand but has been resisted in the English courts, which have preferred the institutional constructive →

trust. While there were hints that a remedial trust could eventually develop (see the comments of Lord Scott in ***Thorner v Major*** [2009]), the current position is that England and Wales do not use a constructive trust as a remedy for a wrong: ***Polly Peck International plc (in administration) No 2*** [1998] and has been clearly rejected in ***Angove's Pty Ltd v Bailey*** [2016], which involved mistaken payments. Although it is unclear why the mistaken payment was held on trust, the *obiter* comments by Lord Sumption on the issue of remedial constructive trusts are informative.

Traditional constructive trusts

A breach of a fiduciary obligation will give rise to a constructive trust. Fiduciary relationships generally arise where there is a situation of 'trust and confidence' between the parties. A fiduciary relationship can arise in a variety of situations, such as solicitor/client; accountant/client. Where such a relationship exists, the fiduciary owes an obligation to the principal to carry out his or her fiduciary duties correctly. The following are examples of where a breach of a fiduciary obligation has created a constructive trust:

1. solicitor: ***Lipkin Gorman v Karpnale*** [1991];
2. trustee: ***Keech v Sandford*** (1726);
3. company directors: ***Guinness v Saunders*** [1990];
4. intermeddlers with a trust: ***Mara v Browne*** [1896];
5. recipients of trust property: ***BCCI v Akindele*** [2000];
6. persons who assist in the breach of a trust: ***Twinsectra v Yardley*** [2002];
7. secret commissions and bribes: ***FHR European Ventures LLP v Cedar Capital Partners*** [2014];
8. breach of contractual obligations: ***Ashburn Anstalt v Arnold*** [1989].

LOOKING FOR EXTRA MARKS?

Note that these categories are not closed. Judicial statements indicate that even a thief who obtains property raises the necessary fiduciary relationship to create a constructive trust: ***Westdeutsche Landesbank Girozentrale v Islington LBC*** [1996]. The law in relation to mistaken payments and the creation of a trust was stated in ***Chase Manhatten Bank NA v Israel-British Bank*** [1981], which created a trust of such payments. In the recent decision of ***Angove's Pty Ltd v Bailey*** [2016] the Supreme Court confirmed that mistaken payments were held on trust, but sadly the reason is unclear. This may create the opportunity for academic and legal debate.

Categories 1–7 are dealt with in detail in later chapters so are only identified here for you to see the interwoven nature of equitable principles.

Contractual obligations giving rise to constructive trusts

A contractual relationship does not necessarily create a fiduciary relationship, so it would be incorrect to say that it is imposed as a fiduciary. However, the constructive trust has been used as a method of giving a remedy for a breach of contractual obligations.

Ashburn Anstalt v Arnold [1989] stated that a constructive trust can be imposed where the court is 'satisfied that the conscience of the owner of the land had been affected so that it would be inequitable to allow him to deny the claimant an interest'. However, this decision is based on its own particular facts and has been doubted in ***IDC v Clark*** [1992].

LOOKING FOR EXTRA MARKS?

The imposition of a trust for the breach of a personal obligation may be a step too far. See the decision in a commercial context of ***Yeoman's Row v Cobbe*** [2008], which seemed to shut the door on their imposition, although Lord Scott's later statements in ***Thorner v Major*** [2009] seemed to reopen it.

Trusts of the family home

When relationships break up the most common battle is over the ownership of the family home. In this part of the chapter we consider how implied trusts apply to family property. When a home is legally owned by two or more people at law they will own the property as joint tenants. There is a presumption that they will also own the beneficial interest as joint tenants. The burden will be on the person trying to rebut that presumption to prove that the beneficial interest is owned differently: ***Stack v Dowden*** [2007]. If there is only one legal owner then it is for the claimant to establish a beneficial interest first, before it can be quantified: ***Lloyds Bank v Rosset*** [1991]. It is clear from recent decisions in cases of single legal ownership that to establish the interest there is a two-stage process: first to establish the beneficial interest and then to quantify the beneficial interest.

Resulting trusts

It has been suggested by the Supreme Court in ***Jones v Kernott*** [2011] that resulting trusts are no longer applicable to the allocation of beneficial interests in family property. The law on resulting trusts would consider that any contribution made prior to or at the time of purchase of the home (***Curley v Parkes*** [2004]) would be used to allocate a beneficial interest in the home. A point to note is that when there is a mortgage over the property, the person who takes the mortgage out is held to make that contribution on his or her own behalf: ***Cowcher v Cowcher*** [1972].

Quantifying the share of the home under a resulting trust

The share is in direct proportion to the contribution. This is the 'bank balance' approach to allocating shares in the home; if there was a 10 per cent contribution to the purchase this will give rise to a 10 per cent interest in the property.

LOOKING FOR EXTRA MARKS?

Until the decision in ***Jones v Kernott*** is followed and applied in the courts, the role of resulting trusts is unclear. For a review of the decision, it may be worth looking at ***Crossco No 4 Unlimited v Jolan*** [2011] to see how courts are responding to the case.

Constructive trusts and the family home

An interest in the family home may be gained when it would be 'unconscionable' for the legal owner to deny that another person should have some claim to the ownership of the home. It was accepted in ***Gissing v Gissing*** [1971] that contributions other than financial can create an interest in the home. Lord Bridge in ***Lloyds Bank v Rosset*** [1991] stated that this is based upon the common intention of the parties. This can be found in two ways:

1. express common intention constructive trust;
2. inferred (implied) common intention constructive trust.

As stated in ***Stack v Dowden*** [2007], it is clear that there is a two-stage procedure:

1. establish a beneficial interest;
2. quantify the beneficial interest.

See Figure 9.1.

Figure 9.1 Process of constructive trust in the family home

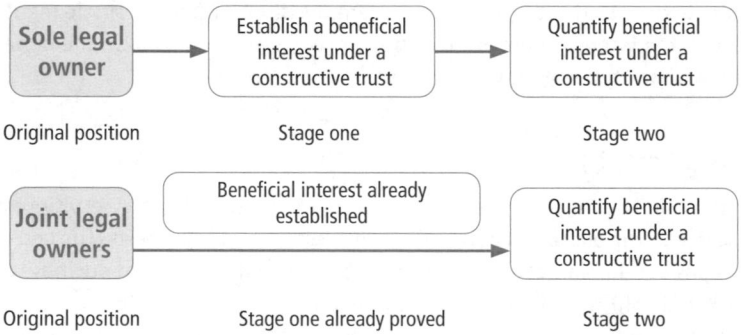

Express common intention trusts

An express common intention constructive trust will arise when, at the time of acquisition (but exceptionally later), the parties have expressed a shared common intention to share the interest in the home:

1. The intention must be express.
2. The intention must be common.
3. The common intention must relate to the acquisition of a share in the beneficial interest of the family home.

Express

In ***Springette v DeFoe*** [1992] Dillon LJ said that the interest:

> cannot mean an intention which each happened to have in his or her own mind but had never communicated to each other.

The express agreement can be 'imperfectly or imprecisely remembered' as Lord Bridge said in ***Lloyds Bank v Rosset*** [1991]. The courts are not looking for legal language, but language clear enough to form the necessary intention on which to base a proprietary interest.

Common

The intention must be common. It must be shared by both parties and not the view of only one of the parties. In ***Springette v DeFoe*** [1992] Dillon LJ stated that as the parties' intention was not expressed it would be difficult to find that their intention was 'common'.

Sharing the home

The parties' intention must be to share the home, not just to share their lives. Thus, an agreement to pay rent would not help to establish an interest in the family home: ***Thomas v Fuller-Brown*** [1988]. It must concern gaining an interest in the family home. In ***Eves v Eves*** [1975], lies to the young claimant about why she was not to be registered on the legal title gave the courts enough evidence that there had been a discussion about owning the house and not just sharing a life together.

LOOKING FOR EXTRA MARKS?

It could be suggested that the fact that one party lies is explicit evidence that there is no intention to share. See 'Key debates' at the end of the chapter.

Detrimental reliance

Once an express common intention is found, the person seeking to establish the existence of a constructive trust must prove that he or she relied on that agreement to his or her detriment. The reliance must be subsequent to the express intention, and not something that was being done before and as part of the normal tasks of a couple: ***Lloyds Bank v Rosset*** [1991]. The conduct from which reliance can be found is broad in *this* category of constructive trust. In cases such as ***Eves v Eves*** [1975] and ***Grant v Edwards*** [1986] the courts look for some action that the other would not have done 'but for' believing he or she had an interest in the home (see Table 9.2).

Table 9.2 Conduct following an express agreement

CASE	CONDUCT WHICH HAS SUFFICED TO CREATE AN INTEREST FOLLOWING AN EXPRESS AGREEMENT
Eves v Eves [1975]	Had children, cleaned, and decorated home. It seemed significant to the court that she undertook heavy manual work on home.
Grant v Edwards [1986]	'Made a very substantial contribution to the housekeeping and the feeding and bringing up of the children . . . [using] her earnings in that way.'

In considering whether there has been detrimental reliance, the courts try to distinguish between actions which are 'truly' detrimental and those which are merely demonstrations of 'love and affection'. In ***Lloyds Bank v Rosset*** [1991] the actions of Mrs Rosset were no more than would be expected from a wife. See also ***Pettitt v Pettitt*** [1970].

REVISION TIP

A common mistake for students in exams is to leap straight into the discussion of detrimental reliance, using the cases explained earlier. Students will then note that there has been no express agreement. To an examiner this indicates a poorly thought-out answer and perhaps a misunderstanding. If there is no agreement, then the relevance of contributions other than directly financial may only be relevant *to the quantification* of the interest. See the section 'Quantifying the share under a constructive trust', p .

Inferred common intention constructive trusts

In the absence of an express agreement, the common intention is to be inferred from the conduct of the parties. This area has been the subject of much judicial and academic discussion. As a matter of precedent, the House of Lords' decision in ***Lloyds Bank v Rosset*** [1991] states that there is only one type of conduct which allows the courts to infer that the parties intended to share the beneficial interest in the family home—direct financial contributions (see Figure 9.2). This has been cast into doubt by later persuasive authority on the point.

Figure 9.2 Inferred common intention

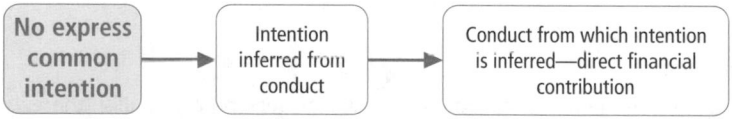

Gissing v Gissing [1971] stated that in the absence of express statements, the question of the parties' intention was an objective one. Lord Bridge went further in ***Lloyds Bank v Rosset*** [1991], where he 'doubted anything else' but contributions which are referable to the acquisition of the property would be sufficient to infer the common intention. Thus, payments at the time of acquisition will apply, such as paying a deposit, but the difference between this and a resulting trust is that later payments to the mortgage will also be sufficient. If there is no such payment, then this category of trust will fail (see Table 9.3).

Table 9.3 Illustrative cases

CASE	CONDUCT THAT HAS NOT GIVEN AN INTEREST UNDER AN INFERRED CONSTRUCTIVE TRUST
Pettitt v Pettitt [1970]	Husband had laid out the garden, built walls, and done substantial work in the home
Thomas v Fuller-Brown [1988]	Designing and building a two-storey extension to home inferred just work in lieu of rent
Gissing v Gissing [1971]	Contributions to children's clothes, her own clothes, and laid the lawn
Hussey v Palmer [1972]	Claimant paid for an extension which increased the value of the house; she gained an interest in the home

LOOKING FOR EXTRA MARKS?

In ***Gissing v Gissing*** [1971], although there was a later express agreement the court held that this did not reflect the parties' intention at the time of acquisition of the home. It may be worth considering whether there is a gender stereotype in cases such as ***Pettitt v Pettitt*** [1970]. Be prepared to comment on cases in essays. Also, the case of ***Burns v Burns*** [1984] can be seen as the high point of the inferred constructive trust concept in the consideration of indirect, and perhaps non-financial, contributions being considered in establishing a constructive trust in the home. ***Lloyds Bank v Rosset*** [1991] has firmly rejected this move. However, obiter comments in ***Stack v Dowden*** [2007] and ***Jones v Kernott*** [2011] suggest that the intention to create a beneficial interest can be inferred (or imputed) based on non-financial or indirect financial contributions to the home. In ***Geary v Rankine*** [2012] the Court of Appeal referred favourably to the judgments in ***Stack v Dowden*** and ***Jones v Kernott***, confirming it as a two-stage test, the first part as to the acquisition of a beneficial interest to be 'deduced objectively from their conduct' (para 20). Here the courts were not convinced that there was a shared intention. More recently, the Court of Appeal confirmed the approach of the 'whole circumstances' in seeking the common intention in ***O'Kelly v Davies*** [2014]. It appears that the courts are taking the stance that the test is not now as narrow as the decision in ***Lloyds Bank v Rosset***. This area will remain in confusion until a case clearly on this point is decided by the Supreme Court.

REVISION TIP

It is important to note that the statements in the cases mentioned do not change the ruling in ***Lloyds Bank v Rosset***, on the issue of *establishing* an equitable interest. As it was not an issue in ***Stack v Dowden*** the comments of the Lords there are *obiter*. Also, the decisions in cases such as ***Geary v Rankine*** [2012] which applied the principles of ***Jones v Kernott*** to the creation of a trust and ***Thompson v Hurst*** [2012], which followed the principles of ***Lloyds Bank v Rosset***, are of the lower court. You should take guidance from how your institution deals with this issue as there is not space to fully discuss the debate here.

Quantifying the share under a constructive trust

Having established the property interest under a constructive trust the courts will then quantify the interest. Unlike the 'bank balance' approach of resulting trusts, the issue of quantification in respect of constructive trusts of the family home is more problematic. As the trust is based upon the conscience of the party, the 'equity required to do justice' will vary. A recent decision where the creation of a trust was based on the comments in ***Stack v Dowden*** was ***O'Kelly v Davies*** [2014]. So, it may be that the law in this area is changing to a more flexible approach.

Starting point

If the parties are joint legal owners, the starting position for the courts will be that 'equity follows the law' and they share the beneficial ownership: ***Stack v Dowden*** [2007]. Where there is sole legal ownership the law presumes that it is owned solely by the legal owner. The person trying to rebut these presumptions can produce evidence to the contrary.

Evidence

While parties may agree to share their home they rarely, in the flush of romance, discuss just how the home will be divided should they separate. If such an agreement is made, then the courts will give effect to that express agreement: ***Springette v DeFoe*** [1992]. This will apply regardless of actual contributions: ***Clough v Killey*** [1996].

In an inferred common intention constructive trust, the evidence will be based upon the contributions made by the beneficial claimant: ***Gissing v Gissing*** [1971]. However, for both types of constructive trust these are starting positions for allocating interests.

The courts take what has been called a 'broad-brush approach' to quantifying the share and will look at the whole course of dealing between the parties to allocate interests. Cases such as ***Midland Bank v Cooke*** [1995] and ***Drake v Whipp*** [1996] have suggested that 'the whole course of dealing' between the parties should be considered which 'should not be confined to acts of direct contributions'. In ***Oxley v Hiscock*** [2004], Chadwick LJ suggested quantifying interests in the family home based on principles of 'fairness' at the end of the relationship or based on principles of proprietary estoppel: ***Yaxley v Gotts*** [2000].

Stack v Dowden [2007] reviewed this area, while calling for changes in how to establish a beneficial interest; it rejected decisions based on fairness (see Lord Neuberger at 144), but Baroness Hale set out very clearly in her judgment what factors may be considered. The approach taken in ***Oxley v Hiscock*** was approved by the Supreme Court in ***Jones v Kernott*** [2011].

LOOKING FOR EXTRA MARKS?

There is currently a Cohabitation Rights Bill before Parliament and it may be worth considering if the prospective legislation, which may never be enacted, would improve the situation for cohabitees.

REVISION TIP

In explaining this area, it is essential that students are very clear that a two-stage approach is taken when there is a sole legal owner. First, it is necessary to establish a beneficial interest, using the principles in ***Lloyds Bank v Rosset***. The second step, which also applies when there are joint legal owners, is to establish the beneficial share: ***Stack v Dowden***.

Proprietary estoppel

If the intention to create a trust cannot be found, the courts retain the ability to find an estoppel (see recently ***Southwell v Blackburn*** [2014]). It is important to note that proprietary estoppel can be the basis of an action (therefore a sword and a shield). The courts look for:

- an assurance, which can be a unilateral statement; and
- reliance of the claimant: see ***Pascoe v Turner*** [1979].

Detriment which makes conduct unconscionable

Assurance can be active or passive, such as allowing another to work on your property, knowing that he or she believes by such actions he or she will gain an interest in the home. The reliance can be not seeking alternative arrangements for accommodation or work: ***Gillett v Holt*** [2001]. This area was reviewed in a commercial context in ***Yeoman's Row v Cobbe*** [2008] and in a family situation in ***Thorner v Major*** [2009].

Remedies

The remedies available for estoppel are the 'minimum equity to do justice': ***Jennings v Rice*** [2002]. This can be the payment of financial compensation, as in ***Dodsworth v Dodsworth*** (1973) to a transfer of full ownership: ***Thorner v Major*** [2009].

Conclusion

The imposition of implied trusts has a varied and complex basis. A resulting and constructive trust can be applied to any property but has particular practical relevance in relation to the family home.

However, be aware that implied trusts is a huge topic, which can be examined in a variety of areas: as a remedy for breach of trust, enforcing property rights, failure of trusts, and protecting business interests.

KEY CASES

CASE	FACTS	PRINCIPLE
Barclays Bank v Quistclose [1970] AC 567	Money was lent for the payment of dividends. The payments were not made, and the company went into liquidation.	The money given to pay dividends was held on a primary trust to pay dividends and when that failed the secondary trust (resulting) was to repay the lender.
Jones v Kernott [2011] UKSC 53	Property was bought in joint names and the parties later separated. On the allocation of property rights, the courts had to determine how the share could be determined.	As the parties already had a beneficial interest as legal joint tenants the only issue was to consider the size of the beneficial interest. The courts considered that resulting trusts were not the suitable approach to take in family situations such as this, and approved the approach taken in ***Oxley v Hiscock*** [2004].
Lloyds Bank v Rosset [1991] AC 107	Property was purchased with a mortgage in the name of Mr Rosset only. Extensive renovation work was supervised by Mrs Rosset. The bank claimed possession of the home when the mortgage was defaulted. Mrs Rosset tried to establish an equitable interest in the home by way of constructive trust.	To establish an interest under a constructive trust it must be proved that there was: • an express declaration that the beneficial interest would arise, followed by detrimental reliance; or • financial contributions to the purchase of the home, which could be post-acquisition, from which the courts could infer a common intention as to beneficial ownership.
Shepherd v Cartwright [1955] AC 431	Property was purchased by a father for his legitimate child.	The court presumes that this is a gift and no equitable interest arises for the father unless he can prove a contrary intention.
Patel v Mirza [2016] UKSC 42	The case involved insider dealing, so was based outside the issues of equity. Why it is important is in discussing the use of illegality as evidence.	The reliance model of illegality in ***Tinsley v Milligan*** was no longer the correct test but should be one based on the broader issues of policy, proportionality, and public interest.

KEY DEBATES

Topic	Constructive trusts and common intention
Academic/author	Lawson
Viewpoint	That the cases where one party lies to another about his or her interest, such as ***Eves v Eves***, suggest that the intention is anything but to share beneficially.
Source	Lawson, 'The Things We Do for Love: Detrimental Reliance in the Family Home' (1996) 16(2) LS 218. See also Gardner, 'Rethinking Family Property' (1993) 109 LQR 263.

Topic	Reform of trusts in the family home
Academic/author	Hughes et al
Viewpoint	Excellent summary of the proposals for reform.
Source	Hughes et al, 'Come Live with Me and Be My Love' [2008] Conv 197.

Topic	Quantification of share in the family home
Academic/author	Dixon
Viewpoint	Does ***Stack v Dowden*** change anything in the imputation or inference of how the beneficial interest should be shared? Also considers the subsequent Privy Council decision.
Source	Dixon, 'Never Ending Story—Co-ownership after *Stack v Dowden*' [2007] Conv 456.

Topic	Commonwealth approaches to sharing the family home
Academic/author	Moffat
Viewpoint	A summary of the approach in other jurisdictions which will form a base for comparative essays.
Source	Moffat, *Trusts Law*, 6th edn (2015), pp 647–60.

Topic	The basis of resulting trust and the role of intention
Academic/author	Swadling
Viewpoint	The ongoing debate between Professor Swadling and Professor Chambers in relation to the function of intention as a basis for a resulting trust.
Source	Swadling, 'Explaining Resulting Trusts' (2008) 124 LQR 72.

Topic	The *Quistclose*-type trust in commercial context
Academic/author	Goodhart and Jones
Viewpoint	The ***Quistclose*** trust raises questions as to how property is held. The development of the trust is an essential development in commerce.
Source	Goodhart and Jones (1980) 43 MLR 489. Generally, see Moffat, *Trusts Law*, 6th edn (2015), pp 760–74 for an excellent summary of the issues.

EXAM QUESTIONS

Problem question

Anne and Iain buy a house for £100,000. Anne takes out a mortgage for £80,000 in her name. Anne pays £18,000, while Iain pays the remaining £2,000. When they move in Iain tells Anne that he thinks couples should share everything. Anne replies, 'That is a lovely idea'. Iain later wins £18,000 on the lottery and gives this to Anne to buy a car.

Iain takes on all the household duties so that Anne can pursue her career. While Anne is pregnant Iain takes over paying the mortgage. Iain agrees to be the primary carer of their child so that Anne can continue her work.

After ten years Anne now wants to sell the house and travel the world, without Iain.

Advise Iain on his interest in the home.

Essay question

The imposition of a resulting trust for a settlor may be contrary to their every intention. Discuss the situations when a resulting trust can arise and if they are justified.

Online resources

For an outline answer to this essay question, as well as multiple choice questions, bonus material and interactive key cases, please visit the online resources.

Concentrate Q&As

For more questions and answers on equity and trusts, see the *Concentrate Q&A: Equity & Trusts* by Rosalind Malcolm.

Go to the end of this book to view **sample pages**.

Variation of trusts 10

KEY FACTS

- A trust may be varied by a power within the trust itself, by the collective consent of the beneficiaries, by the court, through its inherent jurisdiction, or by statute.
- The power of the courts to intervene will depend on whether the variation relates to administrative or managerial matters, or a reorganization of the beneficial interests.
- The **Variation of Trusts Act (VTA) 1958** gives the courts a wide jurisdiction to vary a trust for the benefit of those beneficiaries unable to consent.
- A benefit under the **VTA 1958** will typically be financial but the court can also take into account non-financial benefits.

Introduction

As a trust can operate for many years, there may be occasions where it is useful or necessary to vary the terms of the trust. The most common reason for varying the terms of a trust is to minimize beneficiaries' liability to pay tax. The key issue in variation of trusts is consent—either by the beneficiaries or, where necessary, by the courts. Where this consent does not exist, trustees who do not follow the terms of the trust will be liable for breach of trust. However, it will often be impossible for all the beneficiaries to consent. Therefore, the majority of this chapter will focus on the circumstances in which the courts may approve a variation on their behalf.

Methods of varying the terms of the trust

A trust can be varied by:

- the terms of the trust instrument;
- the consent of beneficiaries;
- the court's inherent jurisdiction; or
- statutory provisions.

The trust instrument

The provisions of the trust may expressly provide trustees with the power to vary the terms of the trust. This allows trustees to modify the terms of the trust to adjust to changing circumstances without having to receive the consent of the beneficiaries or use trust assets in gaining court approval for such variations. While this might appear to give trustees free rein to remould the trust as they see fit, in ***Society of Lloyd's v Robinson*** [1999] Lord Steyn stated that a power to vary the terms of a trust must be exercised for the purpose for which it was granted and not beyond the reasonable contemplation of the parties. Therefore, the extent to which the trustees are free to vary the terms of the trust will depend on the terms on which the power was granted.

EXAMPLE 1

Richard establishes a trust for Jackie for life, remainder to Eleanor. The trust includes a power to the trustees to vary the terms of the trust 'where necessary for the efficient administration of the trust'. If after 20 years' dedicated service the trustees propose to include a new term in the trust to provide them with an annual salary, would they succeed?

Arguably, they would not. The power to vary refers to changes improving the efficient administration of the trust. The trustees are already bound by their fiduciary obligations to carry out their responsibilities. Therefore money should not influence the exercise of their responsibilities! The trustees, of course, remain free to pursue remuneration through other methods—for example, **s 29 Trustee Act 2000** or court-approved payments (see chapter 11).

Beneficiary consent: the rule in *Saunders v Vautier*

Collectively, the beneficiaries can use the rule in ***Saunders v Vautier*** (1841) to end the trust, at which point they may choose to take the property absolutely or resettle it on more favourable terms. This rule can only be applied where:

- all the beneficiaries are together absolutely entitled to the trust property;
- all beneficiaries agree to ending the trust; and
- all beneficiaries are *sui juris*—ie adults (over 18) with the legal capacity to give consent.

There are two important limitations on the rule in ***Saunders v Vautier***:

1. Beneficiaries cannot use the threat of ending the trust as a weapon to force trustees to act in accordance with their instructions: ***Stephenson (Inspector of Taxes) v Barclays Bank Trust Co Ltd*** [1975]. If this were permitted, trustees would effectively be prevented from discharging their fiduciary obligations to the beneficiaries by personally considering and deciding how their best interests are served.
2. *All* beneficiaries must give their consent. If the beneficiaries include children, beneficiaries who cannot legally consent, or others who do not yet exist, the rule in ***Saunders v Vautier*** will not apply.

As any change to the terms of the trust requires the collective consent of all beneficiaries, variation will not always be possible. However, in certain circumstances the court will be able to provide approval for those beneficiaries who cannot do so.

The court's inherent jurisdiction

The courts have an inherent jurisdiction to vary the terms of a trust where the consent of all the beneficiaries cannot be obtained. As Romer LJ stated in ***Re New*** [1901], this is a jurisdiction which is to be exercised 'with great caution, and the court will take care not to strain its powers'. The central concern of the courts is to act only when it is required and, otherwise, to avoid interfering with the intentions of the settlor.

What sort of variations could be approved?

The court will only approve variations relating to the administration and management of the trust. It will not generally intervene in the reorganization of the beneficial interests of the beneficiaries (see Figure 10.1).

In what circumstances will the court approve a variation?

Following the decision of the House of Lords in ***Chapman v Chapman*** [1954], the court's jurisdiction is restricted to two situations: 'emergency' and 'compromise'.

Figure 10.1 The court's inherent jurisdiction

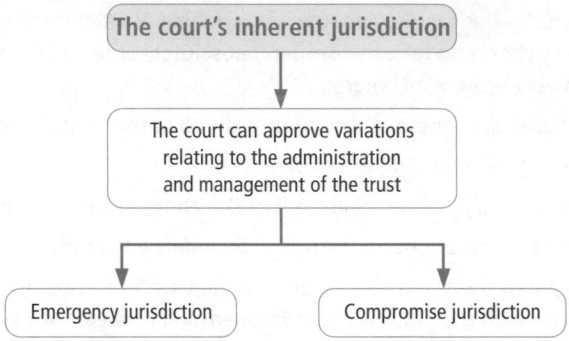

'Emergency'

'Emergency' can be understood in its literal context, as in ***Re Jackson*** [1882], where the trustees needed permission to use trust money to make repairs to prevent a trust property from collapse. However, a more accurate understanding of an 'emergency' is something not anticipated by the settlor: ***Chapman v Chapman*** [1954]. This means that the court will intervene if, *by not taking action*, it would frustrate or interfere with the settlor's intention.

For example, in ***Re Tollemache*** [1903], the court refused to approve a variation merely because it was of financial benefit to the beneficiaries. However, it is interesting to contrast this decision with the reasoning of the Court of Appeal in ***Re New*** [1901]:

RE NEW **[1901] 2 CH 534**

It was proposed that a company, in which the trust already had shares, be reorganized to allow for further growth. It was undisputed that this would be of benefit to the beneficiaries. However, the trustees did not have the power to invest in these new shares and applied for a variation to the terms of the trust from the court.

While the Court of Appeal approved the variation, Romer LJ emphasized that it was not within the court's inherent jurisdiction to interfere merely because a change would be of benefit to the beneficiaries. Instead, *as the proposed variation would not alter the trust's property but only its nature* (ie the *type* of holding), the court was satisfied that its intervention actually *supported* the settlor's intention of leaving shares in this company on trust.

Maintenance provisions—where a settlor has established a trust and directs that the income should be accumulated for a period of time, the court will approve the insertion of a term providing for the maintenance of a beneficiary, on the basis that a settlor would not have established a trust to benefit a beneficiary in the future ensuring their financial position in the meantime: ***Havelock v Havelock*** (1881).

'Compromise'

Originally, 'compromise' was defined widely to allow the court to approve variations to the rights of the beneficiaries: ***Re Downshire Settled Estates*** [1953]. This allowed the court to approve of tax-saving and financially advantageous bargains between different classes of beneficiaries.

However, such a power was difficult to reconcile with the narrower 'emergency' jurisdiction of the courts, and in ***Chapman v Chapman*** [1954] the House of Lords adopted a more restrictive approach. Lord Morton argued that the court only had the jurisdiction to intervene in '*genuine disputes*' over the beneficial interests. He stressed that, in such circumstances, the court could not be said to be interfering with the beneficial interests because the existence of a dispute meant that they were not already clear. Therefore, all the court was doing was *clarifying* the settlor's intentions.

Why is the court's inherent jurisdiction so narrowly defined?

In ***Chapman v Chapman***, Lord Simonds argued that if the courts were to exercise a wider jurisdiction, this should be authorized by the legislature and not claimed by the courts for themselves. This restrictive approach was criticized by the Law Reform Committee in its 1957 report *The Court's Power to Sanction Variation of Trusts* (Cmnd 310), which provided the impetus for the **VTA 1958**. This Act, together with the various other statutory provisions, has now largely replaced the court's inherent jurisdiction with a wider authority to approve changes to the terms of a trust.

Statutory provisions

The courts have also been given statutory authority to vary the terms of a trust in a number of circumstances (see Table 10.1).

Table 10.1 Statutory powers to vary a trust

STATUTE	COURT'S POWER TO VARY
Section 53 Trustee Act 1925	To vary the terms of a trust 'for the maintenance, education, or benefit of the infant'.
Section 57(1) Trustee Act 1925	To approve changes to the administration and management of trusts where it is 'expedient' to do so. Note: this section does not allow the courts to interfere in the *beneficial interests* under a trust: ***Re Downshire Settled Estates*** [1953].
Section 1 Variation of Trusts Act 1958	This wide power allows the court to approve 'any arrangement . . . varying or revoking all or any of the trusts, or enlarging the powers of the trustees of managing or administering any of the property subject to the trusts'.

The Variation of Trusts Act 1958

The **VTA 1958** allows the court to provide consent for certain types of beneficiary where they cannot do so for themselves. Thus, any variation still requires the consent of all other existing *sui juris* beneficiaries. In ***Re Steed's Will Trusts*** [1960], Evershed MR described the Act as conferring 'a very wide and indeed revolutionary discretion' to the courts to vary the terms of a trust.

In order to answer a question on the application of the **VTA 1958**, you will need to consider the following questions (see Figure 10.2):

Figure 10.2 The Variation of Trusts Act 1958

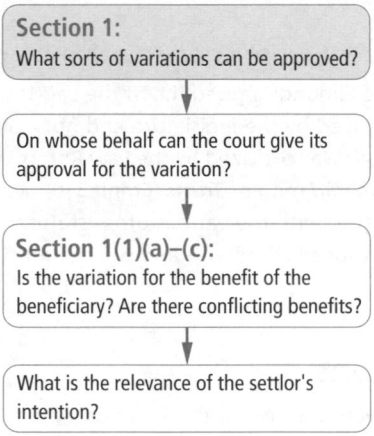

What sorts of variations can be approved?

Section 1 VTA 1958 gives the courts a wide power, so that, unlike other methods of variation, the court can deal with matters relating to both:

- administrative and managerial aspects of the trust; and
- all other terms, including those relating to the beneficial interests under the trust.

However, the court will *not* give its approval for variations which represent, in effect, a complete **resettlement** of the property on new trusts. In ***Re Ball's ST*** [1968], Megarry J explained that 'If an arrangement changes the whole substratum of the trust, then it may well be said that it cannot be regarded merely as varying that trust'. In ***Ridgwell v Ridgwell*** [2007], Behrens J accepted that a variation that created an additional life interest that deferred the entitlement of the **remaindermen** children did not fundamentally alter the basis of the original trust. Compare this decision with the following case:

RE T'S ST **[1963] 3 WLR 987**

A mother held a life interest in half the trust's property, the remainder going to her two children. The other half of the trust's property was to be split between her two children when they reached 21. The mother believed that one of her daughters was irresponsible and immature and applied for a variation to the trust which would transfer her daughter's quarter-share to a new protective trust under which she would hold a life interest. Wilberforce J rejected this proposal as it fundamentally altered the daughter's position under the trust from an absolute interest to a mere life interest.

LOOKING FOR EXTRA MARKS?

The courts' powers under the **VTA 1958** are essentially supportive ones. When discussing the **VTA 1958** in an essay, it is useful to be able to discuss this policy and not just recite the relevant decisions. If you read the judgments in ***Re Ball's ST*** [1968] and ***Re T's ST*** [1963], you will see that the court does more than simply approve or reject proposed variations. In both cases, the court contributes advice on how a successful application can be made. For example, in ***Re T's ST*** [1963], while Wilberforce J was unwilling to approve the proposed application, he was prepared to grant a revised order which *postponed* the vesting of the daughter's absolute interest and created an interim **protective trust** which could be extended should the daughter's behaviour warrant it.

On whose behalf can the court give its approval for the variation?

The **VTA 1958** does not change the fact that all *sui juris* beneficiaries must consent to any proposed variation. In general, the parties to an application under the **VTA 1958** should include the settlor (if still alive) and all beneficiaries. The courts can only give consent on behalf of *four* types of beneficiaries identified in **s 1(1) VTA 1958**.

Section 1(1)(a): infants and those incapable of giving consent

This group will include minors and those persons unable to consent, for example beneficiaries of unsound mind.

Section 1(1)(b): unascertained persons

Under this subsection, the court can give approval for:

Any person (whether ascertained or not) who may be entitled, directly or indirectly, to an interest under the trusts as being at a future date or on the happening of a future event a person of any specified description or a member of any specified class of persons, so however that this paragraph shall not include any person who would be of that description, or a member of that class, as the case may be, if the said date had fallen or the said event had happened at the date of the application to the court.

The meaning of this subsection can be broken down into two parts:

1. It covers those who *may be entitled* at a future date or on the happening of a future event.

KNOCKER V YOULE **[1986] 1 WLR 934**

Property was held on trust for a woman's children. Under the trust, there was a remote chance that the children's Australian cousins could become entitled. The children sought to vary the trust and approval was sought from the court on behalf of the cousins, as it was impractical to obtain the consent of all of them.

The court refused to give its consent on their behalf. In interpreting the phrase 'may be entitled' in **s 1(1)(b)**, Warner J argued that regardless of how unlikely it was that they would become entitled, they still had an interest and their consent was needed to any change.

Section 1(1)(b) does not include those beneficiaries who only have a remote chance of benefiting—they must still consent. Instead, **s 1(1)(b)** covers those beneficiaries whose future *status* may entitle them to an interest. Therefore, a trust which benefits a future spouse would be included as the beneficiary may never marry (***Re Clitheroe's ST*** [1959]). Likewise, a trust which benefits the next-of-kin of a beneficiary would be included as it remains uncertain who the next-of-kin will be until the beneficiary dies (***Re Suffert*** [1961]).

These situations can be distinguished from the unborn beneficiaries dealt with by **s 1(1)(c)** where the question revolves around their *existence* rather than a particular *status*.

2. The proviso to **s 1(1)(b)**:

The second half of **s 1(1)(b)**—beginning 'so however'—contains a proviso which provides that at the time the application is made, it will be assumed that the future date or event has occurred. If, on that basis, there are persons who satisfy the contingency, those persons will have to consent personally, and the court will not do so on their behalf.

RE SUFFERT **[1961] CH 1**

A woman held a life interest under a trust, with the remainder to be passed either to those appointed in her will or, in the absence of a will, to her next-of-kin under the rules of intestacy. When she sought to vary the terms of the trust, she had three adult cousins who were her next-of-kin. The court applied the proviso and considered who would have an interest if, at that point, the woman was assumed to have died. On that basis, it held that it would not provide consent for the cousins.

EXAMPLE 2

Michael establishes a trust for his wife, Catherine, with the remainder to be divided equally between those members of his family who are members of the armed forces. In default of appointment, the capital is to be divided among his nieces and nephews.

Should Catherine wish to vary the terms of the trust, all of Michael's adult nieces and nephews would have to give their consent. Under **s 1(1)(a)**, the court would have the jurisdiction to provide consent for any infant nieces and nephews. Under **s 1(1)(b)**, consent could be given on behalf of those unknown beneficiaries who may at some future time become members of the armed forces. In addition, the court will assume that, at the time of the application, Catherine has died. Therefore, if, at that time, one of Michael's brothers is an Army Lieutenant, the court will apply the proviso in **s 1(1)(b)** and require that the brother also consent to any change.

Section 1(1)(c): unborn beneficiaries

Many trusts seek to provide benefits for future generations of a family. This section allows the court to consent to changes on behalf of those not yet born.

Section 1(1)(d): discretionary beneficiaries under a protective trust

Protective trusts are defined by **s 33 Trustee Act 1925**. If the principal beneficiary's interest is forfeited due to certain events, for example his or her bankruptcy, the property will instead be held on discretionary trust for others, such as the beneficiary and his or her family. As long as the principal beneficiary has not yet forfeited his or her interest, this section allows the court to provide consent on behalf of those who would be entitled under the discretionary trust.

Is the variation for the benefit of the beneficiary?

Section 1 VTA 1958 states that for those beneficiaries under **s 1(1)(a)–(c)** (but not those under **s 1(1)(d)**), any variation must be for their benefit.

'Benefit' has been broadly defined by the courts to include not only financial advantages (eg the reduction of inheritance tax as in ***Re Druce's ST*** [1962]) but also non-financial advantages (see Table 10.2):

Table 10.2 Examples of non-financial benefits accepted by the courts

CASE	NON-FINANCIAL BENEFIT ACCEPTED BY THE COURT
Re T's ST [1963]	Delay to entitlement approved to protect an 'immature and irresponsible' beneficiary from squandering benefits
Re Holt's ST [1968]	Delay in entitlement approved to ensure children were advanced in maturity and careers before becoming independently wealthy
Re Weston's ST [1969]	Proposal to move trust (and beneficiaries) to Jersey for financial advantage rejected in favour of allowing the children to grow up in England
Re Remnant's ST [1970]	Proposal to remove a forfeit clause for those children who married a Roman Catholic approved as preventing family conflict
Re Y Trust [2019]	Proposal to revise definitions of 'issue' and 'descendant' to allow children born into homosexual relationships, illegitimate children, and children adopted over the age of two to be included approved as supporting a strong and cohesive family support structure

The courts' discretion to assess the 'benefit' of a variation is extremely wide and potentially very subjective. This problem is accentuated when the court has to weigh financial benefits against non-financial ones. While this discretion allows the court to consider all the circumstances of a case, it is an unfortunate feature of variation cases that many are heard in private and not reported. Therefore, it is difficult to establish any clear principles determining how that discretion should be exercised.

What is the relevance of the settlor's intention?

In the case of ***Re Steed's WT*** [1960], the settlor's intention to protect her housekeeper from her 'sponging brother' was used to refuse an application by the beneficiary to vary the trust.

However, this case was later distinguished in ***Goulding v James*** [1997].

GOULDING V JAMES **[1997] 2 ALL ER 239**
The testatrix left her daughter, June, a life interest, with the remainder to go to June's son, Marcus, should he reach the age of 40. Marcus's children (of which he had none at the time) would take the remainder if Marcus died before June. June and Marcus applied to the court under s 1(1)(c) VTA 1958 for approval on behalf of Marcus's unborn children to vary the trust. Under their proposal, Marcus and June would take 45 per cent of the estate absolutely, with the remaining 10 per cent held on trust for Marcus's children. While this would benefit the children, it was argued that the testatrix had set up the trust specifically to protect June's interest from her husband, Kenneth, whom she mistrusted. She had also delayed Marcus's benefit as she thought him a 'free spirit' who needed to settle down (Marcus was living in an artistic community in Nantucket at the time). The Court of Appeal approved the variation. The settlor's intention could only be considered insofar as it related to the interests of the beneficiary on whose behalf the court was asked to give consent. As the testatrix's concerns related to June and Marcus, her intentions were irrelevant to the question of whether consent should be given on behalf of Marcus's unborn children.

LOOKING FOR EXTRA MARKS?

Goulding v James renders the settlor's intention largely irrelevant. However, it remains unclear what weight the court would give to that intention should it relate to the interest of the beneficiary the court is being asked to consider. You could gain valuable credit in an exam by being able to analyse the conflicting reasoning. In 'Variation of Trusts: Settlors' Intentions and the Consent Principle in *Saunders v Vautier*' (1997) 60 MLR 719, Luxton argues that if the effect of varying a trust under the VTA 1958 is akin to the operation of the rule in ***Saunders v Vautier***, the court is providing proxy consent for the beneficiary and so, logically, it should only consider questions of relevance to that beneficiary. This would exclude the question of the settlor's intention entirely. However, neither ***Re Steed's WT*** nor ***Goulding v James*** goes quite that far. Instead, we are left with a compromise, wherein the settlor's intentions may sometimes be relevant but rarely conclusively.

KEY CASES

CASE	FACTS	PRINCIPLE
Chapman v Chapman [1954] 2 WLR 723	Raised the question of the court's inherent jurisdiction to vary a trust to the financial advantage of the beneficiaries.	Defined and narrowed the court's inherent jurisdiction to vary a trust to cases of emergency and the resolution of 'genuine disputes' over beneficial interests. Led directly to the enactment of the VTA 1958.

CASE	FACTS	PRINCIPLE
Goulding v James [1997] 2 All ER 239	The court approved the variation of a trust under the **VTA 1958** on behalf of as yet unborn children, despite extrinsic evidence that the settlor's intentions regarding the *sui juris* beneficiaries ran contrary to the changes.	The settlor's intention is only of relevance insofar as it relates to the beneficial interest of the beneficiary on whose behalf the court is asked to consent. However, it will not necessarily outweigh financial benefits.
Re Ball's ST [1968] 1 WLR 899	The court approved a variation dispensing of the settlor's life interest in favour of life interests for his two sons.	The court cannot approve variations which amount to a 'resettlement' of the trust on entirely different terms.
Re Weston's ST [1969] 1 Ch 223	Proposal to move trust (and beneficiaries) to Jersey for financial advantage rejected in favour of allowing the children to grow up in England.	'Benefit' under the **VTA 1958** can include non-financial as well as financial benefits.

KEY DEBATES

Topic	How consistent has the courts' approach to variation of trusts been?
Academic/author	Harris
Viewpoint	Harris provides an excellent overview of the entire area. There has been relatively little written on this area—some extra reading on your part could really improve your marks.
Source	Harris, *Variation of Trusts* (1975).

Topic	What is the relevance of the settlor's intention under the VTA 1958?
Academic/author	Luxton
Viewpoint	***Goulding v James*** distinguished ***Re Steed's WT*** to allow a more restrictive approach to be taken to the settlor's intention. However, this still imposes unsatisfactory constraints upon the court's discretion to vary a trust for the benefit of the beneficiaries.
Source	Luxton (1997) 60 MLR 719.

EXAM QUESTIONS

Problem question

Scott and his wife, Laura, have life interests in the Summers Trust. The remainder is shared equally between their four children, Ben, Connor, Deborah, and Eve, on the condition that they are married at the time their interest vests. The trust states that if any of the children do not marry, their share will pass to their siblings.

Scott and Laura are tired of the wet weather in the United Kingdom and are seriously considering emigrating to Australia. They would like the trustees to be able to invest in residential property in Australia so that they might spend some time there to decide whether they wish to move permanently.

They also wish to help all their children by removing the marriage condition in the trust and inserting a condition that the children will not become entitled until they are 25 years old.

Ben is 23 and married.

Connor is 20 and gay.

Deborah is 16 and a devout Christian. She has broken off all contact with her gay brother and opposes the change on religious grounds.

Eve is 14 and severely autistic. As she finds it extremely difficult to form close personal relationships, her parents are concerned that she will never marry.

Advise Scott and Laura whether the court will give permission for these variations.

Essay question

Discuss the extent to which the courts should take the settlor's intention into account when deciding whether to approve variations under the **VTA 1958**.

Online resources

For an outline answer to this essay question, as well as multiple choice questions and interactive key cases, please visit the online resources.

Concentrate Q&As

For more questions and answers on equity and trusts, see the *Concentrate Q&A: Equity & Trusts* by Rosalind Malcolm.

Go to the end of this book to view **sample pages**.

Trustees' duties and powers

11

KEY FACTS

- Trustees' duties are obligatory and must be carried out.
- Trustees' powers are entirely discretionary.
- Trustees are in general not entitled to **remuneration**, but the **Trustee Act 2000 (TA 2000)** provides for the remuneration of trust corporations and trustees acting in a professional capacity.
- Trustees are the archetypal fiduciary and are subject to strict duties designed to prevent any risk of conflict between their duties and their own personal interests.
- When a beneficiary is entitled to an income from trust property, trustees have a duty to invest. This duty is predominantly dealt with by the reforms of the **TA 2000**.
- Trustees have a duty to provide beneficiaries with information about the trust, but this is not absolute.
- Powers of maintenance and advancement allow trustees to assist certain beneficiaries before their entitlement vests.

Introduction

This chapter deals with the main duties and powers of trustees. Rather than rigidly separating duties and powers, this chapter presents the duties and powers of trustees in a way which reflects how they might arise during the operation of a trust. Therefore, after dealing with the initial questions of the appointment, removal, and payment of trustees, the chapter turns to issues arising on appointment to the trust and then those likely to arise during the administration of the trust.

The appointment and removal of trustees

Anyone with the capacity to hold property can be a trustee, for example adults of sound mind and corporations. Trustees are typically appointed by the settlor or testator in the trust instrument or will. If a person is named as a trustee but is unwilling to accept the role, that person may disclaim (refuse) the trust. This should be done by a deed. A trustee cannot disclaim *part* of the trust—acceptance of part of the trust is acceptance of the whole: ***Re Lord and Fullerton's Contract*** [1896]. A trust should typically have no more than four trustees (although the settlor may expressly require more, and the court may authorize further trustees where appropriate).

- Trusts of realty (trusts including land) should have a minimum of two trustees.
- Trusts of personalty (trusts which involves only personal property) may operate with a single trustee.

How can additional trustees be appointed?

- An express power in the trust instrument.
- **Section 36(6) Trustee Act 1925**—as long as there are no more than three trustees, additional trustees may be appointed by either the person expressly given the power to do so (**s 36(6)(a)**) or, if there is no such person, the other trustees (**s 36(6)(b)**).
- **Section 19 Trusts of Land and Appointment of Trustees Act (TOLATA) 1996**—where all beneficiaries are *sui juris* and collectively absolutely entitled to the trust property, they may direct the trustees to appoint an additional trustee of their choosing. This power cannot be exercised where (i) the trust instrument has expressly conferred a power to appoint trustees to someone else; or (ii) there are already more than three trustees.
- **Section 20 TOLATA 1996**—beneficiaries may direct trustees to appoint a substitute if a trustee becomes mentally incapable of carrying out his or her role. (**Section 20** only applies where the power under **s 36 Trustee Act 1925** is not exercised.)
- **Section 41 Trustee Act 1925**—the court may appoint an additional trustee where it is impracticable or inexpedient for others to act without the court's involvement.

How can trustees be removed?

REVISION TIP

The rules relating to the appointment of trustees are uncontroversial and you are unlikely to be asked to discuss them in any detail. However, if you are answering a problem question in which it seems that the trustees have acted inappropriately, you may gain extra credit for discussing whether the beneficiaries or the courts can remove the trustees from their position.

Retirement

Trustees can only retire in certain circumstances. If their retirement is ineffective, their liability to the trust will continue. Trustees can retire in the following ways:

- The trust instrument expressly allows trustees to do so.
- It is intended to *replace* the retiring trustee.
- **Section 39 Trustee Act 1925**—a trustee may retire if:
  - there are at least two remaining trustees or a trust corporation;
  - the remaining trustees or person with the power to appoint trustees consents by deed to the retirement.
- **Section 19 TOLATA 1996**—unless the trust instrument expressly confers the power to appoint trustees to someone else (**s 19(1)(a)**), where all beneficiaries are *sui juris* and collectively absolutely entitled to the trust property, they may direct a trustee in writing to retire (**s 19(2)(a)**). **Section 19(3)** places conditions on the use of this power:
  - reasonable arrangements must have been made to protect any rights of the trustee in connection with the trust;
  - there must be at least two remaining trustees or a trust corporation;
  - either the trustee is to be replaced by another or the remaining trustees consent by deed to his or her retirement; and
  - the retiring trustee has made a deed declaring his or her retirement.
- The court may exercise its inherent jurisdiction to supervise trusts to permit a trustee to retire. This jurisdiction does not require the consent of the remaining trustees.

How can trustees be replaced?

- **Section 36(1) Trustee Act 1925**—lists eight situations in which a trustee can be replaced, for example death, retirement, unfitness to act. The power can be exercised by a hierarchy of persons in the following order:
  - person expressly given the power (**s 36(1)(a)**) or, if there is no such person,

  - the surviving trustees or the personal representative of the last surviving trustee (s 36(1)(b)).
- **Section 19 TOLATA 1996**—beneficiaries may direct the trustees in writing to appoint a trustee of their choosing, subject to the same conditions set out in relation to retirement (see the section 'Retirement', p *).
- **Section 41 Trustee Act 1925**—the court may replace a trustee where it is impracticable or inexpedient for others to act without the court's involvement.

Removal by the court

The court may exercise its inherent jurisdiction to remove a trustee. Its primary motivation will be the welfare of the beneficiaries. Therefore, a trustee's dishonesty may warrant her removal, as might hostility between the trustees and beneficiaries, even though, in the latter case, the trustees have committed no wrong: ***Letterstedt v Broers*** (1884). However, as each case is decided on its facts, minor errors (***Isaac v Isaac*** [2005]), or the expense of replacing a trustee (***Re Wrightson*** [1908]) may persuade the court not to remove a trustee.

Payment of trustees

Generally, trustees are not entitled to be remunerated for their services. The rationale for this rule is that financial motives should not be allowed to intrude upon the trustee's fiduciary obligations to beneficiaries. However, it is common practice for trust instruments to include an express remuneration clause. Where there is no express remuneration clause, trustees will be entitled to remuneration in the following circumstances (see Figure 11.1).

Figure 11.1 The remuneration of trustees

Sui juris **beneficiaries collectively consent to trustees' remuneration**

Court's inherent jurisdiction to remunerate trustees

Note: this is only used in exceptional circumstances (***Re Duke of Norfolk's ST*** [1982])

Section 29 Trustee Act 2000

Trustees acting in a **professional capacity** are entitled to **reasonable** remuneration, provided the other trustees consent in writing

Note: **lay trustees** are still **not** entitled to payment unless authorized by other means

Section 31 Trustee Act 2000

All trustees may recover expenses properly incurred in the course of their duties

Duties on taking up the role of trustee

Upon accepting a position as trustee, a trustee must do the following (see Figure 11.2):

Figure 11.2 Duties on taking up role of trustee

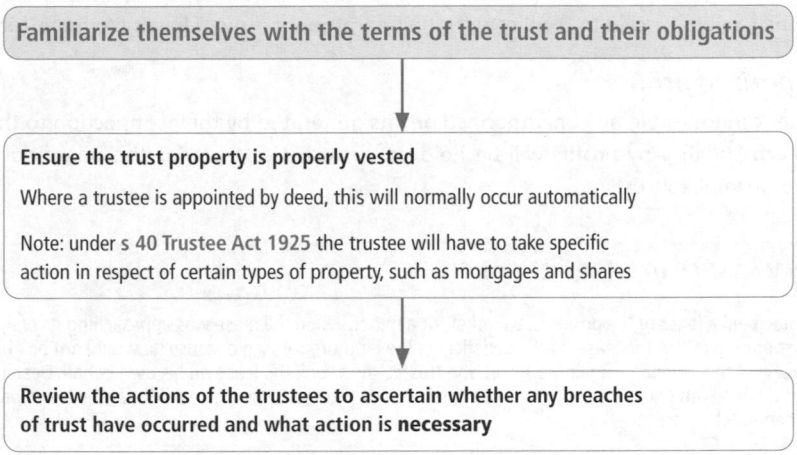

The administration of the trust

In administering a trust, the trustees must act unanimously, unless the trust instrument allows otherwise: ***Luke v South Kensington Hotel Co*** (1879). This rule offers a degree of protection to beneficiaries by preventing majority decision-making.

Fiduciary duties

In ***Bristol and West Building Society v Mothew*** [1996], Millett LJ described the fiduciary relationship in the following terms:

> A fiduciary is someone who has undertaken to act for or on behalf of another in a particular matter in circumstances which give rise to a relationship of trust and confidence. The distinguishing obligation of a fiduciary is the obligation of loyalty.

Trustees owe fiduciary duties to beneficiaries, and there are a number of relationships which are also well established as fiduciary in nature, including solicitors and clients, and directors and their company. However, the question of whether a relationship is fiduciary in nature will ultimately depend on the facts. Thus, in ***Reading v Attorney-General*** [1951], a sergeant who used his position and uniform to help smugglers avoid detection was held to have breached his fiduciary obligation to the Crown. In ***Imageview Management Ltd v Jack*** [2009], a footballer's agency company was considered to owe fiduciary duties to their clients because the nature of their role as agents demanded that their own personal interests must always take second place to their clients' interests.

Fiduciaries have a number of duties designed to prevent any conflict arising between the interests of the trustee and those of the beneficiaries. These duties are strictly enforced by the courts. While this can sometimes be said to lead to the unfair treatment of innocent fiduciaries, the exacting nature of these duties is designed to discourage them from undertaking any action which might be said to conflict with their paramount duty of loyalty to beneficiaries.

Unauthorized profits

Fiduciaries cannot retain any unauthorized profits generated by their connection to the trust: ***Bray v Ford*** [1896]. Any profits will be held on constructive trust for the beneficiaries (see chapter 9 on implied trusts):

KEECH V SANDFORD **(1726) SEL CAS CH 61**

The trustee held a lease of the profits of a market for a minor. When the lease was approaching its end, the trustee sought to renew the lease for the beneficiary. The landlord refused because he would not be able to enforce any of the covenants against a minor. The trustee then took the lease on his own behalf. Despite the fact that the landlord would not have renewed the lease for the minor, the court held that the lease was held for the benefit of the trust.

It will not make a difference if the fiduciary generates a profit for both himself *and* the trust:

BOARDMAN V PHIPPS **[1967] 2 AC 46**

In his fiduciary capacity as solicitor to a trust, Boardman obtained information about a company in which the trust had invested. He realized that the company could be made more profitable and purchased a controlling share to enable him to carry through his plans. All of the competent trustees and the beneficiaries had been made aware of this opportunity, but due to the trust's restrictive investment powers, the trustees could not make the purchase themselves. Through his hard work, the company made substantial profits for both himself and the trust. Despite this, the House of Lords held on a three to two majority that Boardman held his profits on constructive trust for the trustees.

Note: Boardman was able to retain a portion of the profits on a ***quantum meruit*** basis for his efforts. However, this does not alter the fact that all of the profits were held on trust.

If a fiduciary makes a profit from his or her company's dealing with the beneficiary, his or her share of the profits will be subject to a constructive trust for the beneficiary: ***Williams v Barton*** (1927).

Bribes

A fiduciary who receives a bribe from a third party is clearly in breach of the fiduciary duty not to make an unauthorized profit. However, the extent of the remedy available to the beneficiary in such circumstances has been questioned. In ***Lister & Co v Stubbs*** (1890), the Court of Appeal held that the claimant could not establish a *proprietary* interest in bribes received by their fiduciary, as those monies had never belonged to the company. However, in ***Attorney-General for Hong Kong v Reid*** [1994] the Privy Council held that the claimant was able to establish a proprietary interest in the bribe monies received by Reid on the basis of the equitable maxim that *equity sees as done that which ought to be done*. This meant that the defendant held the property purchased with the bribe money (which had increased in value) on constructive trust for the claimant. Both approaches can be considered controversial: ***Lister & Co v Stubbs*** reduces the extent to which fiduciaries can be held accountable by beneficiaries and seems to run contrary to the principle that fiduciaries should not be allowed to profit from their position; ***Attorney-General for Hong Kong v Reid*** clearly seeks to send a strong message that any exploitation of a fiduciary relationship will not be tolerated, but did so through the creative use of an equitable maxim which trampled upon 100 years of established legal principle!

This debate was reopened in ***Sinclair Investments (UK) Ltd v Versailles Trade Finance Ltd (in administration)*** [2011] when the Court of Appeal declined to follow ***Attorney-General for Hong Kong v Reid*** and reasserted that a beneficiary will only have a *personal* claim against a fiduciary in respect of property which neither belonged to the beneficiary nor was acquired by taking advantage of an opportunity that rightfully belonged to the beneficiary. However, just a few years later in ***FHR European Ventures LLP v Cedar Capital Partners LLC*** [2014], the Supreme Court confirmed the approach taken in ***Attorney-General for Hong Kong v Reid***. In a careful and thorough review of the authorities, Lord Neuberger argues that the importance of ensuring fiduciary loyalty is the key to understanding the rules in this area and not the question of whether the bribe money belonged to the principal. As such, accepting a bribe should be considered to fall within the general principle that an agent who acquires a benefit through their fiduciary position is to be treated as having acquired it *on behalf of their principal*. This approach provides the principal with both proprietary and personal remedies from which to choose and means that the value of bribes *and* any subsequent additional profit can now be potentially recovered.

Trustees' dealings with trust property

Trustees who sell trust property have an overriding duty to obtain the best price. In ***Buttle v Saunders*** [1950], an injunction was awarded preventing a trustee from accepting an offer to purchase property for reasons of morality when a higher offer had been received.

The self-dealing rule

The sale of trust property to a trustee is **voidable** by a beneficiary. Here the nature of the fiduciary relationship operates to prevent the *risk* of a trustee putting his or her own commercial interests before the fiduciary obligation to obtain the best price for the trust. This rule is strictly enforced and, in general, it does not matter if the property is purchased in good faith and for full value (***Ex p James*** (1803)) or even after the trustee retires (***Wright v Morgan*** [1926]), unless a significant period of time has since elapsed (***Re Boles and British Land Company's Contract*** [1902]).

One interesting exception occurred in ***Holder v Holder*** [1968]:

HOLDER V HOLDER **[1968] CH 353**
The defendant had been appointed as an executor of his father's will. He sought to renounce this position but had carried out some minor administrative tasks, which rendered this ineffective. However, he played no further part in the administration of the estate. When the other executors placed two of his father's farms for sale at auction, the defendant purchased them. However, one of the beneficiaries sought to have the purchase set aside on the basis that the defendant was a fiduciary. The Court of Appeal refused, arguing that there was no conflict of interest as the defendant had paid a fair price and had not authorized the sale.

The decision in ***Holder v Holder*** [1968] sits oddly with the courts' generally strict approach to fiduciary duties, and it is often questioned whether these rules need to be relaxed. The Court of Appeal's approach in this case might be said to be more typically *equitable* in character as it pays much closer attention to the whole circumstances of the case and broader questions of fairness than the more usual strict application of rules would allow. In this sense, ***Holder v Holder*** [1968] has much in common with the minority approach taken in ***Boardman v Phipps*** [1967], in which Lord Upjohn argued that a real conflict of duty and interest must be identified before the rule is applied.

The fair dealing rule

A trustee's purchase of a beneficiary's equitable interest in property will not be voidable as long as the trustee acts honestly, makes full disclosure to the beneficiaries, and pays a fair price: ***Coles v Trecothick*** (1804).

The trustee must not compete with the trust

The fiduciary obligations of trustees towards beneficiaries entail that they should not compete with the trust: ***Re Thomson*** [1930].

REVISION TIP

The consequences of a breach of a fiduciary relationship can extend beyond the liability of the fiduciary herself. See chapter 12 to explore this issue further.

LOOKING FOR EXTRA MARKS?

The question of how strictly fiduciary duties should be enforced raises many questions about the nature of the fiduciary relationship and the courts' attitude towards them. Impress your examiners with a good knowledge of these issues: read Jones, 'Unjust Enrichment and Fiduciary's Loyalty' (1968) 84 LQR 472; Conaglen, 'The Nature and Function of Fiduciary Loyalty' (2005) 121 LQR 452; and Collins, 'The No-conflict Rule: The Acceptance of Traditional Equitable Values?' (2008) 14 Trusts & Trustees 213.

The duty of investment

Whenever property is held on trust to benefit both **life tenants** and remaindermen, the trustees have a duty to invest the trust property in order to generate an income for the life tenant.

The previous law contained in the **Trustee Investments Act 1961** (as amended) favoured an overly protective approach to investment which was ill-suited to deal with the complexities of the modern financial world.

The **Trustee Act (TA) 2000** significantly widens the investment powers of trustees while enhancing protection for both beneficiaries and trustees; broader investment powers that enable trustees to provide better returns for beneficiaries are balanced with guidance to trustees on how to exercise their investment powers appropriately.

The duty to act even-handedly

Investment is about the *management of risk*. When considering their duty of investment, trustees must consider both the need to provide an income for life tenants and how to preserve and ideally increase the capital for remaindermen. ***Nestle v National Westminster Bank plc*** [1993] confirms that trustees have a duty to act even-handedly towards the different classes of beneficiary:

NESTLE V NATIONAL WESTMINSTER BANK PLC [1993] 1 WLR 1260

Georgina Nestle, a remainderman of a trust, received £269,203. However, she argued that if the funds had been properly invested, the capital would have been worth £1 million. While the court held that the bank had clearly misunderstood the extent of its investment powers, the policy it had undertaken had produced some savings in terms of estate duty. Even though the funds' overall growth was slow, the court was of the opinion that the trustees had not breached their duty to act even-handedly.

Staughton LJ added that the duty of even-handedness was one to be exercised in light of all the circumstances. Therefore, if a life tenant was living in poverty while the remainderman was already wealthy, the trustees could invest in such a way as to produce a greater income for the life tenant, as long as this did not unduly jeopardize the capital.

LOOKING FOR EXTRA MARKS?

The defendant in *Nestle* escaped liability despite being shown to have discharged its duties very poorly. Stauch and Watt, (1998) 62 Conv 352, argue that the court incorrectly conflates breach with loss, so that where some small gains could be shown, no breach of trust could be said to have occurred. They argue that the issue of breach must be determined separately from any consideration of loss and consider how such losses might be appropriately evaluated in an investment context.

The Trustee Act 2000: a modern approach to investment

Consider the following issues when addressing a question on investment.

The **TA 2000** provides a set of default provisions for trustee investments. All of the provisions in relation to investment, including the **s 1** duty of care, can be expressly altered or excluded by the trust instrument (see Figure 11.3).

Section 1: the duty of care

Section 1 TA 2000 imposes a statutory duty of care upon trustees and plays a key role in controlling the greater powers the Act grants to trustees. **Section 1** states:

Figure 11.3 Central investment issues in the Trustee Act 2000

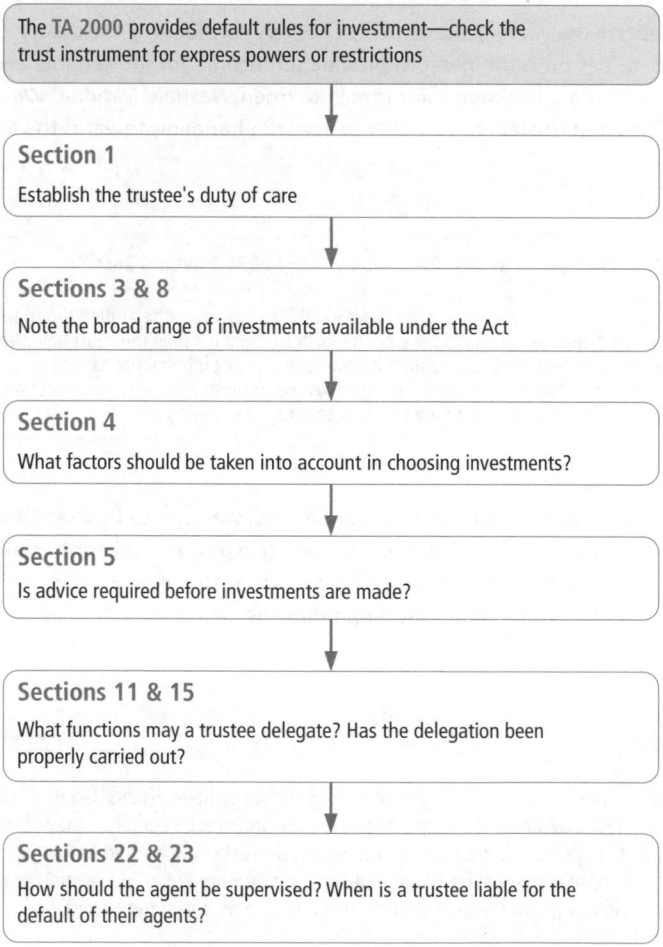

1. Whenever the duty under this subsection applies to a trustee, he must exercise such care and skill as is reasonable in all the circumstances, having regard in particular:

   (a) to any special knowledge or experience that he has or holds himself out as having, and

   (b) if he acts as a trustee in the course of a business or profession, to any special knowledge or experience that is reasonable to expect of a person acting in the course of that kind of business or profession.

There are a number of things to note about this duty of care:

Section 1 codifies the previous common law duty of care, which was to act as an 'ordinary prudent man of business': ***Speight v Gaunt*** (1881). It is useful to read **s 1** alongside the previous common law guidance. In ***Speight v Gaunt***, the House of Lords approved Lindley LJ's description of this test in ***Re Whitely*** (1887) as 'such care as an ordinary prudent man would take if he were minded to make an investment for the benefit of other people for whom he felt morally obligated to provide'. In ***Richards v Wood*** [2014], the Court of Appeal confirmed that this previous test had not been materially altered by **s 1**. Therefore, a couple who had sold property subject to a trust below a suggested market asking price but within a range accepted by professional valuers was held to have acted reasonably in the circumstances, as an ordinary prudent man would have.

- The duty of care is an objective one—a trustee's personal view will not excuse liability unless it was reasonable in the circumstances.
- The duty of care varies according to the expertise of the trustee. Therefore, a professional trustee will be expected to meet a higher standard of conduct than a lay trustee.
- Remember: the duty of care applies to all trustees' powers under the Act, unless altered by the trust instrument (**Sch 1 TA 2000**). It also applies to a number of powers under the **Trustee Act 1925**, such as the **s 19** power to insure trust property.

REVISION TIP

Students often set out the relevant provisions of the **TA 2000** but then forget to apply the **s 1** duty of care; for example, trustees must supervise their agents under **s 22**. However, just because an agent steals trust money does not mean that the trustees will be liable for the loss, unless they have failed to supervise with reasonable care and skill.

Sections 3 and 8: the scope of trustees' investment powers

Section 3(1) TA 2000 confers a 'general power of investment' upon trustees to 'make any kind of investment that he could make if he were absolutely entitled to the assets of the trust'.

Section 8(1) gives trustees the *power* to acquire freehold or leasehold land in the United Kingdom as (i) an investment; (ii) for occupation by the beneficiary; or (iii) any other reason.

The **TA 2000** embraces a much broader definition of investment than previously operated. The previous law, contained in the **Trustee Investments Act 1961**, only allowed investment from a list of proscribed 'authorised investments'. In addition, the ability of trustees to invest in land was previously very restrictive. **Section 8** makes it clear that 'investment' can now include capital as well as income growth.

Ethical investments

A common aspect of problems on trustee investments is whether trustees can pursue an ethical investment policy. This question was considered in ***Cowan v Scargill***.

COWAN V SCARGILL **[1984] 2 ALL ER 750**

The trustees of a pension fund for coal miners were divided on how best to invest. One side, led by Arthur Scargill, argued that the pension's fund should not be invested in companies abroad and especially not with industries which competed with the coal industry. This policy would avoid helping the competition and risking miners' jobs in an increasingly competitive energies market. However, his plan was rejected by Megarry V-C, who said that trustees must put aside their own personal views: '[u]nder a trust for the provision of financial benefits, the paramount duty of the trustees is to provide the greatest financial benefits for the present and future beneficiaries.'

Despite this general rule, there are a number of ways in which an ethical investment policy may be legitimately pursued:

- The trust instrument expressly imposes an ethical investment policy.
- In ***Cowan v Scargill***, Megarry V-C suggested (*obiter*) that where beneficiaries collectively held strong views on the matter, these might be taken into account.
- In ***Harries v Church Commissioners*** [1992], Sir Donald Nicholls V-C considered that *charitable trusts* might be able to avoid investments which clashed with their ethical objectives, even if this caused a loss.
- Trustees should be able to pursue an ethical investment policy as long as they consider the best financial interests of the beneficiaries first, ie the wealth of investment opportunities should make it possible to invest ethically without affecting the beneficiaries' best financial interests. However, adopting an ethical policy without considering the best financial interests of the beneficiaries will be a breach of trust: ***Martin v City of Edinburgh District Council*** [1988].

Sections 4 and 5: controlling trustees' choice of investments

Sections 4 and 5 TA 2000 provide trustees with guidance on how to manage their investment choices. In choosing investments, under **s 4(3)**, trustees must have regard to the 'standard investment criteria' of:

- suitability; and
- the need for diversification.

Suitability: the Explanatory Notes of the **TA 2000** state that trustees must consider the suitability of proposed investments in general and in particular. This means that they should first consider whether the type of investment (eg shares) is suitable for the trust. They must then consider whether, for example, shares in a particular company are appropriate for the trust.

Diversification: this section reflects the **TA 2000**'s adoption of the 'modern portfolio theory' set out in the first instance decision of ***Nestle v National Westminster Bank plc*** [1993]. Hoffmann J stated that:

> Modern trustees acting within their investment powers are entitled to be judged by the standards of current portfolio theory, which emphasises the risk level of the entire portfolio rather than the risk attaching to each investment taken in isolation.

This encourages trustees to formulate an investment strategy that balances riskier investments (which could bring greater returns) with more secure investments (which will produce lower returns but expose the trust fund to less risk). If trustees give due consideration to this, they will not be judged for the failure of individual investments.

The Act does not *require* diversification, merely that trustees consider whether there is a need. For example, it may be more sensible for a smaller trust to invest in largely low-risk investments, whereas a bigger trust fund has the scope to take more risks, as long as those risks are appropriately balanced.

Section 4(2)—trustees must review their investment strategy 'from time to time'. This encourages trustees to be diligent in responding to changing circumstances. For example, if a trust generated its income from purchasing and renovating property for resale, a drop in property values would reasonably require trustees to consider reinvesting at least part of the trust fund elsewhere.

Section 5(1)—trustees should take and consider 'proper advice' from someone 'reasonably believed to be qualified . . . by his ability in and practical experience of financial and other matters' (**s 5(4)**) whenever considering or reviewing their investments.

Section 5(3)—advice is not required if the trustee reasonably concludes that it is unnecessary or inappropriate to seek advice. For example, this exception might apply where the trustee is professionally experienced in investment.

Sections 11 and 15: the power of delegation

The responsibilities of trustees are often onerous, especially for the ordinary lay trustee. Allowing certain roles to be delegated allows trustees to ensure that the trust is properly managed.

Section 11 outlines the roles which can be *collectively* delegated by trustees. Note: the *individual* delegation of trustees' functions is still governed by **s 25 Trustee Act 1925**.

Section 11(2) lists the functions which non-charitable trusts *cannot* delegate. These include the distribution of trust assets, the discretion to decide whether payments or fees should be made out of the trust fund (eg claims for maintenance and advancement), and the power to appoint trustees. Note: this means that trustees' power of investment *can* be delegated.

Schedule 1, para 3—the **s 1** duty of care applies in selecting an agent. ***Fry v Tapson*** (1885) establishes that trustees should not employ agents to carry out tasks outside their ordinary course of business.

Section 15 places special requirements on the delegation of 'asset management functions'. These are functions which include the investment, acquisition, management, and disposal of trust property (**s 15(5)**). Where such a function is delegated, **s 15** requires:

- an agreement in or evidenced by writing (**s 15(1)**);
- preparation of a written policy statement for agents to provide guidance on how to carry out their role (**s 15(2)(a)**);
- that the agreement should contain a term ensuring that an agent complies with the policy statement (**s 15(2)(b)**).

Sections 22 and 23: review of agents and liability for their default

Section 22 states that trustees must keep their agents' actions under review and, if necessary, intervene. In ***Appleby Corporate Services (BVI) Ltd v Citco Trustees (BVI) Ltd*** [2016], a trustee failed to check regularly on an investment manager's actions, despite evidence that the trust was suffering losses over a five-year period. The trustee was held liable for failing to supervise its agent appropriately and was ordered to restore the trust fund to the value it had at the time the trustee should first have identified a problem.

Section 23 states that the trustees will be liable for the defaults of their agents if they have failed to satisfy the duty of care in appointing or reviewing their agents.

The duty to provide information

If beneficiaries are to hold trustees to account, they clearly require access to information about the trust. But what is the extent of trustees' duty to provide such information?

Trustees do not have to give reasons for how they use their discretion

Trustees frequently have to exercise their discretion in carrying out their duties. For example, trustees may have a duty to take advice before making an investment, but they must ultimately decide whether or not to follow the advice. Another common example is the trustees' discretion to choose which members of a class to benefit in a discretionary trust.

The case of ***Re Beloved Wilkes' Charity*** (1851) established that *trustees do not have to give reasons for the use of their discretion*. While this limits trustees' accountability, it also allows trustees to fulfil their role as fiduciaries:

- For trustees to act impartially, they must be free of pressure from beneficiaries.
- In the context of family trusts, protecting trustees from having to explain their decisions may prevent family conflict.

Note: Lord Truro added that where there is evidence of bad faith or dishonesty or the trustees provide reasons for their actions, the court can intervene and evaluate their conclusions.

If trustees are not required to give reasons for the use of their discretion, to what information are beneficiaries entitled?

Other information about the trust

Accounts

All trustees must keep accounts and make them available to the beneficiaries: ***Pearse v Green*** (1819). This includes beneficiaries under a **discretionary trust**, although this right may be limited where they are part of a large class: ***Murphy v Murphy*** [1999].

Information about the trust

The beneficiaries' right to information was originally based on their proprietary interest in the trust: ***O'Rourke v Darbishire*** [1920]. This entitled beneficiaries to access all 'trust documents'.

In ***Re Londonderry's Settlement*** [1965], Salmon LJ attempted to define 'trust documents':

1. they are documents in the possession of the trustees as trustees;
2. they contain information about the trust, which the beneficiaries are entitled to know;
3. the beneficiaries have a proprietary interest in the documents and, accordingly, are entitled to see them. If any parts of a document contain information which the beneficiaries are not entitled to know, I doubt whether such parts can be truly said to be integral parts of a trust document.

However, this definition does little to clarify the scope of the term 'trust documents'. In addition, the court stressed that the beneficiaries' right to see 'trust documents' did not include:

- documents which might reveal how the trustees had exercised their discretion;
- confidential information, including the agendas of trustee meetings and correspondence among trustees or beneficiaries.

A more workable and conceptually satisfying approach has been advocated by the Privy Council in ***Schmidt v Rosewood Trust***:

SCHMIDT V ROSEWOOD TRUST **[2003] 3 ALL ER 76**

The claimant sought disclosure of the accounts and information on trust assets in relation to a discretionary trust. The trustees resisted the claim on the basis that as a mere potential beneficiary under a discretionary trust, the claimant had no proprietary claim to see the requested documentation.

Lord Walker stated that while the beneficiaries' right to information *could* be described as a proprietary interest, such an interest was neither sufficient nor necessary to found the claim. Instead, the beneficiaries' right to information was better described as *an aspect of the court's inherent jurisdiction to supervise the administration of trusts*.

Following ***Schmidt***, beneficiaries no longer have an automatic right to demand information. This could also be said to permit trustees to be secretive, as the cost of litigation may discourage beneficiaries from complaining.

However, the Privy Council's approach means that the court could potentially order the disclosure of *any* documentation it deems relevant, thus enhancing the accountability of trustees.

Schmidt also offers the court the flexibility to respond to different circumstances by allowing the court to balance the interests of trustees, beneficiaries, and any third parties. See ***Breakspear v Ackland*** [2008], where the court refused to disclose a settlor's **letter of wishes** on the basis it would cause family conflict.

The ability of beneficiaries to hold trustees to account effectively remains debateable. However, interestingly, the case of ***Dawson-Damer v Taylor Wessing LLP*** [2017] suggests that beneficiaries might also be able to access personal information held by trustees through Data Protection legislation, including information that trustees might otherwise be entitled to withhold. While such an approach may risk the sort of family conflict the court is keen to avoid, it is to be hoped that this might also help prevent trustees from being able to hide poor decisions from scrutiny.

LOOKING FOR EXTRA MARKS?

The unsettled nature of the law in this area makes it a prime subject for an essay question on the accountability of trustees. Improve your marks by demonstrating knowledge of both the current law and calls for greater accountability. Kirby P argues for greater accountability in his minority judgment in the Australian case ***Hartigan Nominees Property Ltd v Rydge*** (1992). A good discussion of the debate can also be found in Sir Gavin Lightman's article 'The Trustees' Duty to Provide Information to Beneficiaries' [2004] PCB 23.

The duty to distribute

Trustees are under a duty to distribute the trust property in accordance with the terms of the trust. Failure to distribute or distributing the trust property to the wrong person is a breach of trust: ***Re Diplock*** [1948]. The law provides a variety of options for trustees who are uncertain about who the beneficiaries of a trust are or the extent of their entitlement.

Applying to the court for directions

Trustees can apply to the court for directions if there is any uncertainty as to how the trust should be carried out. Moreover, if the trustees follow the court's directions, they will not be liable for any losses arising from that advice.

What if the trustees cannot find the beneficiaries?

REVISION TIP

These different methods protect trustees should a missing beneficiary appear. Remember: while the trustees will be protected from liability for breach of trust, the beneficiary may pursue his share of the trust against the other beneficiaries (see Figure 11.4).

Figure 11.4 Managing a trust with missing beneficiaries

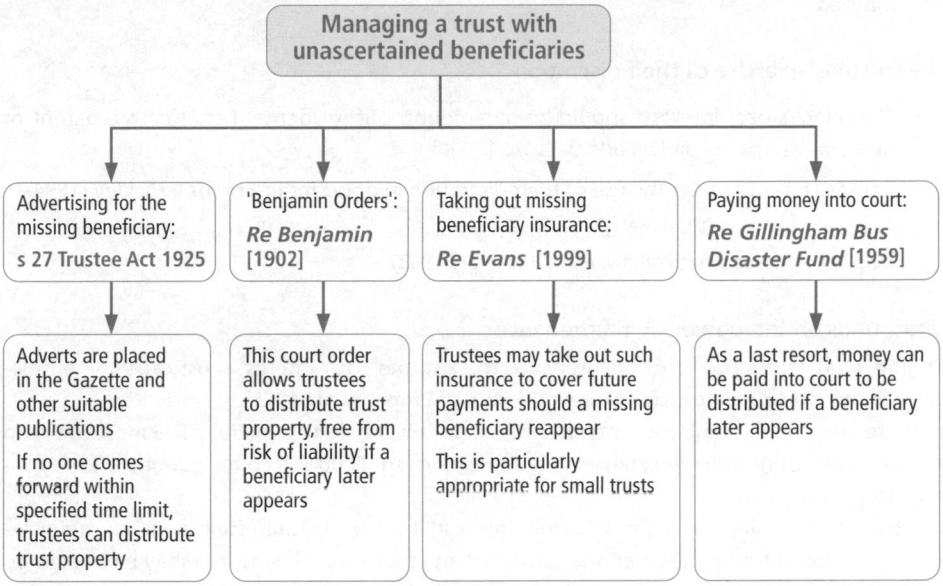

Powers of maintenance and advancement

During the administration of a trust, trustees may be asked to assist beneficiaries financially before their interest vests. The trustees can do so, at their absolute discretion, through their powers of maintenance and advancement.

Maintenance

The power of maintenance allows trustees to use the **income** from their interest to provide for the maintenance of a minor beneficiary. Maintenance powers can arise from:

- express provision in the trust instrument;
- **s 53 Trustee Act 1925** (see chapter 10);
- **s 31 Trustee Act 1925**.

Section 31 Trustee Act 1925

- For trusts created after 1 October 2014, **s 8 Inheritance and Trustees' Powers Act (ITPA) 2014** amends **s 31(1)(i)** so that trustees may apply *part or all* of the income for the 'maintenance, education or benefit' of a minor beneficiary 'as [they] may think fit'. For trusts created before, the power is to be exercised according to what is reasonable in all the circumstances.

- Payments will typically be made to the minor's parents or guardians, unless the minor is married.

The trustees' exercise of their discretion

- The minor's best interests should be paramount, but incidental benefits to a parent or guardian are permissible: ***Fuller v Evans*** [2000].
- Trustees must consider the use of their discretion in good faith: ***Bryant v Hickley*** (1894).
- Trustees must consider the use of maintenance powers periodically—money should not be paid over automatically: ***Wilson v Turner*** (1883).

Limitations on the power of maintenance

Section 31(3)—for a power of maintenance to exist, the trust interest must carry the entitlement to the intermediate income (see **s 175 Law of Property Act 1925**).

There are a small number of interests which do not satisfy this section. The most common is the contingent pecuniary testamentary disposition, eg '£200,000 to my daughter, Lesley, on her 21st birthday'.

If the income is already subject to a prior interest, it cannot be used for maintenance, for example 'My shares for Laura, when she turns 25. Until that time, the income shall be appointed to Clara'.

The power of maintenance can be excluded by a contrary intention on the part of the settlor (eg ***Re Erskine's ST*** [1971]).

Contingently entitled adults

Section 31(1)(ii)—adults with a contingent trust interest are automatically entitled to the income from that interest, subject to any contrary intention. However, they will only be entitled to the income arising from the time they reach majority (ie 18). For example, if Patrick is left 500 shares on trust for when he turns 30, he will be entitled to the dividends on the shares from the age of 18.

Advancement

The power of advancement allows trustees, at their absolute discretion, to appoint part of a beneficiaries' entitlement to the **capital** of the trust before it vests absolutely. Advancement powers can arise from:

- express provision in the trust instrument;
- **s 53 Trustee Act 1925** (see chapter 10);
- **s 32 Trustee Act 1925**.

Section 32 Trustee Act 1925

Trustees may apply part of the beneficiary's capital interest for the 'advancement or benefit' of a minor or adult beneficiary (**s 32(1)**). ***Pilkington v IRC*** [1964] defines 'advancement or benefit' as 'any use of money which will improve the material situation of the beneficiary'.

The trustees' exercise of their discretion

- Trustees must consider whether to exercise their power of advancement and not simply appoint money without thought.
- If trustees make an advancement for a specific purpose, they must check whether that purpose has been carried out: ***Re Pauling's ST*** [1964] (see Table 11.1).

Table 11.1 Case examples of 'advancement or benefit' accepted by the courts

CASE	EXAMPLE OF 'ADVANCEMENT OR BENEFIT'
Re Williams WT [1953]	To purchase a house for the beneficiary
Roper-Curzon v Roper-Curzon (1871)	To help a beneficiary in their career
Lowther v Bentinck (1874)	To pay off debts
Pilkington v IRC [1964]	To provide tax advantages for the beneficiary
X v A [2006]	To satisfy a beneficiary's moral obligation to donate to charity

Limitations on the power of advancement

- **Section 32(1)(a)**—for trusts created after 1 October 2014, **s 9 ITPA 2014** amends **s 32(1)(a)** so that a beneficiary's *entire* interest can be advanced. However, for trusts created before that date, no more than *half* of the beneficiary's share in the capital can be advanced.
- **Section 32(1)(b)**—any advancements made will be deducted from the beneficiary's final entitlement.
- **Section 32(1)(c)**—no advancements can be made where there is a *prior interest* on the capital, unless that person exists, is an adult, and consents in writing.
- The power of advancement is defeated by evidence of a contrary intention, such as a direction to accumulate: ***IRC v Bernstein*** [1961].

KEY CASES

CASE	FACTS	PRINCIPLE
Bristol and West Building Society v Mothew [1996] 4 All ER 698	A solicitor's negligence in wrongly advising the claimant was held not to be a breach of his fiduciary obligations.	The core obligation of a fiduciary is loyalty. Fiduciaries must act in good faith and avoid conflicts of interest.
Cowan v Scargill [1984] 2 All ER 750	The court refused to sanction an investment policy which put the economic interests of the mining industry ahead of the best financial interests of the beneficiaries of a pension scheme.	In general, trustees must consider the best financial interests of the beneficiaries when choosing investments.
Keech v Sandford (1726) Sel Cas Ch 61	When a landlord refused to renew a lease held on trust for an infant beneficiary, the trustee took it over. It was held that the trustee held the lease on constructive trust for the beneficiary.	Trustees cannot retain any profits deriving from their connection with the trust.
Nestle v National Westminster Bank plc [1993] 1 WLR 1260	The claimant argued unsuccessfully that the value of her interest should have been greater and that the defendant's overly cautious investment strategy constituted a breach of trust.	Trustees must treat all beneficiaries even-handedly. Trustees are to be judged on their investment policy overall rather than on individual failures—modern portfolio theory.
O'Donnell v Shanahan [2009] EWCA Civ 75	Two directors of a company entered into a personal property investment deal when the original deal brokered by the company fell through, depriving the company of its commission.	Fiduciaries must avoid conflicts of interest with their principal. Opportunities that arise through a fiduciary relationship are properly considered the property of the principal and full consent must be obtained before a fiduciary may take any advantage of them.
O'Rourke v Darbishire [1920] AC 581	A claimant alleged that he was the beneficiary of a trust and sought access to relevant documents pertaining to how the 'trust' had been managed.	Beneficiaries are entitled to see trust documents, as long as they do not reveal reasons for trustees' use of their discretion or confidential information.
Schmidt v Rosewood Trust [2003] 3 All ER 76	A claimant sought access to a wide range of documents relating to two trusts under which he claimed a discretionary interest.	Beneficiaries' access to information is an aspect of the court's inherent jurisdiction to supervise the trust. The court must balance the interests of trustees, beneficiaries, and third parties in deciding whether to order disclosure.

KEY DEBATES

Topic	Why Are Trustees' Fiduciary Duties So Strictly Enforced?
Academic/ author	Webb and Akkouh
Viewpoint	Fiduciaries' core obligation of loyalty requires fiduciaries to be deterred from any potential conflict of interest.
Source	Webb and Akkouh, *Trusts Law* (2017), ch 10 provides an extremely accessible discussion of this complicated area.

Topic	What is the impact of the Trustee Act 2000?
Academic/ author	Clements
Viewpoint	The **Trustee Act 2000** was urgently needed to address problems with the previous law and to allow trustees to operate effectively in the modern financial world.
Source	Clements [2004] 2 Web JCLI.

Topic	Should beneficiaries have greater access to information about the trust?
Academic/ author	Lightman
Viewpoint	The beneficiaries' ability to enforce the trust requires access to information. Greater accountability is needed.
Source	Lightman [2004] PCB 23.

Topic	What are the consequences of the decision in *FHR v Cedar Capital Partners*?
Academic/ author	Whayman
Viewpoint	The policy-focused decision in ***FHR*** is welcome but the issue of what legal principles can underpin this approach remain to be answered.
Source	Whayman (2014) Conveyancer 518.

EXAM QUESTIONS

Problem question

Jan and Beth hold £500,000 on trust for Toby with the remainder for Lisa. They have little knowledge of investments. A friend recommends Paul, a computer engineer, as someone who could manage their investments. Paul recently inherited £10,000 and, after investing it, made a profit of £2,000.

Jan and Beth employ Paul, who makes the following investments in May 2012:

1. £200,000 in a range of unit trusts;
2. £100,000 in shares in Carfax, a leading UK bank;
3. £150,000 in villas to rent out on the Spanish Costa del Tan;
4. £50,000 in investment capital for IP-Ops, a computer repair company owned by Paul.

In May 2013, Paul tells the trustees that the unit trusts and villas are performing well, and that IP-Ops has had an extremely profitable first year of business. However, following a drop in consumer confidence, the shares in Carfax Bank have lost 25 per cent of their value.

The trustees instruct Paul to move the Carfax investment to a more stable company.

Three months later, the trustees meet with Toby and Lisa and inform them of the trust's performance. On investigation, Toby discovers that Paul has not yet sold the Carfax shares, which have now lost another 25 per cent of their value.

The beneficiaries are concerned that the trust is being poorly managed. Advise the beneficiaries.

Essay question

> It is an inflexible rule of a Court of Equity that a person in a fiduciary position . . . is not, unless otherwise expressly provided, entitled to make a profit; he is not allowed to put himself in a position where his interest and his duty conflict (Lord Herschell in ***Bray v Ford*** [1896]).

Critically discuss whether fiduciary duties are enforced too strictly in England and Wales.

Online resources

For an outline answer to this essay question, as well as multiple choice questions and interactive key cases, please visit the online resources.

Concentrate Q&As

For more questions and answers on equity and trusts, see the *Concentrate Q&A: Equity & Trusts* by Rosalind Malcolm.

Go to the end of this book to view **sample pages.**

12 Remedies for breach of trust

KEY FACTS

- Beneficiaries will have a claim against a trustee in breach.
- Liability between trustees is joint and several.
- A remedy can be provided for breach of a trust or fiduciary obligation.
- The fiduciary obligation can arise in a variety of factual situations.
- Remedies can be against the trustee or third parties.
- The remedy can be personal or proprietary.
- The remedy can be at common law or in equity.

Introduction

A breach of the trustee/fiduciary obligation will lead to a remedy. This chapter will explain the personal and proprietary remedies available to the claimant:

- A personal claim means that the claim is made against the trustee/fiduciary personally; it is not based upon the recipient having the property in his or her possession.
- A proprietary claim is based upon the defendant having the property or its replacement in his or her possession and being required to return it, or its substitute, to the claimant.

The claimant, after identifying the breach, can use the tracing process to identify whether to make a proprietary or personal claim and to identify who the claim may be against.

REVISION TIP

The first step in an answer is to identify the breach, who committed the breach, and where the property is held. This will enable your answer to take the correct approach.

Figure 12.1 illustrates the possible routes for a claimant.

Figure 12.1 Possible routes for remedy

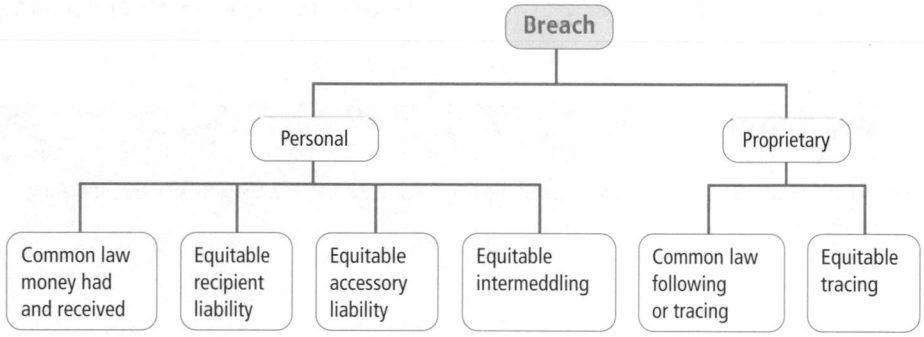

Personal actions

Against the trustee

Trustees have certain powers and duties under a trust (see chapter 11). These powers and duties can lead to a breach, where:

1. there is a failure to carry out a duty;
2. a trustee acts outside his or her powers;
3. a trustee acts without the required standard of care.

If there is more than one trustee, you should identify which of the trustees the claim is against. A trustee is not **vicariously** liable for the actions of other trustees. However, a failure to act with due care (that exercised by the prudent and reasonable person (***Speight v Gaunt*** (1883)) or a breach of the statutory duty of care contained in **s 1 Trustee Act 2000**) is a breach in itself. Breaches include:

- leaving one trustee in sole control of the trust property; and
- inaction or standing by while other trustees breach their duty: ***Styles v Guy*** (1849).

Trustees are not responsible for breaches that occur *before* they became a trustee or for breaches which occur after they have retired. However, every trustee who participates, actively or passively, in the breach is **jointly and severally** liable for any loss. So, although there is no vicarious liability, the fact that you have not exerted control over the actions of your fellow trustees—your inaction—may be a breach in itself, incurring liability.

A trustee also has core fiduciary duties (see chapter 11) which will also lead to remedies. A breach of trust duty is compensatory. A breach of a fiduciary duty is restitutionary in nature. If there is more than one breach it is important to identify the losses which flow from each breach: ***Target Holdings Ltd v Redferns*** [1995]. If one breach creates a profit (eg an unauthorized investment generates a profit), this cannot be offset against losses caused by a different breach.

The claims are made directly against the trustee—a personal action—to compensate the claimant for losses caused by the breach in the same way as an action for damages for a breach of a contractual obligation. This issue was recently reviewed in the case of ***AIB Group v Mark Redler & Co Solicitors*** [2014].

REVISION TIP

In structuring your answer, having established the breach and the liability, consider whether there are any defences available to the defendant.

Defences

Against a claim by beneficiaries

A trustee may be granted relief or an **indemnity** from the breach. The following are situations which will provide the defendant trustee with a defence to an action for breach of trust.

Exemption clauses

The trust documents may include an exemption clause. Such clauses usually cover breaches which occur despite the trustee acting with all care, but if widely drafted it could include negligent breach. Where the trustee is a professional, the courts are less likely to allow a broadly drafted exemption clause to allow a trustee to avoid liability for gross negligence: ***Armitage v Nurse*** [1998].

Consent and acquiescence

Consent of the *sui juris* beneficiary in the breach will provide a defence to the trustee against claims by that beneficiary but not against other beneficiaries who may have suffered a loss. **Section 62 Trustee Act 1925** provides the court with a discretion to impound the beneficial interest of a beneficiary who has encouraged or acquiesced in a breach. This will be used to pay compensation to the beneficiaries who did not participate in the breach: ***Re Pauling's ST*** [1964].

Judicial discretion

Section 61 Trustee Act 1925 provides wide discretionary power for the courts to grant relief if the trustee in breach has acted honestly and reasonably: ***Santander UK plc v RA Legal Solicitors*** [2014]. However, the court will also take into account the effect of any breach on the beneficiary so that even an honest and reasonable trustee may still be refused relief: ***P & P Property v Owen White & Catlin LLP and others*** [2018].

Time barred

Section 21 Limitation Act 1980 bars claims made after six years, although this does not apply if there has been fraud: **s 21(1)(a) Limitation Act**. If the basis of a claim is recipient and accessory liability (see 'Recipient liability and accessory liability' at p) then **s 21(1)(a)** does not engage: ***Williams v Central Bank of Nigeria*** [2014].

Against a co-trustee's claim

As the trustees are jointly and severally liable for their breaches, a claimant may decide to bring a claim against all of the trustees or just one—usually the richest. As the breach may also include a trustee's inaction, this could be said to be inequitable—the beneficiary may target the wealthiest rather than the most culpable. However, the trustee may have a claim against his or her fellow trustee which is independent of the beneficiary's claim.

The trustee who has been required to pay compensation may be able to require the other trustees to contribute to his or her costs. The following situations may provide some relief:

- A co-trustee may be ordered to indemnify a trustee for the compensation he or she has paid out where:
  - there has been a fraud by the co-trustee;
  - the co-trustee has breached for his or her own benefit: ***Bahin v Hughes*** (1886);
  - a solicitor has exercised a controlling influence on a lay trustee: ***Re Partington*** (1887).
- The **Civil Liabilities (Contribution) Act 1978** grants the courts powers to order co-trustees to contribute to the losses claimed if it is 'fair, just and reasonable'.

The remedies against the trustee may be adequate as long as the trustee is solvent. However, if there are no available remedies or the trustee is unable to compensate the beneficiary, the most appropriate remedy for a claimant may be against a third party to the trust (refer to Figure 12.2 and Figure 12.3 at the end of the chapter).

Personal actions against third parties

Actions may be brought against those who are not appointed as trustees—termed 'strangers' as they are strangers to the trust. The actions may be personal or proprietary and available at common law or in equity.

Common law personal claims

The remedy for money had and received is based upon a remedy in the law of restitution. The law of restitution has developed immensely over the last decades and the scope of this book means that it cannot be fully developed here. The basic requirements are that:

- property is *received* in an unmixed form;
- the claimant is the legal title holder.

The basic principle is that the law will identify property which the recipient has or had in his or her possession. Property that is identified as belonging to the claimant will be followed into the possession of the recipient. The courts may require that the property be returned to the claimant (the proprietary remedy). However, for reasons explained later, the claimant may elect to take the personal remedy of requiring the recipient to account for the benefit received, the restitutionary value.

REVISION TIP

In order to identify the person who must compensate, the claimant must prove that the defendant actually has or had the claimant's property. Students often become confused about the interplay between the following and tracing *process* and the *proprietary remedies* which may follow this process.

Tracing or following is used to locate the property, after which the claimant will usually be able to elect which remedy to pursue against the defendant.

The liability for the claim is strict; once the breach has been established it is 'unjust' for the recipient to retain that benefit.

LIPKIN GORMAN V KARPNALE **[1991] 2 AC 548**

A solicitor removed clients' money from the client account and used the money for gambling at the Playboy Club. This was a breach of the solicitor's fiduciary obligations. The Playboy Club had received that money under a void contract (gambling contracts were void at the time). As the Playboy Club had no legal claim to the money it was required to return its value to the 'real' owner.

The Playboy Club was unaware of the breach by the solicitor. It was the fact that it had received the money that gave rise to the claim for restitution. The club had to return the value received (subject to defences).

Defences to the claim

Equity's darling

An absolute defence to any claim is that the recipient obtained the property as a **bona fide** purchaser for valuable consideration without notice, or 'equity's darling'.

- *Bona fide*: this is a question of fact for the courts to decide. If the party can prove that he or she acted 'without notice' then he or she is likely to be bona fide.
- *Purchaser for valuable consideration* requires that the receipt forms part of a valid contract, which is only valid if there is consideration.

Change of position

The 'change of position' defence is a development by the courts which has softened the impact of the strict liability of restitutionary claims; having identified the property **'in the hands'** of the recipient, that recipient may be able to retain some benefit. The extent will be measured by how much the recipient has 'changed his or her position' in reliance of the receipt: ***Lipkin Gorman v Karpnale Ltd*** [1991] (see Table 12.1).

Table 12.1 What constitutes change of position?

CHANGE OF POSITION	SUCCESS?
Paying off a mortgage: ***Scottish Equitable v Derby*** [2000]	Unsuccessful as the mortgage payment was not a change of position
Paying off a mortgage: ***Boscawen v Bajwa*** [1996]	Successful—the claimant can be 'subrogated' to the mortgage provider. This means that the claimant takes the place of the mortgage lender. The debt that was paid is now owed to the claimant. This was recently confirmed in ***Bank of Cyprus UK Ltd v Menelaou*** [2015]
Paying out winnings from gambling: ***Lipkin Gorman v Karpnale Ltd*** [1991]	Successful—the club had acted in good faith and paid out money in reliance of the bets placed

REVISION TIP

This defence has been developed in response to a common law claim, but it has also been suggested as a defence for an equitable claim.

Equitable personal claims

In addition to the common law claim, there are claims which can be made in equity. The courts treat the intermeddler, recipient, or assistant *as if he or she were a trustee* in the following situations:

- a person who intentionally intermeddles with a trust;
- the recipient of trust property; and
- a person who assists in a breach of trust.

Intermeddling

A person who makes a deliberate decision to interfere with trust property and the duties of a trustee will be considered a '*trustee de son tort*': ***Mara v Browne*** [1895]. This means that that person acts in relation to the trust property as if they were a trustee. The meddling is not itself a breach, but that person will be liable for any later breaches as if they had been a properly appointed trustee.

Recipient liability and accessory liability

This is often referred to as 'stranger liability'. The 'stranger' refers to the fact that the person on whom liability is imposed is not appointed a trustee, nor does he or she elect to intermeddle with the trust. Although not appointed a trustee, the courts have imposed upon such a person a liability as extensive as a trustee properly appointed.

The origins of stranger liability come from the statements in ***Barnes v Addy*** (1874), where Lord Selborne said that liability shall not arise unless the stranger 'receives and become chargeable with some part of the trust property, or unless they assist with knowledge in a dishonest and fraudulent design on the part of the trustees'.

The 'stranger' will become liable 'as if he or she were' a constructive trustee, although they are not constructive trustees; ***Williams v Central Bank of Nigeria*** [2014] UKSC 10 (see Millett LJ in ***Paragon Finance v Thakerar*** [1999], where he stated that they were 'persons whose trusteeship is merely a formula for giving restitutionary relief'). This is because the stranger's conscience is so affected that equity will not 'suffer a wrong without a remedy'.

The relevant knowledge required to establish such liability is an area of much academic and judicial debate. A starting point can be the decision in ***Baden, Delvaux and Lecuit v Société Générale pour Favoriser le Développement du Commerce et de l'Industrie en France*** [1989] (referred to now as ***Baden***). However, this has been modified by subsequent decisions. ***Baden*** set out five categories of knowledge that may be relevant:

1. actual knowledge;
2. wilfully shutting one's eyes to the obvious;
3. wilfully and recklessly failing to make such enquiries as an honest and reasonable man would make;
4. knowledge of circumstances which would indicate the facts to an honest and reasonable man; and
5. knowledge of circumstances which would put an honest and reasonable man on enquiry.

The first three categories are often referred to as *actual knowledge* and the latter two as *constructive knowledge*: ***Agip (Africa) Ltd v Jackson*** [1990]. Whether the knowledge needs to be dishonest, which would affect the conscience of the defendant, has been problematic; however, the courts struggle with exactly what equates to knowledge and dishonesty.

Recipient liability

This is when the 'stranger' actually receives trust property into their possession. It was once labelled 'knowing receipt', which raises issues of what knowledge is required to impose liability. If the stranger has the requisite knowledge, then a constructive trust will arise on the property.

In ***BCCI v Akindele*** [2000] the Court of Appeal relied upon the decision in ***Belmont Finance Corpn v Williams Furniture Ltd (No 2)*** [1980] and Nourse LJ referred to the constructive trust being based upon whether it was 'unconscionable' for the recipient of trust property to retain the benefit of receipt.

On the facts of ***Akindele*** [2000] it is difficult to see exactly what 'unconscionable' means. One factor may be that in a commercial context there is a need to encourage commercial flexibility. It is worth keeping in mind as you study this area that the financial markets are important to the British economy. Many of the debates and decisions are aimed at oiling the financial market.

LOOKING FOR EXTRA MARKS?

Read a summary of ***Re Montagu's Settlement*** [1987] and ***Belmont Finance*** [1980] on the different and conflicting interpretations of knowledge in relation to recipient liability. The decision of the Court of Appeal in ***BCCI v Akindele*** [2000] was questioned by Lord Millett in the House of Lords in ***Twinsectra v Yardley*** [2002]. The concept of 'unconscionability' has been seen in other areas: see ***Pennington v Waine*** (2002). As equity acts *in personam* the issue of unconscionability is a very live issue in creating rights. It is a thread in many areas of equity.

Accessory liability

This has been called both 'dishonest assistance' and 'knowing assistance'. The change in labels reflects the problem of defining what knowledge is needed to impose liability for an accessory. It may be wrong to call such a person a constructive trustee as the property never vests in the 'stranger'. The label stems from the fact that liability is imposed upon accessories 'as if they were trustees'.

In ***Royal Brunei Airlines Sdn Bhd v Tan*** [1995], Lord Nicholls in the Privy Council stated that the accessory would be liable if he or she acted dishonestly which 'means simply not acting as an honest person would in the circumstances. This is an objective standard.' He admitted that honesty had a strong subjective element and suggested that 'a court will look at the circumstances known to the third party at the time; having regard to the personal attributes of the third party, such as his experience and intelligence, and the reason why he acted as he did'.

This decision was interpreted by the House of Lords in ***Twinsectra v Yardley*** [2002]. A majority of the House *seemed* to equate Lord Nicholls's *ratio* with that of the ***Ghosh*** test in criminal law. Lord Hutton's judgment suggests that a person is dishonest if:

- his or her actions are seen as dishonest by the standards of the ordinary reasonable person (the *objective element*); and
- the defendant realized that by those standards he or she was dishonest (*the subjective element*).

However, Lord Millett's strong dissenting judgment took an alternative view of Lord Nicholls's judgment in ***Royal Brunei***. In ***Barlow Clowes International v Eurotrust International*** [2005], the Privy Council, with Lord Hoffmann, a member of the majority in ***Twinsectra***, on the panel, sought to 'clarify' the test in ***Twinsectra***. The two-stage test is there but follows Lord Millett's explanation. The Privy Council, a persuasive authority, was followed by the Court of Appeal in ***Abou Rahma v Abacha*** [2006] and more recently in ***Starglade v Nash*** [2010], where the court asked the same first question but then imbued the reasonable person with the 'characteristics' of the defendant. It is unsatisfactory that there should be conflicting persuasive and binding authority; this will hopefully be avoided in future after the decision in ***Willers v Joyce*** [2016] which now allows the Pricy Council to state that their decisions are intended to be binding in domestic courts.

LOOKING FOR EXTRA MARKS?

The Court of Appeal in ***Group Seven Limited*** v ***Notable Services LLP*** [2019] has reviewed this area in the light of the decision on dishonesty in ***Ivey v Genting Casinos*** [2017] and seemed to equate some of the discussion as being 'blind eye knowledge'. We might consider if this is a reflection of the old *Baden* criteria?

Conclusion

Personal remedies can be against a fiduciary/trustee who is in breach but also against those indirectly associated with a breach, those who receive trust property, or those who assist in the breach of duty.

Proprietary claims

An alternative would be to make a proprietary claim to vindicate the property rights of the claimant. If the property belonging to the claimant can be identified, then it will be returned to the claimant. Note that it is the property interest you have in an object not the object itself that is being claimed.

There are a number of advantages to bringing a proprietary claim:

- If the trustee/recipient has become bankrupt the beneficiary takes **priority** over other creditors.

- Any increase in value of the property taken by the trustee is recoverable.
- There are no time limitations to bring a proprietary claim.

The first step is to identify the property in the hands of the trustee, or a third party, as being the trust property, which will then help you decide on a personal or proprietary (or combination of both) claim.

LOOKING FOR EXTRA MARKS?

Much judicial and academic ink has been spilt over the issue of whether a fiduciary who accepted bribes and secret commissions was subject to a personal claim or proprietary remedy. This matter has been masterfully summarized by Lord Neuberger delivering the decision of the Supreme Court in ***FHR European Ventures LLP v Cedar Capital Partners*** [2014] (see chapter 11).

The tracing (following) process

It is important that the following rules are seen as a process. The aim for the claimant is to find who now has possession of the property which is being reclaimed. Once the property interest has been identified then the claim is made.

REVISION TIP

If the trust property has remained unchanged then the courts *follow* the asset into the hands of the trustee, or third party. If the property has changed in nature, then the courts *trace* the property. These are often called the equitable remedies of following or tracing, but they are in fact a process by which the property is identified: ***Westdeutsche Landesbank Girozentrale v Islington LBC*** [1996].

Example 1

In breach, a trustee spends £5,000 to buy a horse.

If the seller of the horse is a bona fide purchaser for valuable consideration without notice ('*equity's darling*') there is no claim against that purchaser for the money. So, the money has now become a horse. The property that is being claimed is the horse: its nature has changed but the property rights in it are the same.

REVISION TIP

It is important to note that in the tracing process the purpose is to identify the property. Once the property has been identified the next step is to see if the claimant's best interest is to bring a proprietary remedy—if the value of the property has increased—or a personal remedy—if the value has gone down. Once identified, to protect the personal claim an equitable ***lien*** can be placed on the property (similar in principle to that of a mortgage), which will give the claimant a priority over claims on *that* property: ***Foskett v McKeown*** [2001].

Common law proprietary claim

When a party receives property to which that party is not legally entitled, he or she is under an obligation to return the property to the rightful owner. The party may receive this property because:

- it is received under a void contract; or
- it is received without the recipient giving valuable consideration.

The law will follow the property to the recipient, into the hands of another, by the process identified earlier. The liability for this claim is strict: once the property is found in the hands of the recipient, the property must be returned, subject to defences. A common law claim requires that:

- the claimant has legal title (so a beneficiary cannot use this remedy, but a trustee can); and
- the property is unmixed.

Following at common law cannot be used when the property has been **mixed** with another person's property: ***Agip (Africa) Ltd v Jackson*** [1990]. This means that the property claimed has been combined with another person's property. The common example is where money is taken in breach and placed in a bank account with the recipient's own money. But the principle applies to all property.

However, the *clean* substitution of one property for another does not prevent the claim: ***Taylor v Plumer*** (1815). In this case the claimant's money was used to buy bonds and bullion; Lord Ellenborough said that 'the product or the substitute for the original thing still follows the nature of the thing itself'.

LOOKING FOR EXTRA MARKS?

Compare the tracing process with the protection of suppliers of materials to a company (creditors) offered under a (***Romalpa***) retention of title clause: ***Aluminium Industrie Vaasen BV v Romalpa Aluminium Ltd*** [1976]. In this way the supplied goods never become the property of the company and should the company be liquidated the goods are reclaimed by the seller: ***Hendy Lennox Ltd v Grahame Puttick Ltd*** [1984].

Problems arise when the property supplied with such a clause is used to manufacture goods. In ***Re Peachdart Ltd*** [1984], leather supplied was deemed to have been mixed in the production of handbags; although the leather was legally physically recognizable, it had lost its identity. See also ***Borden UK Ltd v Scottish Timber Products Ltd*** [1981].

REVISION TIP

The principle with the retention of title is exactly the same as common law tracing. The seller retains the legal title. You may see in the cases that the buyer may hold a position as **bailee** or agent; but keep in mind what the purpose of the clause is—to retain a property interest.

Equitable proprietary claim

In contrast to following at common law, tracing in equity does not 'stop at the doors of the bank': ***Chief Constable of Kent v V and another*** [1983]. Tracing in equity is therefore more flexible than following at common law as it can be used to trace property into mixed funds. The problem is identifying how much of the mixed property belongs to the claimant.

Essential elements for an equitable proprietary claim

From ***Re Diplock*** [1948] it is clear that to use equitable tracing there must be two requirements:

- a fiduciary relationship; and
- an equitable interest.

In a trust situation there will be a fiduciary relationship between the trustee and the beneficiary. In chapter 9 we identified classic relationships where a fiduciary relationship exists. However, it has become increasingly easy to establish a fiduciary relationship. Lord Browne-Wilkinson in ***Westdeutsche Landesbank Girozentrale v Islington LBC*** [1996] stated that a thief creates a 'fiduciary relationship' when he or she takes property belonging to another.

It is not necessary that the equitable interest pre-exists the acquisition of property by another. This leads to a 'chicken-and-egg' situation in relation to the two requirements for equitable tracing, which may be more apparent than real. This may be why Lord Millett doubted whether a fiduciary relationship was even necessary: ***Foskett v McKeown*** [2001].

REVISION TIP

Once a constructive trust has been established this gives the claimant a right to trace the property in equity. Therefore, if property is found in the possession of a recipient with the requisite knowledge to create recipient liability, the recipient becomes a trustee and the claimant can decide to make a proprietary claim, not merely a personal one. This is the point at which the personal claim and the proprietary claim overlap. Often students are uncertain as to which claim to pursue; the answer for a claimant is usually financial. Which claim will give the best financial result? See Figures 12.2 and 12.3 at the end of the chapter.

Where there has been a breach of trust the claimant must identify where the remedy lies. There will always be a personal remedy against the trustee but a common problem, especially in exams, is that the trustee has become bankrupt or has disappeared. In this situation, the personal claim may be worthless.

TERMINOLOGY TIP

Students sometimes say in this situation that there is no personal claim. This is not true. There is a personal claim—it is just not worth pursuing.

Identifying who has the property

The rules in the tracing process need to be understood as falling into two categories:

- claims against the fiduciary (trustee); and
- claims between two 'innocent' claimants.

REVISION TIP

Always identify who has the property that is being claimed. The claim may be made against the fiduciary or trustee in breach, but it may sometimes happen that the trustee has mixed two trust funds' monies in the same account or purchased property with a mixed fund, so two innocent parties' money has been used.

Chapter 9 established that property which is purchased with the funds of two people is shared between them in proportion to their contribution under a resulting trust. ***Sinclair v Brougham*** [1914] presumes between all parties tracing their property that it is shared **rateably**: *pari passu*. The same reasoning applies to tracing claims where more than one person's money has been used to purchase property subject to a tracing claim, regardless of whether the claim is against the fiduciary or another innocent claimant. The courts are seeking to identify the property that is owned by the beneficiary. If the property being traced is an asset that has been purchased or exchanged for the trust property, the basic principle is to identify how much of the asset belongs to the trust and how much to an innocent contributor, a recipient, or a trustee in breach.

So, if a trustee takes a painting from the trust property and exchanges the painting and his or her own gold watch for a car, the courts would need to ascertain in what proportion the car belonged to the trust and to the trustee in breach. It is more common in exam questions that the value is represented in monetary figures. This is the process of tracing.

Claim against a trustee in breach

The rules in relation to claims against a trustee in breach will be explained by working through an example.

REVISION TIP

In an exam, be clear where the money is coming from and where it is going. It may be useful in your answer plan to draw an accounting table of the sums you are dealing with. This is one suggested layout, but any method that can help you identify who owns what share of property is helpful. Carefully planning the answer in this way will pay dividends.

Payments into an overdrawn account

In breach of trust, a trustee takes £2,000 from Trust Fund A and places it into his current account which has an overdraft of £1,000 (see Table 12.2).

Table 12.2 Overdrawn account

BALANCE IN THE CURRENT ACCOUNT AFTER TRANSFER	TRUSTEE'S INTEREST	TRUST A'S INTEREST
£1,000	*–£1,000*	£2,000

The money to pay the overdraft has been dissipated; there is no asset into which to trace the property.

LOOKING FOR EXTRA MARKS?

It has been suggested that 'backwards tracing' may provide an answer for payments into an overdrawn account. This means that if the overdraft was caused by purchasing an asset for the trustee then the claimant should have a claim on that asset. In ***Bishopsgate Investment Management Ltd v Homan*** [1995], Leggatt LJ rejected the principles, but Dillon LJ said that it was arguable whether the facts could allow an inference that there was an intention by the trustee to repay the overdraft with trust money. This view found favour in ***Foskett v McKeown*** and was discussed by the Privy Council in ***Federal Republic of Brazil v Durant International Corpn*** [2015].

The presumptions of honesty

(a) Trustee in breach takes £2,000 from Trust Fund A and places it into his current account, which has an existing balance of £1,000.

At this point the money in the account would be shared one-third for trustee and two-thirds for Trust Fund A because this is the proportion in which they made the contributions.

REVISION TIP

In an exam question, commonly the trustee will spend the money in the account, because otherwise, although the trustee may be imprudent with the trust money, there is no difficulty in reclaiming the money.

Re Hallet's (1880) deals with the situation where money is taken from the trustee's account. The court uses a presumption of honesty, meaning that the trustee is deemed to spend his or her *own money* first. So, when the trustee then buys a painting for £1,500, the painting would be purchased in the same proportion as the contribution: two-thirds by trustee and one-third by Trust A. This rule will be applied even if the value of the painting increases: ***Re Tilley's WT*** [1967]. The beneficiary is protected as the fund is safe and identifiable and the share of the painting is identifiable. The remedy is not to punish the trustee but to protect the property of the trust fund (see Table 12.3).

Table 12.3 *Re Hallet's*

BALANCE IN THE CURRENT ACCOUNT	TRUSTEE'S INTEREST	TRUST A'S INTEREST
£3,000 (after transfer)	£1,000	£2,000
–£1,500 (purchase of picture)	*£1,000*	*£500*
£1,500 (after purchase)	0	£1,500

(b) If the balance in the bank (in example (a)) was then dissipated by the trustee, the courts may reverse the application of ***Re Hallet's*** (1880) by using ***Re Oatway*** [1903].

REVISION TIP

A common mistake made by students in exams is to apply ***Re Oatway*** immediately. More marks will be gained for explaining the presumption in ***Re Hallet's***, and how that would affect distribution of property rights, then explaining how ***Re Oatway*** modifies that.

Applying ***Re Oatway*** (1903)—trustee in breach takes £2,000 from Trust Fund A and places it in his current account, which already has £1,000 in it. Then he purchases a painting worth £1,500. He then spends the balance of the bank account on a world cruise (see Table 12.4).

Table 12.4 Re Oatway

BALANCE IN THE CURRENT ACCOUNT	TRUSTEE'S INTEREST	TRUST A'S INTEREST
£3,000 (after transfer)	£1,000	£2,000
–£1,500 (purchase of picture)		*£1,500*
£1,500 (after purchase of picture)	£1,000	£500
–£1,500 (purchase of cruise)	*£1,000*	*£500*

This means that the money used to buy the painting, which remains an identifiable asset, was in fact that of the trust. So, the painting is owned by Trust A and the money dissipated is only £500 of Trust A's money and the bulk is the trustees' money. This preserves the property of the trust fund as much as possible. If the painting has increased in value, there will be a proprietary claim. If the painting has reduced in value, the claimant can place an equitable lien over the property to the value of the money taken (not the money spent on the painting) to protect any personal claims the claimant may make.

The aim is to protect the interest of the (innocent) beneficiary and ensure that the wrongdoer risks the loss. The presumption would be that (still trying to be honest) the trustee in fact spent the trust fund money and dissipated his own. This then secures the trust funds against the asset. It is unclear from ***Re Oatway*** whether all the money from the account needs to be dissipated or if the beneficiary will be allowed to 'cherry-pick' the rules to apply and ensure the most returns for his claim: see Rimer J in ***Shalson v Russo*** [2003]. The ability to 'cherry-pick' was rejected in ***Turner v Jacob*** [2008] when there were funds remaining in the account to cover the loss.

TERMINOLOGY TIP

'Dissipated' means that there is no asset to attach a property right to, not that the property is worthless. For example, the money has been spent on a holiday or a meal. It does not mean that shares or other property purchased with the trust money now have no value.

The seller of the painting cannot be made to return the money as the seller is 'equity's darling'. This is an absolute defence for the seller. However, if the money had been donated to a charity or given as a gift, the equity's darling defence would not apply. The trust can trace 'into the hands' of the innocent volunteer.

Later payments into the account by the trustee in breach

The rule in ***Roscoe v Winder*** [1915] is that if a trustee in breach mixes his or her own, later-acquired, money in the same bank account with trust money, the presumption is that this is *not* a repayment of the money used in breach. The presumption will only be rebutted if there is clear evidence that the intention of the trustee was to repay the money taken in breach.

The trustee takes £500 he won on the lottery and places it into the account that has £1,000 of Trust A money remaining in it after the trustee spent £1,000 on a holiday (see Table 12.5).

Table 12.5 Lowest immediate balance

BALANCE IN THE ACCOUNT	TRUSTEE'S INTEREST	TRUST A'S INTEREST
£2,000		£2,000
–£1,000 (spent on a holiday)	0	*£1,000*
+£500 (lottery winnings)	£500	
£1,500	£500	£1,000

The trustee has the property right in this money and is not deemed to repay the beneficiary unless there is evidence of that intention: ***Roscoe v Winder*** [1915]. This may seem an anomaly to the 'presumption of honesty' but the claim is proprietary and as such the £500 was never the property of the trust. On this basis, it makes sense that Trust A cannot claim that the £500 represents its property. It has no pre-existing property right in the £500 that the court will protect. Its personal claim remains intact.

Two innocent volunteers mixed funds in a bank account

The rules that operate between two innocent parties are different in some aspects. If the trust property remains identifiable then the property is shared rateably as between the trustee and the trust fund: ***Sinclair v Brougham*** [1914].

The trustee takes £1,000 from Trust B and places that in the account which already has £750 of Trust A funds in it (see Table 12.6).

Table 12.6 Innocent volunteers mixed fund

BALANCE IN THE ACCOUNT	TRUSTEE'S INTEREST	TRUST A'S INTEREST	TRUST B'S INTEREST
£1,750 (after transfer)	0	£750	£1,000

The position is now that there is a mixed fund between two innocent parties. Different rules apply in relation to how they are dealt with between each other compared with how the trustee is dealt with in relation to them. If the trustee now spends the money in the bank the rule in ***Clayton's Case*** (1817) will apply. This states that, in a current account, money is assumed to be taken on a 'first in, first out' basis. This means that between the two innocent parties the money that was in the account first will be the first to be spent. This is a simple accounting issue.

Following on from that, the trustee spends £1,500 on shares, which, since purchase, have reduced in value and are now worth £500. Trust A had its money in the account for several months before Trust B had its money placed in the account (see Table 12.7).

Table 12.7 *Re Clayton's*

BALANCE IN THE ACCOUNT	TRUSTEE'S INTEREST	TRUST A'S INTEREST	TRUST B'S INTEREST
–£1,500 (purchase of shares)	0	*£750*	*£750*
£293	0	0	£293

As Trust A was the first to have money in the account the 'first in, first out' rule from ***Clayton's Case*** (1817) will take that money first, then the balance will come from Trust B.

The remaining money in the bank belongs to Trust B. This rule can work harshly, for example if Trust A will be exhausted on this interpretation but Trust B still has a significant amount left.

If this does cause an inequitable result, then the rule in ***Clayton's Case*** can be set aside: ***Barlow Clowes v Vaughan*** [1992]. Although ***Clayton's Case*** was stated to be the default position in ***Barlow Clowes v Vaughan***, the court found that this could not have been the intention of the contributors. One option is to consider that the money is contributed subject to a 'rolling charge' (the North American approach) so funds are allocated proportionately at each withdrawal or at the final stage regardless of when contributions and withdrawals were made. This found approval in ***Shalson v Russo*** [2003].

Innocent volunteers who receive trust property

'Innocent volunteer' also applies to situations where a person receives property under an invalid contract, such as the Playboy Club in ***Lipkin Gorman*** [1991]. Tracing will identify the property in the possession of the innocent recipient. Once it has been found in the possession of the recipient, liability is strict.

Defences available to the innocent volunteer

Re Diplock [1948] suggested that in this situation the innocent volunteer may claim that it would be unconscionable to return the property. The personal claim against the trustee in breach remains (***Ministry of Health v Simpson*** [1951]), but the proprietary claim may fail. This is the same principle as the change-of-position defence in common law claims. In ***Boscawen v Bajwa*** [1996] it was stated that the common law defence of change of position could apply to the equitable claims.

Figure 12.2 Summary of potential claims in common law

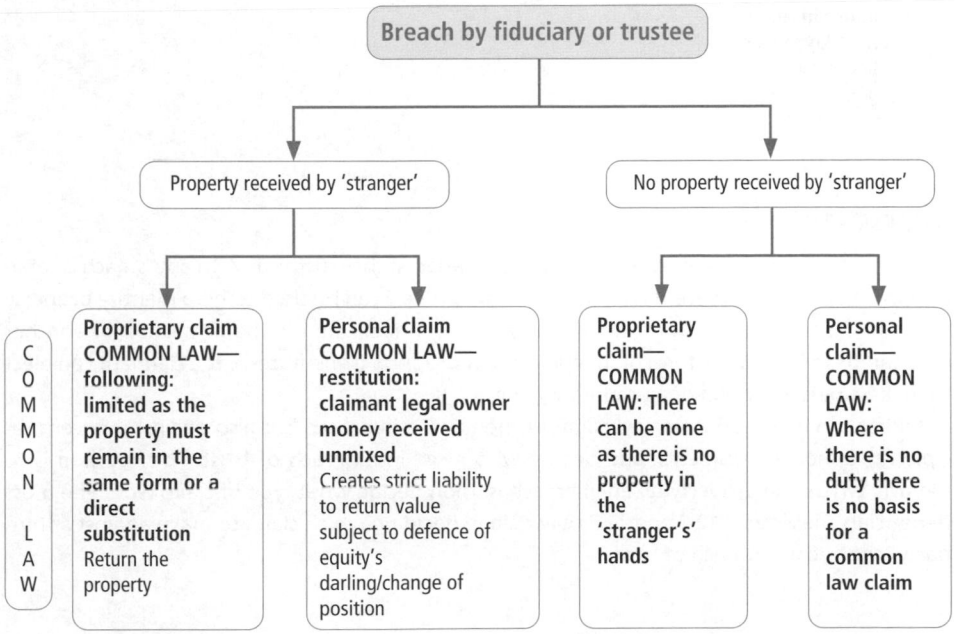

Figure 12.3 Summary of potential claims in equity

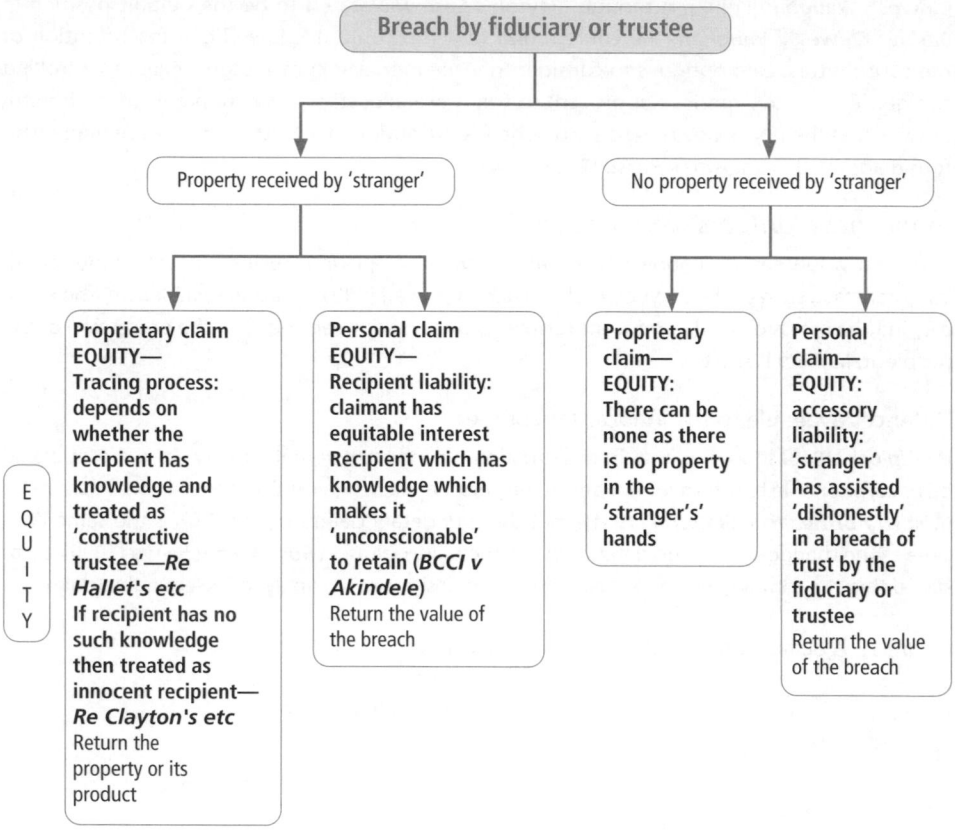

Conclusion

The remedies for breach of trust can be personal against the trustee as with any breach of obligation. In addition to these claims, a proprietary process can be used to help identify property taken in breach of trust. Once the property has been identified in the possession of another (this can be in its original form or in replacement property (substitutes)), the claimant can elect to make a personal claim or a proprietary one.

Claims can be brought not only against the trustee in breach but also against innocent recipients, dishonest recipients, and people who assist in a breach of trust. The key step is to identify where the property taken in breach is, then decide what type of claim would be most beneficial. The Figures 12.2 and 12.3 may help in deciding which claim to make against a third party involved in a breach of trust.

KEY CASES

CASE	FACTS	PRINCIPLE
Agip (Africa) Ltd v Jackson [1990] Ch 26	A senior officer innocently signed a forged payment order. The forger, an accountant, was employed by the company. Payment was made by innocent banks. The forgery was discovered too late to stop payment.	Where there had been no mixing the property could be traced at common law. Money was transferred by electronic transfer so there was no physical asset which could be traced. The fraudulent accountant owed a fiduciary duty to the company. He would be liable to account as constructive trustee as he knowingly assisted in the fraud.
BCCI v Akindele [2000] 4 All ER 221	Money was loaned on very favourable terms. BCCI collapsed, and the creditors tried to claim against the money paid to Chief Akindele for his assistance in fraud.	The level of dishonesty needed to create liability as constructive trustee was 'such that it would make it unconscionable for them to retain the receipt'.
Foskett v McKeown [2001] 1 AC 102	Deposits paid for property were used to pay for insurance premiums by M. M committed suicide and over £1 million was paid on the insurance policy. The claimant traced the money into the insurance payment.	The claimant was entitled to a charge over the payment, with interest paid on that amount, but his claim was not restricted to this (as the Court of Appeal had found). He could claim a proportion of the payment equivalent to his contribution.
Lipkin Gorman v Karpnale Ltd [1991] 2 AC 548	A solicitor removed clients' money from the client account and used the money or gambling at the Playboy Club. This was a breach of the solicitor's fiduciary obligations. The Playboy Club had received that money under a void contract (gambling contracts were void at the time). As the Playboy Club had no legal claim to the money it was required to return its value to the 'real' owner.	The liability to repay the solicitor was strict but subject to a defence of change of position. The argument by the Playboy Club that it was equity's darling failed as its contract was void under the existing gambling laws of the time.
Twinsectra v Yardley [2002] 2 AC 164	Money was lent to Sim, acting for Yardley, for the sole purpose of buying property. In breach, Sim paid the money to Yardley's solicitor, Leach. He released it to Yardley. On default Leach was sued for dishonest assistance.	The loan was made as a ***Quistclose*** trust. The case decided on the 'combined test'. Has D transgressed the standards of conduct? Does D realize the transgression? Note: the test was 'reviewed' by the ***Privy Council in Eurotrust v Barlow Clowes*** [2006].

KEY DEBATES

Topic	Meaning of dishonesty in accessory liability
Academic/author	Lord Millett
Viewpoint	The liability should be objective and not have a subjective element.
Source	Lord Millett's dissenting judgment in ***Twinsectra v Yardley*** [2002]. For an overview of the issues, see Pearce and Barr, *Pearce and Stevens' Law of Trusts and Equitable Obligations*, 7th edn (2018), pp 719–45.

Topic	Strict liability for recipient liability
Academic/author	Birks
Viewpoint	Liability should be strict subject to defences as with common law money had and received.
Source	Birks [1989] LMCLQ 296.

Topic	Backwards tracing
Academic/author	Matthew Conaglen
Viewpoint	Considers the policy in relation to backwards tracing.
Source	'Difficulties with Tracing Backwards' (2011) 127 LQR 432

EXAM QUESTIONS

Problem question

Jack, a solicitor for Badger & Co, takes £3,000 out of the customer account. He spends £2,000 at the local casino, Fungirls & Co. He places the remaining £1,000 in his bank, which already has a balance of £500. He takes £1,000 and buys a painting from his friend Augustus, which is now worth £2,000. The remaining £500 in his account, he spends on a holiday weekend in France.

Advise Badger & Co as to its remedies.

See the Outline answers section in the end matter for help with this question.

Essay question

The rules on common law and equitable tracing should be united into a coherent system of rules. Discuss.

Online resources

For an outline answer to this essay question, as well as multiple choice questions and interactive key cases, please visit the online resources.

Concentrate Q&As

For more questions and answers on equity and trusts, see the *Concentrate Q&A: Equity & Trusts* by Rosalind Malcolm.

Go to the end of this book to view **sample pages**.

13 Equitable remedies

KEY FACTS

- Equitable remedies are discretionary.
- Equitable remedies are granted where common law remedies would be inadequate.
- Equitable remedies can be granted at full trial or at an interim stage before a full trial.
- Equitable remedies operate *in personam*, against the defendant personally.

Introduction

The common law provides the remedy of **damages** as of right for any breach. However, damages may not always provide a suitable or adequate remedy. For example, if a person was trespassing on your land then money would not be the suitable remedy as the trespass itself has caused no financial loss. As 'equity will not suffer a wrong without a remedy' over the years the courts have developed a number of equitable remedies to address the limitations of the common law response. As these remedies have been developed to ensure fairness, they are not available as of right, but are always granted at the discretion of the court. This chapter considers the range of equitable remedies which have been developed by the courts:

1. specific performance;
2. injunctions;
3. rescission;
4. rectification; and
5. account.

Specific performance

In most situations where there is a breach of contract, the loss suffered will be capable of being compensated by a common law award of damages. However, in some cases, the court may choose to compel the defendant to perform his or her original obligation under the contract by making an order for specific performance. Typically, such an order will be made where monetary damages would not provide an appropriate remedy or compensate for the loss suffered. As this equitable remedy compels the completion of an obligation, it would be inappropriate to grant an order of specific performance without a full hearing. Therefore, specific performance is only available at full trial and cannot be awarded at an interim stage.

Unique

Damages will be considered inadequate when the obligation the claimant seeks to enforce is unique. A simple illustration of this can be found in contracts for the sale of land. Although an award of monetary damages may allow you to purchase *similar* land, you will never be able to replace the land that you were originally promised.

The courts have interpreted what is 'unique' broadly. It does not mean that the goods are literally unique but that they are effectively unique in the context of the contract:

- ***Sky Petroleum v VIP Petroleum*** [1974]: a contract to supply petrol could be specifically enforced. The issue had arisen during a national petrol shortage, making it impossible to find an alternative supplier. The risk from the refusal to deliver—that the claimant might go out of business—meant that the remedy was necessary.

- ***Behnke v Bede Shipping Co Ltd*** [1927]: delivery of a ship was granted specific performance because the ship was of 'peculiar and practically unique value to the plaintiff', which could not easily seek an alternative supplier of that kind of vessel.

REVISION TIP

It is very important in a problem exam question that you apply the law to the facts. For example, a contract for a car will not usually be unique, but if the purchaser needs to buy a specific car, perhaps one that was a prop in a James Bond film, then that car may be said to have a unique quality.

A common problem for good students who know the law is a failure to advise the client—that is, not just stating what the law is but also applying it to the facts of the case before you.

Considerations in granting an order

It is important to remember that equitable remedies are discretionary. So, even if the situation appears to warrant specific performance, there are certain circumstances in which the court will refuse to make such an order.

Supervision

Even if the court believes that there is a unique quality to the obligation sought to be enforced, it will not award specific performance if the performance of that obligation would require the constant supervision of the court. This means that if the claimant would have to continually return to the court for successive orders, the remedy would essentially be ineffective. In ***Co-operative Insurance Society Ltd v Argyll Stores Ltd*** [1988], Argyll Stores decided to close its store in a shopping centre owned by the claimant as it was losing money. The lease agreement required it to remain open during normal business hours. The House of Lords reversed the Court of Appeal decision to grant specific performance, as to enforce the contract would require the constant supervision of the courts.

Personal services

The courts are reluctant to enforce a contract for a personal service for many reasons. It is reluctant as it may turn a contract for service into a contract of slavery: ***De Francesco v Barnum*** (1890). This reluctance is now statutory based in **s 236 Trade Union and Labour Relations (Consolidation) Act 1992**:

> no court shall . . . by way of an order for specific performance . . . compel an employee to do any work.

However, this only applies to employee contracts. The courts distinguish between contracts '*of service*' and '*for service*'. An example may help to illustrate the difference.

EXAMPLE 1

Mark is hired by Lois to build her a conservatory. This is a contract *for* service. The task is discrete and clearly defined (see ***Posner v Scott-Lewis*** [1987] discussed later). It would be relatively easy to require the promised performance to be completed by an order for specific performance.

EXAMPLE 2

Mark is hired to work in Lois's factory which produces window frames. This is a contract of service. There is an ongoing employer–employee relationship which is unlikely to be enforced.

REVISION TIP

Do not leap to the conclusion that a person is an employee. Apply the facts. Consider what the person is being required to do.

In ***Posner v Scott-Lewis*** [1987] a leasehold covenant required the landlord to employ a resident porter to carry out clearly specified duties at a block of flats. The court considered that the terms were sufficiently clear and ascertainable.

Compare this with ***Warner Bros Pictures Inc v Nelson*** [1937], where the actress Bette Davis was contracted to work exclusively for Warner Bros Pictures. The courts would not compel her to work, by an order of specific performance, as it was akin to 'slavery'.

However, even if it is a contract for service the courts may still decide not to give specific performance. It may be that the service can easily be performed by another. In Example 1, it is likely that damages would be adequate to pay for a replacement supplier of conservatories. This stance can be explained by the equitable maxim 'equity will not act in vain'. If a defendant is forced to perform a task, he or she may not perform the task to a high standard. If being forced to complete the obligation would lead the defendant to deliberately perform badly, an order of specific performance is unlikely to be an effective or appropriate remedy and the court may decide that it is easier to award damages from the outset.

Defences

Hardship

If the grant of specific performance would cause hardship to either party, then the court may not grant specific performance: ***Patel v Ali*** [1984].

Mistake and misrepresentation

The courts may refuse to rescind a contract for misrepresentation and leave the claimant to a remedy of damages. The courts will generally hold the defendant to the performance of his or her contract unless it causes real hardship: ***Tamplin v James*** (1880).

Conduct of claimant

In line with the equitable maxim that those who seek equity must come with clean hands, the conduct of the claimant may bar an order for specific performance. The claimant must prove that he or she has either performed, or is willing and able to perform, his or her obligations: ***Cornish v Brook Green Laundry*** [1959].

Delay or laches

Although generally in equity time is not of the essence, in balancing the equity between the parties, unreasonable delay may defeat equity. What is unreasonable will depend on the facts, particularly the object matter of the contract: ***Lazard Bros v Fairfield Property Ltd*** (1977). Where time is of the essence, specific performance will not usually be granted after the date of performance: ***Union Eagle Ltd v Golden Achievements Ltd*** [1997].

Injunctions

Injunctions can be awarded at two stages of the trial process. It is more common for injunctions to be granted at the conclusion of the full trial hearing. These injunctions are known as **perpetual** and act as the final conclusion to the legal dispute. However, in certain circumstances, the urgency of the matter requires swifter action. For example, where the claimant alleges that the defendant is planning to release documents containing trade secrets to a competitor in breach of confidence, by the time the full trial takes place the damage may already have been done and the claimant will have been deprived of an effective remedy. In this situation, the claimant would seek an interim injunction to stop the defendant acting before the full trial.

Interim injunctions are temporary in nature and will typically last until the conclusion of a full trial hearing. It is vital that such orders are temporary as they are often granted before the court has had the opportunity to hear all the arguments and evidence relating to the claim.

TERMINOLOGY TIP

Do not be confused if you come across references to 'interlocutory' injunctions in textbooks, articles, and cases. Until recently, interim injunctions were known as 'interlocutory' injunctions.

Injunctions are a more flexible type of equitable remedy than specific performance because they can perform different roles. There are three broad types of injunctions:

1. Prohibitive injunctions—these prevent a defendant from doing something and therefore stop a breach of an obligation.
2. Mandatory injunctions—these compel a defendant to do something (and therefore work in a similar way to specific performance).

3. *Quia timet* injunctions—these may be either prohibitory or mandatory and are made where the harm alleged has not yet happened but is feared by the claimant or threatened by the defendant.

Perpetual injunctions

Prohibitive injunctions

Prohibitive injunctions prevent a breach of an obligation. This can include a breach of confidence, such as information obtained during employment. It can include very wide powers to prevent disclosure of information on a worldwide basis, where the release of such information would create serious risk of personal injury. This can be seen in the case of ***Venables v News Group Newspapers*** [2001], where the identity and whereabouts of one of the killers of the toddler Jamie Bulger were not to be published. This was the only way to protect the claimant's rights under the **Human Rights Act 1998**.

REVISION TIP

In an exam, consider that if one remedy does not achieve your purpose another one would. In ***Warner Bros Pictures Inc v Nelson*** [1937], an injunction was ordered against an actress to prevent her from working for any other film company for the duration of her contract with Warner Bros. The claim for specific performance was denied but the claimant achieved its aim with an injunction.

Mandatory injunctions

Mandatory injunctions at full trial require the performance of an obligation in the same way as specific performance. If the obligation is contractual then specific performance is the more common remedy. There may also be a 'restorative' mandatory injunction. This will be given where a wrong has been done which may have been prevented by a prohibitive injunction. A mandatory injunction may be ordered to undo the wrong: ***Jones v Stones*** [1999].

Interim injunctions

Prohibitive injunctions

For a grant of an interim injunction, the courts are making a decision without the benefit of a full trial. To make sure that they have considered the grant carefully they follow the guidelines set out by Lord Diplock in ***American Cyanamid Co v Ethicon Ltd*** [1975]:

- there is a serious question to be tried;
- damages are inadequate;
- the balance of convenience requires the grant of an injunction.

LOOKING FOR EXTRA MARKS?

To fully understand the importance of Lord Diplock's test it is worth understanding what the test was prior to ***American Cyanamid***. The claimant was required to show a strong **prima facie** case that rights had been infringed, that damages were inadequate, and that justice required the grant. This was a heavy burden on the claimant to prove that it was more than likely that it would obtain a full injunction at trial.

Serious question to be tried

The courts will only consider such an order if there are serious issues at stake. In ***Morning Star v Express Newspapers*** [1979], the *Morning Star* newspaper objected to the publication of the *Daily Star*, claiming that people would confuse the two. The judge felt that 'only a moron in a hurry' would make the mistake and that there was no case to answer. This issue was recently discussed in ***Kenson Contractors Ltd v Haringey LBC*** [2019] and the relationship with the balance of convenience which illustrates how these tests are applied in practice.

Adequacy of damages

Essentially, the test for all equitable remedies is, 'Would money compensate?'. There are two stages to the test:

1. Would money be able to compensate, and would the defendant be in a position to pay?
2. If it later appears that the injunction has been given incorrectly then the undertaking by the claimant in damages will be an adequate protection.

One consideration would be if the type of damage is irreparable (such as the loss of a right to vote) or the loss is non-pecuniary (such as libel or nuisance), or if damages would be hard to assess (such as the value of goodwill or serious disruption to business). If damages are considered to be adequate the courts will then consider whether the defendant would be unable to pay should the claimant win. If the claimant fails to prove that damages are inadequate the claim will end there.

The claimant will make an undertaking in damages. This means that if it later appears that the injunction was wrongly granted the claimant can compensate the defendant with money. The inability of the claimant to be able to compensate with money will not be determinative of the decision of the grant of an injunction: ***Allen v Jambo Holdings Ltd*** [1980]. If the claimant cannot make an undertaking the courts will go on to consider the balance of convenience.

Balance of convenience

Lord Diplock said that it would be impossible to list the considerations, but in ***Cayne v Global Natural Resources plc*** [1984] it was said that it is not the mere convenience that needs to be weighed but the risk of doing an injustice to one side or the other. Each case turns on its own facts, so these should be carefully considered in any problem question.

Factors which have been considered

If the balance of convenience is equal, the court will maintain the *status quo*. In ***Garden Cottage Foods Ltd v Milk Marketing Board*** [1984] it appears that it is the *status quo ante* (before the defendant began the conduct complained of) which is maintained, which tends to favour the claimant.

As with all equitable remedies, delay may defeat equity. If the claim has been delayed, then it is the *status quo* at the time of claim and not the *status quo ante* that will be maintained. What is an undue delay varies on the facts: ***Shepherd Homes v Sandham*** [1970] (see Table 13.1).

Table 13.1 Factors for the balance of convenience

FACTOR CONSIDERED	CASE
Loss of employment	***Fellowes & Son v Fisher*** [1976]
Damage to business by picketing	***Hubbard v Pitt*** [1976]
Closing a business	***Potters-Ballotini Ltd v Weston-Baker*** [1977]
Protecting confidential material	***X AG v A Bank*** [1983]
Keeping a life-saving drug on the market	***Roussel-Uclaf v GD Searle & Co Ltd*** [1977]

LOOKING FOR EXTRA MARKS?

In ***Series 5 Software Ltd v Clarke*** [1996], a first-instance decision, it was considered that despite the guidelines mentioned earlier, what was required was a review of all the evidence disclosed. This, however, does appear to be a return to the finding of a prima facie case to be answered, which Lord Diplock in ***American Cyanamid Co v Ethicon Ltd*** [1975] had wanted to avoid. If asked to comment on the test, it may be worth noting the High Court's decision in this case.

REVISION TIP

The question of delay must be applied to the facts. In ***Shepherd Homes*** [1970] an unexplained delay of five months prevented the grant. However, in ***Bulmer v Bollinger*** [1977] the word 'champagne' had been used since 1906 by the firm in marketing 'BabyCham', well known to the claimant. However, the delay in the claim did not defeat the order.

Mandatory injunctions

Unlike specific performance, mandatory injunctions can be awarded at an interim stage. The test set out for interim injunctions in ***American Cyanamid Co v Ethicon Ltd*** [1975] will apply, but in balancing the justice of the case the Court of Appeal in ***Locabail International Finance v Agroexport*** [1986] approved the guidance of Megarry J, in ***Shepherd Homes v Sandham*** [1970], that the courts required a 'high degree of assurance' that the grant of an injunction would be found to be the correct decision when the case finally came to court.

The courts take serious note of the balance of convenience between the claimant and the defendant: ***Evans v BBC and IBA*** (1974) (concerning the transmission of party political broadcasts).

REVISION TIP

Always consider the higher burden on the claimant to prove that he or she should be granted an interim mandatory injunction.

In addition to the general remedies, there are remedies which can be sought in the absence of the defendant; these are *ex parte* orders. In considering these orders it is important to take into account the **Human Rights Act 1998** as the defendant is not there to present his or her case, raising issues of a fair trial. The courts still consider that in some circumstances the interests of the parties call for such an *ex parte* application to be allowed. There are more stringent tests for such orders.

Search orders (formerly Anton Piller *orders)*

During the trial process all parties are required to disclose documents that will be relevant to the trial. If the claimant considers that the other party to the litigation will not do so, he or she may ask for a search order. This order is granted without notice because to give notice would possibly defeat the purpose of the order. These mandatory orders require the defendant to permit the search of his or her premises to find documents. Such an order was first used in ***EMI Ltd v Pandit*** [1975], but the leading case on these orders is ***Anton Piller KG v Manufacturing Processes*** [1976]. In this case, Ormrod LJ said that the remedy was one of 'last resort' because of the impact it could have on the defendant's business. In deciding to grant an order there must be:

- an extremely strong prima facie case;
- extremely serious potential (or actual) harm to the claimant;
- clear evidence that the information or items, which are the subject matter of the order, are in the defendant's possession;
- a real possibility that these will be destroyed or removed without such an order; and
- a full and frank disclosure by the claimant of all material matters in the case.

There are procedural safeguards for the defendant set out in the Practice Direction of the Civil Procedure Rules, granting the jurisdiction for these orders in **s 7 Civil Procedure Act 1997**. These include the presence of a supervising solicitor, that the search takes place in office hours, that the defendant or a responsible employee is present, that it is not a fishing exercise, and that only the subject matter listed in the order is taken. The defendant is also protected in that he or she can make an application at short notice to have the order removed or varied: ***Lock International plc v Beswick*** [1989]. These procedural safeguards indicate the balance the court has to make between protecting the interests of both parties and the possible abuse of the order by a claimant.

REVISION TIP

A common mistake is for students to explain, in detail, the procedure for the grant of the order rather than the legal tests for its grant. Ensure that the legal requirements are fully applied.

Freezing orders (formerly Mareva *injunctions)*

These are mandatory orders which will freeze the assets of the defendant. Equity will not act in vain and, if a claimant wins at trial, he or she will want to ensure that the award of damages will be paid. If there is a danger that the defendant may seek to remove or destroy assets to avoid paying damages, a freezing order may be sought. The order will freeze the assets of the defendant, up to the value of the claim, which will be held by the order of the court. This will prevent a defendant removing assets from the court's jurisdiction before trial: ***Mareva Compania Naviera SA v International Bulkcarriers SA*** [1975].

The freezing order is a clear example of the personal nature of the equitable remedy. The claimant gains no property rights over the assets frozen. Additionally, anyone dealing with the property contrary to the order will be personally liable for contempt of court. Thus, if bank assets are frozen the bank manager cannot allow the client access to the money: ***Attorney-General v Times Newspapers Ltd*** [1992].

LOOKING FOR EXTRA MARKS?

Lord Denning had said *per incuriam* that the remedy was proprietary: ***Z Ltd v A-Z and AA-LL*** [1982]. The nature of freezing an asset, perhaps a ship or house, may have the effect of a proprietary remedy. So, is the claim that it is personal illusory?

Section 37 Senior Courts Act 1981, which gives the courts jurisdiction to grant all injunctions, now provides for freezing orders to be made where it is 'just and convenient to do so'. Such an order often accompanies a search order and again is made without notice.

The test set out in ***Derby & Co Ltd v Weldon*** [1990] is that in addition to the ***American Cyanamid*** test it must also be proven that:

- there is a 'good arguable' case;
- the defendant has assets in the jurisdiction; and
- there is a real risk that without the order the assets will be removed or dissipated.

The defendant can keep assets to provide for reasonable living and business costs. It may also be possible to freeze assets outside the United Kingdom: ***Re BCCI SA (No 9)*** [1994]. Guidelines for enforcing these overseas was set out in ***Dadourian Group Int v Sims*** [2006], trying to balance the 'justice and convenience' considerations with the 'risk' to the parties.

Other injunctive orders

Quia timet (because the claimant fears) orders are made at an interim stage and do not require proof of actual harm. Their purpose is to prevent a possible harm from occurring. This may be preventing publication of a story that may harm a person's reputation or interest. The case of ***Venables v News Group Newspapers*** [2001] illustrates an injunction granted when there was no actual harm but the fear of future harm.

Super-injunctions are orders which seek to prevent disclosure of proceedings in court. If the court believes that an injunction will be awarded, then, to protect anonymity of the claimant, and the purpose of the injunction itself, it may prevent disclosure of any details, even that there has been an order. The Committee on Super Injunctions (reported 2011) led by Lord Neuberger noted that super-injunctions are awarded to ensure that there is a correct balance in such a grant between open justice, free speech, and family life: 'Super-injunctions are now only being granted, for very short periods, and only where this level of secrecy is necessary to ensure that the whole point of the order is not destroyed.'

Rescission

Rescission aims to restore *both* parties to their original positions, before the wrong occurred. The wrong which may initiate a claim for rescission may be 'misrepresentation, undue influence, duress and mistake': ***Bainbridge v Bainbridge*** [2016]. It may be to unravel a declaration of trust as in ***Bainbridge v Bainbridge*** [2016] or to undue transfers of land or end a contract. Where a wrong has occurred, the innocent party can ask for the equitable remedy of rescission. However, the right to rescission may be barred in the following circumstances:

- third-party rights—if an innocent third party will be adversely affected by the rescission: ***Phillips v Brooks*** [1919];
- delay—based upon the maxims that delay defeats equity and is a practical point: ***Leaf v International Galleries*** [1950];
- affirmation—when a claimant can rescind a contract but instead decides to continue with the contract: ***Long v Lloyd*** [1958];

- impossibility—if it is impossible to return both parties to their pre-contractual position. However, equity does provide that substantial not precise restoration will suffice: ***Erlanger v New Sombrero Phosphate Co*** (1873).

The important point to be noted in a claim for rescission of transactions is that there must be justice between both parties. This area of law was reviewed recently by the Supreme Court in ***Pitt v Holt*** [2013].

LOOKING FOR EXTRA MARKS?

An interesting issue is whether this remedy creates a proprietary right. If the transaction is set aside then any property in the hands of the wrongdoer can be argued as held beneficially for the innocent party until the transaction is completely unravelled. See the discussion of Rimer J in ***Shalson v Russo*** [2005].

Rectification

Rectification is an equitable remedy which allows a legal document that does not reflect the true agreement of the parties to be appropriately amended. In ***Craddock Bros v Hunt*** [1932] a conveyance of property indicated that it included an area that actually belonged to another house. The court rectified the conveyance. However, it must be noted that the courts are reluctant to vary written documents without good evidence that it is needed: ***City of Westminster Properties Ltd v Mudd*** [1959]. The principles which the courts need to consider were set out in ***Racal Group Services Ltd v Ashmore*** [1995] and were recently summarized in ***Giles v RNIB*** [2014]:

a) Clear evidence of the true intention which is not effected in the instrument to the civil standard of proof.

b) The flaw in the document is not just to the consequences of what they wanted but does not reflect the true intention.

c) It is not enough that all parties agree to the rectification.

Account

The remedy of account will be used to require a fiduciary or agent to repay unauthorized profit, bribes, or profit from a breach of confidence: ***Attorney-General v Blake*** [2000] (see chapter 12).

CONCLUSION

Equitable remedies recognize that not all contracts are for monetary gain, such as holidays or services. Torts are not always easy to compensate with mere money. Where the claimant can prove that this is the situation then equity 'will not suffer a wrong without a remedy'. The evolution of the search order and freezing order indicates that this is an area of development. A common claim by students, and some academics, is that equity is staid and stagnant. It is anything but, as can be seen by the remedies available.

KEY CASES

CASE	FACTS	PRINCIPLE
American Cyanamid Co v Ethicon Ltd [1975] AC 396	There was a potential infringement of a patent.	Court established the principles to grant an interim injunction: • a serious question to be tried; • the adequacy of damages; • the balance of convenience; • special factors to consider.
Anton Piller KG v Manufacturing Processes Ltd [1976] Ch 55	The claimant believed that the defendant had confidential papers belonging to it. The claimant wanted to search the defendant's premises to find them.	'Equity will not suffer a wrong without a remedy' and a search order was granted.
Co-operative Insurance Society v Argyll Stores [1988] AC 1	A lease stipulated that a store should be open during usual business hours. The store was losing money and wanted to close.	If specific performance was ordered the court would be required to supervise compliance with the order. The order was not given.
Lock International plc v Beswick [1989] 1 WLR 1268	The claimant said that the defendants had confidential information taken from the claimant which was being used in competition. The claimant wanted a search order to confiscate the property.	The defendants successfully had a search order discharged as they were not 'fly-by-night video pirates' but respectable business people and likely to comply with disclosure orders.

KEY DEBATES

Topic	Interim orders
Academic/author	Dockray and Laddie
Viewpoint	The nature of the order can be oppressive and have devastating impact on business or persons who have not had a full trial.
Source	Dockray and Laddie, 'Piller Problems' (1990) 106 LQR 601.

Topic	Search orders
Academic/author	
Viewpoint	There may be a risk that orders made without the benefit of a full trial, especially when made without notice, could breach the United Kingdom's obligations under the **European Convention on Human Rights**.
	Chappell v UK (1990) 12 EHRR 1.

EXAM QUESTIONS

Problem question

Hannah contracts with Ahmed to paint a portrait of her mother Joyce, for £5,000 contract price. Ahmed is Joyce's favourite artist. It will be a present for Joyce's birthday on 2 June. He begins the portrait but is then approached by Lars, who offers Ahmed £10,000, if Ahmed will stop the portrait of Joyce and paint Lars in his graduation gown by 1 June. Ahmed informs Hannah that he cannot complete Joyce's portrait.

Hannah had given Ahmed Joyce's diary, containing intimate details of her mother's life, so he could get a 'feel' for her character. Joyce is a politician who is about to stand for re-election. The diaries contain details of several affairs that Joyce had during her life and some details of political indiscretions.

Hannah has been told by her friend that Ahmed has approached a national newspaper to sell some of these details. Ahmed has a bank account in this country and owns homes in Los Angeles and Switzerland.

Advise Hannah on any equitable remedies she may have.

Essay question

The grant of *ex parte* equitable remedies is a breach of fundamental human rights. Discuss.

Online resources

For an outline answer to this essay question, as well as multiple choice questions and interactive key cases, please visit the online resources.

Concentrate Q&As

For more questions and answers on equity and trusts, see the *Concentrate Q&A: Equity & Trusts* by Rosalind Malcolm.

Go to the end of this book to view **sample pages**

Exam essentials

Equity and trusts is a conceptual and challenging area of law; hopefully this book has introduced the essentials of the common areas in your syllabus.

Take a holistic approach to study and be prepared to make the connections between topics. For example, you cannot fully understand how breach of trust can be remedied (chapter 12) without being aware of the trustees' duties (chapter 11). As the remedy can involve the creation of a constructive trust (chapter 9) you would need to understand the essentials for a trust (chapter 3) and the nature of a trust (chapter 2) so that a suitable remedy can be obtained. Do not be put off if you cannot see the big picture in the early days of your study; sometimes this only happens mid-way through the course.

Essays

An essay should not be descriptive but requires that you take a critical approach to the area. Read the 'Key debates' at the end of each chapter which list some of the topical issues. You will also need to read some articles in relation to the essay topic to be able to reach the higher marks. Take the essay question apart and ensure that you answer the question asked, not the one that you wish had been asked. For example:

> The most difficult question one can ask about resulting trusts is why they arise (W Swadling (2008) LQR).

Discuss.

This question uses a quote which you are merely asked to discuss. You must be aware of the academic (often heated) debate in this area. This centres on the role of intention in the recognition of a resulting trust. You must explain the different approaches and then comment on your view of their persuasiveness. The fact that two great equity lawyers cannot agree proves that there is more than one view. Do not just tell the examiner what they say, that is descriptive; comment critically on their views: do you agree with any view; are there good points in both? Use cases to support your argument and illustrate your stance. Make sure that your introduction, which sets out how you will approach the question (eg whether you agree that this is a difficult question or is purely academic), agrees with your conclusion.

Do not go in with a pre-prepared answer on a topic; examiners are experienced in spotting this and it will gain no credit. If you can learn that, then you can learn the law and approach it independently.

Problem questions

The requirements of a good answer to a problem scenario are to advise your client. As you read your problem scenario, highlight, either on the paper or in notes, the material facts; these are the facts which raise legal issues. For example:

Dell is a wealthy elderly gentleman. Having decided to retire to a remote Scottish island for his remaining years, he wishes to give away his property. He takes his portrait of the Queen to his friend Katie, hands it to her, and tells her, 'Look after this and hold it on trust for Luke'.

The first facts do not raise a legal issue; they merely allow the examiner to begin telling a story. The material fact here is that Dell is trying to create a trust of personalty, with Katie as trustee and Luke as beneficiary.

This will lead you to advise on how legal title can be transferred to Katie effectively and how a trust can be created for the benefit of Luke.

Answering the question

Do not begin your answer with an explanation of all the rules in relation to formalities and constitution, how equity may perfect legal title, how equitable interests may be transferred. While what you say may be correct, it will gain little credit from examiners. Instead, begin your answer with a short (a line or two) introduction: 'I will advise Katie whether there is a trust of the portrait for the benefit of Luke.' Then get to your advice: 'As the portrait is a chattel, in order to transfer legal title in Katie it will need to be delivered, which it is when it is handed to Katie by Dell, with the intention that she becomes the legal owner (*Re Cole*). The words here are … '.

Do not tell the examiners all that happened in the cases you are using in your answer; repeating the facts of cases is unnecessary. You should only use the facts of earlier cases when you are distinguishing cases or illustrating why your conclusion is firmly based on this. So, you might say, '*Paul v Constance* shows us that there need be no formal words of trust, and they can arise by clear conduct'. We have read many answers that tell the moving tale of Mr Constance and Ms Paul, their bingo winnings, his personal injury payment, how long they had lived together, etc. While interesting, it is not usually relevant to the advice your client requires.

When you have finished your advice, write a short conclusion on the most likely outcome based on your advice: 'So here it appears that there may be a valid declaration of trust in favour of Luke with Katie holding as trustee.'

And finally

Read the questions carefully; check the rubric, as the examiner may only ask your advice in relation to certain parties, to ensure that your answer can be given in the time allotted.

Do not run over time with any question. If you have three hours for four answers, then stop writing after 45 minutes; leave a page before your next answer in case you get time to go back but move on to the next question. If you only answer three out of four questions, then you immediately reduce your marks by 25 per cent. Practise writing your answers in long hand, so you are ready for the exam room.

Outline answers

CHAPTER 1

Essay answer

- Always read essay questions carefully to identify the relevant issues.
- *Illustrate* the law's adaptation to changing social conditions and *discuss* whether these changes promote certainty or some other goal.
- You cannot cover every possible example, so pick out key areas for discussion. For example:
- *Trusts of the family home*: as levels of cohabitation have increased, there has been an increasing need for the law to adapt. This has revealed tensions between certainty and more welfarist concerns, such as:

Lord Denning and the 'New Model Constructive Trust': ***Hussey v Palmer*** [1972].

Questions over what contributions are relevant to the establishment of a constructive trust (contrast ***Lloyds Bank v Rosset*** [1991], ***Stack v Dowden*** [2007], and recent lower court decisions, such as ***Aspden v Elvy*** [2012], where a more flexible approach is illustrated).

Oxley v Hiscock [2004] argued that the court could quantify the beneficial interest as what was 'fair having regard to the whole course of dealings in relation to the property'. While the House of Lords in ***Stack v Dowden*** [2007] rejected the 'fairness' aspect of this test as too subjective, the case of ***Jones v Kernott*** [2011] confirms the possibility of imputing an intention to the parties of fair shares in certain circumstances.

The degree of uncertainty in this area is illustrated by the increasing calls for legislative reform.

- *Quistclose-type trusts*: the precise conceptual foundations of this trust remain unclear (***Twinsectra v Yardley*** [2002]). While the 'Quistclose' trust clearly attempts to do justice in specific cases, its uncertain foundations lay the ground for further disputes.
- *Formalities cases*: in aiming to prevent fraud, the strict application of the formality requirements often created injustice, leading the court to uphold certain transfers in equity (eg ***Re Rose*** [1952]). However, such cases sit uneasily with the long-established principles of ***Milroy v Lord*** (1862). While problematic decisions like ***Choithram (T) International SA v Pagarani*** [2001] and ***Pennington v Waine*** [2002] attempt to adopt a positive approach to transactions where there is no risk of fraud, the underlying problem of how these approaches will be used creates uncertainty, particularly in the commercial world.
- *Injunctions*: the development of search and freezing orders helps to ensure that claimants will not be deprived of an effective remedy. However, the extensive nature of such orders means the courts must ensure these remedies are not abused.
- Equity has to strike an appropriate balance between certainty and more individualized justice. Innovation is required to adapt to changing social conditions; but without a proper consideration of fundamental principles, the courts risk creating further litigation and confusion.

CHAPTER 3

Problem answer

Trust 1—Certainty of intention

- Anna's bequest uses the word 'trust' but *not* in the legal sense. The bequest is more precatory than imperative (eg ***Re Adams and Kensington Vestry*** (1884) 'in full confidence').
- There will be no trust, but Ruth will still receive the money as a gift.

Trust 2—Certainty of objects

- This is a discretionary trust as the trustees have the power to decide who and how many to appoint.
- The test for certainty of objects—can it be said with certainty that any given individual is or is not a member of the class (***McPhail v Doulton*** [1971])?
- The class to benefit must be 'conceptually certain' (***Re Baden's Trusts (No 2)*** [1973]). Discuss

whether 'trusted work colleagues' would be conceptually certain under the different approaches taken in the Court of Appeal.

- Even if the strict approach of Stamp LJ is used, 'work colleagues' could be interpreted to mean all the employees of the company—a group whose membership could be defined.
- Note: if this approach was adopted, the trust might be *administratively unworkable* if the employees of the multinational company are vast in number (***R v District Auditor, ex p West Yorkshire MCC*** (1986)).
- However, 'work colleagues' might mean those with whom Anna worked directly. While this might satisfy the more liberal approaches of Sachs and Megaw LJJ, it is less likely to meet Stamp LJ's strict requirement that it must be possible to say of anyone whether he or she does or does not fall within the class.
- The greater problem is the inclusion of the word 'trusted', which could have several interpretations: it could relate to work performance or those Anna could trust with a secret. As the bequest does not allow the membership to be defined by someone else, the trust will fail as neither the trustees nor the court would know how to define this group (***Re Tuck's ST*** (1978)).
- The money will be held on resulting trust for the estate.

Trust 3—Certainty of subject matter

- Anna's mention of her 'favourite' jewels suggests that she intends to create a trust of *part* of her jewel collection.
- Unless Anna has physically separated or identified her favourite jewels, this trust will fail for lack of certainty of subject matter and fall into the residue of Anna's estate (***Re London Wine Co*** [1986]).

CHAPTER 4

Problem answer

- Explain how title to shares are transferred at law, needing to comply with the Stock Transfer Act or the Companies Act, assuming they are outside the CREST system. This has not been complied with.
- Equity may perfect title. Apply to the facts:

Evidence of intention to transfer interest in the words 'you can have'.

Is it an intention to give in the future, such as 'you can have . . . '? Explain what is meant by present giving (***Re Freeland*** [1952]).

If it was an intention to give in the present tense, there is no evidence of a change of intention (***Re Gonin*** [1977]).

James has been appointed executor.

- Give a reasoned conclusion on the outcome.
- Explain that to transfer the legal title Sumita should deliver the goods, which are chattels, with the intention to give legal title (***Re Cole*** (1964)) and she has failed to do this.
- The general rule would be that 'equity will not perfect an imperfect gift'.
- However, equity may look upon as done that which ought to be done on the basis of a DMC if the requirements of ***Cain v Moon*** [1896] are satisfied:

Sumita considers that she is going to die soon and in contemplation of that death she has decided to give Ellie her car, as in ***Wilkes v Allington*** (1931).

It seems that there is no express declaration that it is conditional on death. The courts have implied such an intention when the transferor is unlikely to survive (***Sen v Headley*** **[1991]**). It may be that the courts will imply such a contingent intention on the fact that Sumita considers that she is going to die.

There appears to be constructive (symbolic) delivery. In ***Woodard v Woodard*** [1995] it was held that delivery of keys to the car could be enough to transfer the dominion of the property. In addition, Ellie has the registration documents.

A car can form the subject matter of a DMC.

It is suggested that on these facts equity may perfect the transfer to Ellie.

- Give a reasoned conclusion.

CHAPTER 5

Problem answer

Planning your answer

- Identify the property being dealt with—is it land or personalty?

- Identify the interests Kirsty has—legal title or merely the equitable title?

Writing your answer

Blackacre

- Oral declaration of trust in land is valid but unenforceable (s 53(1)(b) LPA 1925). George has an unenforceable beneficial interest on 1 March.
- On 31 March the formalities are complied with and the trust becomes enforceable.

Whiteflower

- Legal title needs to be transferred to Sanjeev in compliance with s 52 LPA 1925 and s 27 Land Registration Act 2002.
- There is a clear intention to create a trust but, as it is a trust in land, it must comply with s 53(1)(b) as under Blackacre.

Shares

- Kirsty wants to dispose of her beneficial interest in shares. She must comply with s 53(1)(c) LPA 1925. Failure to do so makes the transaction void (***Grey v IRC*** [1960]).
- Kirsty is absolutely entitled and *sui juris*. She intends that Charlie is to get the legal and beneficial interest, in which case the Vandervell exception may apply.
- Give a brief conclusion (not a repetition of your answer).

CHAPTER 6

Problem answer

- Identify the relevant issues:

1. The Charities Act 2011, s 5: the trust aims to provide recreational and leisure facilities for the elderly.

- Such trusts must be in the interests of social welfare (s 5(1)).
- To do so, it must satisfy the two basic conditions (s 5(2)):

(a) The trust must benefit a recognized group under the Act—the centre is for the elderly, a group in need by virtue of their age (s 5(3)(b)(i)).

(b) The centre must be aimed at improving the conditions of the group's lives (s 5(3)(a))—the centre addresses something many elderly people lack—facilities allowing them to socialize and get involved in different activities.

- The centre is also for the public benefit, as the elderly in Lincoln would constitute a sufficient section of the community. The trust should be valid.

2. Section 3(1)(b): advancement of education.

- Public benefit? Yes—there is no personal nexus between the settlor and the beneficiaries (***Oppenheim v Tobacco Securities Trust Co*** [1951]).
- Political trust? A political trust cannot be valid (***McGovern v Attorney-General*** [1982]). However, Oliver's wish to help to train lawyers who will challenge the government on civil liberties issues has arguably not been stated as a purpose, but merely as a hope. The main purpose is to help fund the education of law students, perhaps particularly those with an interest in civil liberties. Therefore, this should still be valid.

3. Section 3(1)(d): advancement of health—this head includes the provision of palliative care, such as that provided by hospices.

- Public benefit? Is the hospice a private fee-charging facility? As long as it is not profit-making and does not entirely exclude the poor, it will be considered in the public benefit (***Re Resch*** [1969]).
- *Cy-près?* As the hospice has closed, can the money be applied to another related purpose?
- This is a case of initial failure, as the hospice closed before Oliver's will came into effect.
- Is there a general charitable intention? As the purposes of the gift are not too specific (***Re Rymer*** [1895]) it is probable that the court will allow the money to be applied to the work of another cancer hospice.

CHAPTER 7

Problem answer

- Could the bequest be charitable? In this explanation briefly explain the advantages.
- Not within any of the anomalous exceptions, with a brief explanation only. Do not dwell on what is impossible.
- The gardening club may be an unincorporated association.

- Explain the categories; the ones that are unlikely to be successful should be dealt with in outline only.
- Explain the contractual analysis and what you would want to know about the club: can it dissolve and share assets? Is it part of a larger organization? The contractual analysis would mean that the money could be used for any purpose that the club wishes.
- Explain that if the purpose is important to Johan then the ***Re Denley*** [1969] may be preferable. Explain how ***Re Denley*** works—the ascertainable individuals who will enforce, and so no problem with the beneficiary principle. There is no perpetuity period, so it would seem to fail on this.
- Conclude as to the preferable interpretation.

CHAPTER 8

Problem answer

Planning your answer—look for the clues. There are issues of certainty but focus on the secret trust issues. Clues are dates of conversations about trusts which are not in the will. Obvious clues are: a trust described as being 'on terms they are aware of', 'for purposes known to them', or other similar phrases. Deal with each bequest separately.

Bushmills

- Explain that it appears to be a fully secret trust; set out the basic requirements.
- Explain the *intention* to create the trust and the three certainties. These are quite clear here.
- *Communication*: explain that it can be at any time before death. Explain that this will be acceptable, relating the facts to the relevant law. However, explain the issue with communication to only one intended trustee and the issues in ***Re Stead*** [1900].
- *Acceptance*: Kamjit has been silent; acquiescence. However, it is too late to bind Hamid to the trust and he will take free of the obligation.
- Explain the problems with formalities and fully secret trusts of land.

Badger Bridges shares

- There is a half secret trust as mentioned in the will.
- Deal with the *intention* issues.
- *Communication*: if the communication was before the will there is no problem; however, if it was after the will it may be too late. Expand your discussion on whether Re Keen establishes a strict rule that communication needs to be before the execution of the will or if this is not in fact part of the ratio. If so, the communication can possibly be after the execution of the will. There is not a problem with the letter being in the safe. Pay close attention that the wording of the will and the communications made are consistent; any inconsistency would mean failure.
- If it fails, the legatees cannot take the property for themselves. Explain why. There will be a resulting trust back to the estate.
- *Acceptance*: agreement by one secret trustee as joint tenant or tenant in common should be explained.

CHAPTER 9

Problem answer

- Anne is the legal owner so assumed to be the beneficial owner. The burden is on Iain to prove otherwise. There is no express trust under s 53(1)(b) LPA 1925 so he must rely on implied trust under s 53(2) LPA 1925.
- *Resulting trust*: Iain contributed 2 per cent of the purchase. The money Iain gave to Anne will not give him any interest in the home. While the car may be held by Anne on resulting trust for Iain (a voluntary conveyance of money), it does not gain an interest in the home. Iain may prefer to have 2 per cent of the home rather than 100 per cent of the car, which may devalue.
- A constructive trust may give Iain a larger interest in the home. Deal with each possibility.
- Express common intention. Iain makes an express statement, but Iain is making a statement about how people should share property; Anne has merely stated that she agrees with the idea, not that it is her intention in relation to her own property.
- Additionally, is the statement by Iain about the family home or about property in general?
- If the statement is about the home, apply to the facts, then Iain's detrimental reliance would

seem to create an interest. If the statement is not about the home, then consider an *inferred constructive trust*.

- *Inferred constructive trust*: there has been a financial contribution, both at the outset and additionally with the later mortgage payments.
- Quantifying the interest under the constructive trust: all the work performed by Iain may be considered. Following ***Stack v Dowden*** [2007] the courts will try to find the intention of the parties from their respective actions.
- To finish, explain whether an estoppel would arise from Anne's actions.

CHAPTER 10

Problem answer

- Identify the relevant issues:
- *Wider investment powers*: s 8 Trustee Act 2000 only allows investment to land in the United Kingdom, so the court's permission will be needed.
- Identify the appropriate route: s 57 Trustee Act 1925 allows the court to approve changes to the administration or management of the trust which are 'expedient'.
- Apply: as long as the court does not believe that this enlargement will be to the detriment of the trust, it is likely to consent. The court may also impose any restrictions it deems necessary.
- *Varying the beneficial interests of the trust:*
- Identify the appropriate route: changes to the beneficial interests can only be approved under VTA 1958.
- Apply: will the court give consent for the children?
- The court may consent for Connor, Deborah, and Eve under s 1(1)(b). Note, although Deborah and Eve are minors, the relevant section is *not* s 1(1)(a)—the entitlement of all three depends on them holding a particular *status* (ie married) in the future.
- Ben: the s 1(1)(b) proviso will apply to Ben, so that at the time his parents apply, it will be assumed that they have died. As Ben is currently married, he will be considered to satisfy the marriage condition and, therefore, the court will not consent for him.
- Benefit? The children's accelerated entitlement provides a financial benefit. However, if Connor or Eve do not marry, Deborah would receive a larger share. ***Re Remnant's ST*** [1970] suggests this will not be a problem if there are other broader benefits.
- Deborah's religious objections will likely be outweighed by the benefits to the rest of the family. Approving the variation will create greater family harmony than refusing it.

CHAPTER 11

Problem answer

- Identify the relevant issues:
- *Trustees' duty of care*: as lay trustees, Jan and Beth will not be judged against the standards of professionals. They must exercise reasonable care and skill in the circumstances (s 1 TA 2000).
- *Delegation*: the trustees are permitted to delegate investment powers to Paul under s 11.
- However, there is no evidence that they have satisfied the special requirements for the delegation of asset management functions (s 15). The s 1 duty of care applies to the choice of agent—agents should not be employed outside their area of expertise (***Fry v Tapson*** (1885)). As a computer engineer with only casual experience of investing small amounts of money, it is unlikely that the trustees have acted reasonably.
- *Choice of investment*: s 8 prohibits investment in land outside the United Kingdom. The Spanish villas are unauthorized investments and the trustees must disinvest.
- *Standard investment criteria*: s 13(2) states that Paul must address the SIC, set out in s 4(3):
- *Diversification* (s 4(3)(b)): the investments appear appropriately diverse. Modern portfolio theory states that trustees will not be judged on individual failures (ie the loss on Carfax) if it can be shown that the investment choices sufficiently balance risk with security (***Nestle v National Westminster Bank*** [1993]).
- *Suitability* (s 4(3)(a)): unit trusts and Carfax Bank would appear suitable. While IP-Ops might be suitable *in general*, the fact that Paul owns the company raises a potential conflict of interest.

- *Fiduciary duties*: as an agent, Paul stands in a fiduciary relationship to the trust. Fiduciaries cannot retain profits generated from their connection to the trust (***Boardman v Phipps*** [1967]). Paul will hold the personal profits generated from this investment on constructive trust for the beneficiaries.
- *Retention of Carfax shares*: Paul's failure to move the shares will make him liable to the trust for the further loss in value. However, this also raises the question of whether the trustees have sufficiently supervised Paul with reasonable care and skill (s 22). If the courts decide that they have not, the trustees will also be liable for the further loss.
- *Replacement of trustees*: if the beneficiaries have lost faith in their trustees, they may replace them under s 19 TOLATA 1996, as long as they are both *sui juris* and collectively absolutely entitled to the trust property.

CHAPTER 12

Problem answer

- Identify who has the relevant property. Deal with each potential claim separately.

£2,000 with Fungirls

- This can be done by common law rules as direct receipt of property; no need to complicate.
- Personal claim, which is strict. Subject to defences; it is not 'equity's darling' as it is not a valid contract; change of position can be applied.

£500 picture from Augustus

- The money has been changed into a picture. The money could not be reclaimed from Augustus as he has a defence of 'equity's darling'. There is no evidence of any knowledge to make him liable as a 'stranger'.
- The picture is in the hands of Jack, purchased with the money belonging to the customers (held on trust). The presumption of honesty (***Re Hallet's*** (1880)) would mean that £500 of Jack's money was spent first, then the remaining £500 from the customer's account money. They can claim 50 per cent of the picture, which is now worth £2,000.
- However, Jack goes on to dissipate the remaining balance. ***Re Oatway*** [1903] would allow the principle of Re Hallet's to be reversed. The presumption would be that the £1,000 spent on the picture was actually all the customer account money. They can place an equitable lien over the property to claim the £1,000 and any increase in value.
- The customer account can be reimbursed with the money repaid by Fungirls and possession of a picture.

CHAPTER 13

Problem answer

- Identify, briefly, the wrong(s) which need a remedy: a breach of contract and a potential breach of confidence. Deal with each issue separately.

Breach of contract

- Explain why damages may not be adequate. Ahmed is Joyce's favourite so no other will do, which will mean that it is unique.
- This may be a contract for personal services; explain and apply.
- This may need the supervision of the courts; explain and apply.
- Consider whether any defences apply.
- No date is given but explain that Hannah may prefer an interim remedy.
- Specific performance is not available at an interim stage so a mandatory injunction may be sought. Explain the test for a mandatory injunction and apply.

Breach of confidence

- Explain perpetual and interim injunctions. Interim may be better as there seems a risk of imminent harm.
- Set out each part of the ***American Cyanamid*** [1975] test:

Is there a serious question to be tried? It would seem so.

Damages would not be adequate for the apparent risks.

Discuss the balance of probabilities—apply to the facts.

- To protect any potential award a freezing order may be sought. Set out the test for a grant; do not focus on the procedure but on the legal issues.

Glossary

'Abhors a vacuum' Equity requires that all property is owned by an identifiable object, person, or legal entity.

Acquiescence By agreement; not express but by failure to object.

Advancement (power of) Where beneficiaries have an interest in the capital of a trust, trustees have a power to advance part of the capital for the advancement or benefit of the beneficiary.

Anomalous exception See chapter 7 for non-charitable purpose trusts which have been declared valid.

Assign To transfer an interest, either legal or equitable, in property.

Attorney-General The principal representative of the Crown in legal matters.

Bailee A person who takes possession of property belonging to another.

Bona fide A person who has acted in good faith, with no evidence of knowledge of any wrongdoing.

Capital The trust property itself. Beneficiaries who hold a remainder interest are entitled to the capital of the trust; eg if Phoebe leaves 1,000 shares on trust to Urfan for life, remainder to Mohmin, Urfan will be entitled to the income from the shares for his lifetime. When Urfan dies, Mohmin will be entitled to the shares themselves (ie the capital).

Charity Commission The body responsible for the administration of charities in England and Wales.

Chose in action An intangible property right that is not enforceable by possession, such as a debt under a contract.

Codicil An addition to a will which can change the original terms of the will. The codicil must also comply with the requirements of the Wills Act 1837.

Contempt of court The offence of interfering with or impeding the administration of justice, punishable by fine or up to two years' imprisonment.

Contingency A condition placed on a trust, such as 'to Iain should he pass his exams'.

Damages Monetary compensation given as a remedy as of right on breach of a legal obligation.

Deed A formal contract which can create or transfer an interest or obligation without the need for consideration. The requirements of a deed are set out in s 1 Law of Property (Miscellaneous Provisions) Act 1989.

Dehors Outside—not within the will itself.

Determinable An interest which may be terminated on the occurrence of certain events.

Discretionary trust A type of trust in which the trustees have a duty to apply the trust property among a class of beneficiaries. While the trustees have a duty to distribute, they have the discretion to decide which members of the class to appoint as beneficiaries and in what amounts. This can be compared with a fixed trust, where the beneficiaries and their interests are fixed from the start.

Disposition To dispose of an interest. In this text, to give away or assign.

Dominion Clear evidence of ownership or control.

Donee A person or legal entity who receives a gift. The donor is the person who gives the gift.

Economic duress A common law doctrine which renders agreements entered into as a result of illegitimate economic pressure coercing another's will—voidable.

Ex parte In the absence of one of the parties, in this context usually the defendant.

Executed Legal language used to describe the point at which a will is written and properly formalized. Do not confuse this with the point at which the will becomes effective—ie when the testator dies.

Executor/executrix (masculine/feminine) A person chosen by a testator to administer his or her estate. See also **personal representative**.

Fiduciary A person in a relationship of trust and confidence towards another. While there are established categories of fiduciary, eg trustee/beneficiary and solicitor/client, the categories are not closed.

Imperfect Where an attempt to transfer property legally has failed, the transfer is then said to be imperfect.

'In the hands' In the possession of.

Income The profits derived from property, eg the dividends from shares. **Beneficiaries** who hold a life interest are entitled to the income from the trust property. Compare with **capital**.

Indemnity Payment from one party to another guaranteed to be paid if there is a breach of duty.

Intangible property Property which is not physical in nature, but which can still be owned, eg stocks and shares. See also **chose in action**.

Inter vivos Literally 'in life'. Usually used in relation to this text when a person creates a trust or gives a gift during his or her lifetime.

Interim The period before full trial has been heard.

Joint tenants All property can be co-owned by more than one person. If this is the case, they can own the property as joint tenants or as **tenants in common**. A joint tenancy in property (any property, not just land) means that all the co-owners have an identical interest in property; it is not divided into individual shares. A joint tenant can **sever** his or her joint tenancy at any time and become a tenant in common.

Jointly and severally All trustees are equally liable (jointly) but can also be individually liable for the whole loss (severally).

Letters of wishes A settlor will often include a letter of wishes with a trust instrument, expressing the settlor's preferences regarding how trustees should exercise their discretion, eg to favour the settlor's children over members of his or her wider family when making appointments to a discretionary trust. Trustees should take these wishes into account, but they are not binding.

Lien A legal charge or hold on particular property to secure the repayment of money owed.

Life in being This can be any person alive at the time the trust is created. Often people attach it to the youngest member of the Royal Family, but it can be anyone who is alive.

Life interest An interest in trust property which lasts for the life of the beneficiary; eg if Abigail leaves her shares in Arrowtech to Fraser for life, remainder to Colin, Fraser will hold the life interest and Colin will hold the remainder interest.

Life tenant A person who holds a life interest in a trust. See **life interest**.

Maintenance (power of) A power of trustees to apply any part of the income of a minor's interest towards his or her maintenance, education, or benefit.

Manifested An evidential matter. There should be clear evidence on which to base a legal process; usually in writing is the best evidence.

Mixed Where property does not remain in its unique identifiable form.

Next-of-kin A person's nearest relations.

Perpetual In this context it means granted at full trial. It does not mean that it lasts forever. An injunction may be granted for a specific period or for certain timescales.

Perpetuity Means forever. The law prevents people tying up property interests which cannot be disposed of. One of the features of a property right is that it should be capable of disposal by its owner.

Personal representative The generic word for a person who administers a will.

Personalty Property other than real property, such as pictures, jewellery, and cars (but not exclusively).

Power of appointment In this text, it is the power under a trust to appoint a person to distribute the trust property.

Prima facie At first glance—on the present facts, without a full investigation.

Priority A bankruptcy payment will be made to a person with priority before payments are made to other creditors.

Protective trust A trust which is determinable upon the beneficiary's bankruptcy or other identified event, at which point a discretionary trust arises for the beneficiary and his or her family—see s 33 Trustee Act 1925.

Quantum meruit A Latin phrase meaning 'as much as he has earned'.

Rateably In proportion to their contribution, sometimes referred to as *pari passu*. Note that it does *not* mean equally. If a person contributes 10 per cent to the purchase he or she gets a 10 per cent interest.

Realty Land.

Remainder interest An interest which takes effect after a life interest.

Remainderman A person who holds the remainder interest in a trust. See **remainder interest**.

Remoteness of vesting A rule that property must belong to a legal person within the perpetuity period. The common law rule was that this was a life in being plus 21 years, and there are now different periods set out in the Perpetuities & Accumulations Act 1964 and 2009.

Remuneration Payment for services rendered.

Resettlement Describes when a trust is ended, and its property applied to a new trust. See **settlement**.

Settlement A term used to describe a trust or trust instrument.

Settlor A person who gives (settles) property under a trust.

Severance When co-owners end their joint tenancy and become tenants in common.

Subsisting An interest which exists. In this text, it will differentiate between the creation of a beneficial interest and the transfer (disposition) of an existing interest.

Sui juris A Latin term used to describe beneficiaries who are adults (over 18) of sound mind. You will typically come across this phrase in connection with issues which require the consent of beneficiaries.

Tangible property Physical property, eg a house or a painting. See **intangible property**.

Tenants in common Co-owners of property who have a separate and identifiable interest in property. Unlike a **joint tenant** who has an identical interest to all other joint tenants, a tenant in common has his or her own share of property.

Testamentary A gift or trust made by will (testament).

Testator/testatrix (masculine/feminine) A person who executes a will.

Transferee The person who is intended to receive the property.

Unconscionable/unconscionability It is impossible to give a definitive answer to what this word means. It is a question of fact which equity can apply when the courts exercise their discretion to do justice.

Undue influence An equitable doctrine that renders agreements entered into as a result of another's influence voidable.

Unincorporated association When a group of people form a company, they become incorporated. The company has its own legal identity and can own property in the same way as any individual. An unincorporated association is a group of people who do not have the same legal personality as a company. It is merely a group of people who come together for a purpose. As they have no corporate identity any property owned by the association is owned by all the members of the association.

Valuable consideration Consideration has the same meaning as in contract law. There must be some exchange. Note also that a deed will be sufficient consideration.

Vest When a person, or entity, gains a present legal right.

Vested A present property right either to use and enjoy the property now or to use in the future. It is not conditional on any event as a contingent interest. It is an existing property right which can be enforced at law.

Vicariously Liability which arises for the actions of another.

Voidable If a trust or contract is *voidable*, it is capable of being set aside. However, until that occurs, it remains enforceable. In contrast, if a trust were *void*, it would never have legal effect.

Volunteer A person who has not given valid consideration for the transfer. This may be because it was a gift or because the contract was void or illegal.

Index

A

accessory liability 187–8
account of profits 5, 213
administrative unworkability 37
advancement
presumption of 118–19
trustee powers 174–5
advancement of animal welfare 91–2
advancement of education
'education' defined 82–3
public benefit 83–4
advancement of environmental protection or improvement 91
advancement of health or the saving of lives 87
advancement of religion
public benefit 86–7
'religion' defined 85–6
advancement of the arts, culture, heritage, or science 88–9
amateur sport charities 89
animals
advancement of animal welfare 91–2
purpose trusts 102
Anton Piller orders *see* **search orders**
appointment *see* **powers of appointment**
appointment of trustees
additional trustees 158
by deed 158
arts trusts 88–9
assignments
contracts for valuable consideration to assign 65
direct assignments 64
automatic resulting trust
failure of a contingency 127
failure to dispose of whole beneficial interest 127
money given for a stated purpose which can no longer be carried out 128–9
surplus of funds after a valid purpose trust has completed its purpose 127–8
uncertainty of objects 127

B

bare powers 22
bare trusts 18
beneficial interests *see* **equitable interests**
beneficiaries
advantages of formalities 60
bare trusts 18
certainty of
administrative unworkability 37
automatic resulting trust 127
curing of conceptual uncertainty 36–7
discretionary trusts 32–3
discretionary trusts and fiduciary powers compared 37–9
effect of lack of certainty 37
fixed trusts 32
gifts subject to a condition precedent 33–6
overview 31
charitable trusts distinguished 76
consent to variation of trust 147
duties of trustees
distributions 172–3
fiduciary duties 161–4
information rights 170–2
investments 165
fixed and discretionary trusts distinguished 18
information rights
other information 171–2
reasons for trustee decisions not required 170–1
powers of trustees
advancement 174–5
maintenance 173–4
protective trusts 18
requirements for valid transfer of equitable interests 46
structure of a trust 17
vested and contingent interests distinguished 18–19
beneficiary principle
anomalous exceptions
animals 102
fox-hunting 103

beneficiary principle (*cont.*)
monuments 102
saying of masses 103
general requirements 100
***bona fide* purchaser for valuable consideration without notice** 185
breaches of trust *see* **remedies**
bribes 162–3, 189, 213

C

certainty
advantages of formalities 60–1
importance of three certainties 26
of intention
inferred from conduct 28
inter vivos transactions 61
lack of certainty results in gift 28
link with subject matter 31
precatory and imperative words distinguished 26–8
key cases 39–40
key debates 40
key facts 25
of objects
administrative unworkability 37
automatic resulting trust 127
charitable trusts distinguished 76
curing of conceptual uncertainty 36–7
discretionary trusts 32–3
discretionary trusts and fiduciary powers compared 37–9
effect of lack of certainty 37
fixed trusts 32
gifts subject to a condition precedent 33–6
overview 31
of subject matter
beneficial interests 30–1
effect of lack of certainty 31
link with intention 31
overview 28
property held on trust 28–30
transfers of property 54
'change of position' defence 185
charitable trusts
see also **purpose trusts**
advantages of charitable status 76
charitable purposes
advancement of animal welfare 91–2
advancement of education 82–5
advancement of environmental protection or improvement 91
advancement of health or the saving of lives 88
advancement of religion 85–7
advancement of the arts, culture, heritage, or science 88–9
amateur sport 89
'any other purposes . . . ' 92
general categories 77–8
legal requirements of a valid charitable trust 77
'political purposes' 89–90
public benefit 78–9
recreational and similar trusts 92
relief of those in need 91
relief or prevention of poverty 80–2
trust must have exclusively charitable purposes 79–80
cy-près doctrine 92
general principles 92
types of failure 94–7
key cases 97
key debates 98
key facts 75
legal requirements of a valid charitable trust 77
other types of trust distinguished 76
role of Charity Commission 76–7
Charity Commission 76–7
chattels
formalities for transfer 46
rule in *Strong v Bird* 47
choses in action
formalities for transfer 64–5
general principles 45
class gifts
discretionary trusts 38–9
fiduciary powers 39
clubs *see* **unincorporated associations**
co-ownership
confusion of terms 114
implied trusts
constructive trusts 136–41
overview 135
resulting trusts 135–6
joint tenants
club members 103–4
family homes 135
fully secret trusts 114–15
statutory trusts 20
tenancies in common
club members 103–4
fully secret trusts 114–15

common law
conflict between equity and the common law 3
continuing debate over unified system of rules 4–6
covenants to settle 52–3
equity acts *in personam* 7–8
equity follows the law 8
fusion with equity 3–4
personal actions against third parties 184
problems with the early common law system 2
summary of potential claims in common law 198
tracing 190
consent
defence to personal action against trustee 183
variation of trusts 147
constructive trusts
circumstances in which they arise 21
equity will not suffer a wrong without a remedy 7
family homes
express common intention trusts 136–8
overview 136
modern role of equity 11–12
presumed intention of the parties 21
residuary category of trusts 133–4
traditional constructive trusts 134–5
contempt of court 7–8
contingent interests
automatic resulting trust 127
entitlement to income 174
vested interests distinguished 18–19
contractual obligations
to assign to another 65
breaches giving rise to constructive trusts 135
covenants to settle 52–3
gifts to unincorporated associations 105–7
specific performance 203–4
courts
advantages of formalities 60
authorization of more trustees 158
cy-près doctrine 96
discretionary power to grant relief for breaches of trust 183
origins of equity 2–3
reform by Judicature Acts 1873–75 3–4
variation of trusts
generally cautious approach 147
rationale for restrictive approach 149
relevant circumstances 147–9
relevant variations 147
covenants to settle 52–3
culture trusts 88–9
***cy-près* doctrine**
general principles 92
types of failure
initial failure 93–6
subsequent failure 96

D

defences
personal actions against third parties 185–8
personal actions for breach by trustees 182–3, 185–8
specific performance 205–6
tracing 197
***dehors* trusts**
justification for the enforcement of secret trusts 112
key debates 123
underlying problems 120–1
delay
defence to specific performance 206
doctrine of *laches* 9
disability
charitable trusts 91
disadvantaged persons
charitable trusts 91
discretionary trusts
certainty of objects 32–3
fiduciary powers compared 37–9
fixed trusts distinguished 18
powers given to trustees 21–2
dissolution of unincorporated associations 107–8
donatio mortis causa
contemplation of death 48
delivery 48
examples 49
formalities 47–8
duties of trustees
administration of the trust 161
distributions 172–3
fiduciary duties
dealings with trust property 162–3
fair dealing rule 164
meaning and scope 161–2
non-competing rule 164
self-dealing rule 163–4
unauthorized profits 162–3

duties of trustees (*cont.*)
information to beneficiaries
other information 171–2
reasons for decisions not required 170–1
investments
duty to act even-handedly 165
modern approach to investment 166–7
scope of trustees' investment powers 166–70
statutory widening of powers 165
key cases 176
key debates 177
overview 161
personal actions for breach
defences 182–3
general principles 181–2

E

education *see* **advancement of education**
environmental trusts 91
equitable interests
charitable trusts distinguished 76
family homes
constructive trusts 140
overview 135
resulting trusts 135–6
inter vivos trusts
contracts for valuable consideration to assign 65
declarations that interest held for another 68–71
direct assignments 64
directions to trustee to hold for another 65–6
four ways to benefit another person 64
Vandervell exception 67–8
requirements for valid transfer 46
equitable remedies
account of profits 213
equity 'will not suffer a wrong without a remedy 214
inadequacy of damages 203
injunctions
general principles 206–7
interim injunctions 207–12
perpetual injunctions 207
key cases 214
key debates 215
key facts 202
overview 203
rectification 213
rescission 212–13
specific performance
defences 205–6
relevant considerations in granting order 204–5
where damages will be considered inadequate 203–4
equity
continuing debate over unified system of rules 4–6
flexible approach to implied trusts 126
history and development
conflict between equity and the common law 3
emergence in twelfth century 2
problems with the early common law system 2
reform by Judicature Acts 1873–75 3–4
role of Lord Chancellor 2–3
key cases 13
key debates 13–14
key facts 1
maxims
delay defeats equity 9
equity acts *in personam* 7–8
equity follows the law 8
equity is equality 10
equity looks to intent, not form 9–10
equity sees as done that which ought to be done 10
equity will not permit a statute to be used as an instrument of fraud 10
equity will not suffer a wrong without a remedy 7
general rules of thumb 6–7
he who comes to equity must come with clean hands 8–9
he who seeks equity must do equity 9
modern and highly developed body of legal rules 11–12
'equity's darling' 185
estoppel
equitable principle 50
examples 51
family homes 141
reliance 51
remedies 52
unequivocal promise 51
'every effort' principle 49
exemption clauses 182
express trusts
bare trusts 18
charitable trusts distinguished 76
family homes 136–8

fixed and discretionary trusts distinguished 18
inter vivos and testamentary trusts distinguished 17
private and public trusts distinguished 17
protective trusts 18

F

fair dealing rule 164
family homes
constructive trusts
express common intention trusts 136–8
inferred common intention constructive trusts 138–41
overview 136
importance of implied trusts 126
key cases 142
key debates 142–3
overview 135
proprietary estoppel 141
resulting trusts 135–6
role of equity 7, 11
situations where constructive trusts arise 21, 27
fiduciary powers and obligations
account of profits 213
breaches giving rise to constructive trusts 134
certainty of objects 37–9
defined 22
personal actions for breach by trustees
defences 182–3
general principles 181–2
trustees
dealings with trust property 162–3
fair dealing rule 164
meaning and scope 161–2
non-competing rule 164
self-dealing rule 163–4
unauthorized profits 162–3
financial hardship
charitable trusts 91
fixed trusts
certainty of objects 32
discretionary trusts distinguished 18
formalities
advantages for various parties 60–1
automatic resulting trusts 20
donatio mortis causa 47–8
equity will not permit a statute to be used as an instrument of fraud 10
inter vivos trusts
certainty of intention 61
equitable interests 64–71
interests in land 62–4
key cases 72–3
key debates 73
key facts 59
modern role of equity 12
relevant transactions 60
secret trusts 111
summary of constitution and formalities 71
testamentary trusts 61
transfers of property
chattels 46
choses in action 45
land 45
stocks and shares 45
fox-hunting 103
fraud
equity will not permit a statute to be used as an instrument of fraud 10
justification for secret trusts 111–13
freezing orders
interim injunctions 211–12
modern role of equity 11

G

gifts
benefiting another with property 43
equitable principles to perfect title
covenants to settle 52–3
donatio mortis causa 47–9
estoppel 50–2
'every effort' principle 49
overcoming unconscionability 49–50
rule in *Strong v Bird* 47
of imperfect obligation
exceptions to beneficiary principle 100
unincorporated associations 103
lack of certain intention to create trust 28
presumed resulting trusts 132
subject to a condition precedent 33–6
to unincorporated associations
gift for the members subject to their contractual obligations 105–7
outright gifts 103–4

H

health *see* **advancement of health or the saving of lives**
heritage trusts 88–9

history of equity
conflict between equity and the common law 3
continuing debate over unified system of rules 4–6
emergence in twelfth century 2
problems with the early common law system 2
reform by Judicature Acts 1873–75 3–4
role of Lord Chancellor 2–3
human rights
interim injunctions 210
modern role of equity 11
'political purpose' trusts 89–90
prohibitive injunctions 207

I

illegality
he who comes to equity must come with clean hands 8–9
presumed resulting trusts 132–3
implied trusts
categorization
constructive trusts 20–1
overview 19
resulting trusts 20
statutory trusts 20
constructive trusts
residuary category of trusts 133–4
traditional constructive trusts 134–5
family homes
constructive trusts 136–41
overview 135
resulting trusts 135–6
flexible approach of equity 126
key facts 125
resulting trusts
automatic resulting trust 126–9
presumed resulting trusts 129–33
role of intention 126
inalienability, rule against
charitable trusts 76
purpose trusts 102, 105–8
injunctions
equity will not suffer a wrong without a remedy 7
general principles 206–7
he who seeks equity must do equity 9
interim injunctions
freezing orders 211–12
mandatory injunctions 210
prohibitive injunctions 207–9
quia timet injunctions 212
search orders 210–11
modern role of equity 11
perpetual injunctions 207
super-injunctions 212
intention
certainty of
inferred from conduct 28
inter vivos transactions 61
lack of certainty results in gift 28
link with subject matter 31
precatory and imperative words distinguished 26–8
constructive trusts 21
equity looks to intent, not form 9–10
family homes
express common intention trusts 136–8
inferred common intention constructive trusts 138–41
presumed resulting trusts 20
resulting trusts
intention to benefit another person 126
rule in *Strong v Bird* 47
secret trusts 113
variation of trusts under VTA 1958 154
***inter vivos* trusts**
formalities
equitable interests 64–71
interests in land 62–4
inter vivos and testamentary trusts distinguished 17
interim injunctions
freezing orders 211–12
mandatory injunctions 210
prohibitive injunctions 207–9
quia timet injunctions 212
search orders 210–11
intermeddling 186
intestacy
statutory trusts 20
investments
duty to act even-handedly 165
modern approach to investment 166–7
scope of trustees' investment powers 166–70
statutory widening of powers 165

J

joint tenants
club members 103–4
family homes 135
fully secret trusts 114–15

L

laches
defence to specific performance 206

delay defeats equity 9
land
family homes *see* **family homes**
formalities for transfer 45
inter vivos trusts
evidenced in writing 62
relevant interests 62
rule in *Rochefoucauld v Boustead* 63–4
signed by the settlor 62–3
statutory requirements 62
number of trustees 158
secret trusts 121
specific performance 203–4
statutory trusts 20
voluntary conveyances 130
life-saving *see* **advancement of health or the saving of lives**
limitation of actions
defence to personal actions for breach 183
equitable jurisdiction to decide whether or not a claim is too late 9
loans
constructive trusts 199
presumed resulting trusts 129, 132
Lord Chancellor 2–3

M

maintenance 173–4
mandatory injunctions
interim injunctions 210
perpetual injunctions 207
Mareva injunctions *see* **freezing orders**
masses 103
maxims of equity
concerning the circumstances in which equity will operate
equity is equality 10
equity looks to intent, not form 9–10
equity sees as done that which ought to be done 10
equity will not permit a statute to be used as an instrument of fraud 10
concerning the conduct expected of claimants
delay defeats equity 9
he who comes to equity must come with clean hands 8–9
he who seeks equity must do equity 9
concerning the nature of equity and its jurisdiction
equity acts *in personam* 7–8
equity follows the law 8
equity will not suffer a wrong without a remedy 7
general rules of thumb 6–7
mere powers 22
mistake
defence to specific performance 205
rectification 213
money
requirements for valid transfer 46
monuments 102

N

non-charitable purpose trusts *see* **purpose trusts**
non-competing rule 164

O

objects *see* **beneficiaries**

P

perpetual injunctions 207
perpetuity rules
advantages of charitable status 76
purpose trusts 101–2
personal actions
against third parties
common law claims 184
defences 185–8
against trustees
defences 182–3
general principles 181–2
'political purpose' trusts 89–90
poverty *see* **relief or prevention of poverty**
powers
fiduciary powers 22
mere powers 22
trust powers 21–2
trustees
advancement 174–5
maintenance 173–4
powers of appointment 22
presumed resulting trusts
circumstances in which they arise 20, 129–30
rebutting the presumption
intended gifts 132
mere loans 132
presumption of advancement 131–2
voluntary conveyances 130
presumption of advancement 131–2

privacy (Art 8)
modern role of equity 11
prohibitive injunctions
interim injunctions 207–9
perpetual injunctions 207
proof
presumption of advancement 131–2
secret trusts 118–19
shares in a family home 140
proprietary claims
advantages 188–9
tracing
common law proprietary claim 190
equitable proprietary claims 191–2
importance of rules 189
innocent volunteers mixed funds 196–7
innocent volunteers who receive trust property 197–8
presumptions of honesty 193–6
against trustee in breach 192–3
proprietary estoppel *see* **estoppel**
protective trusts
defined 18
variation of trusts 151, 153
public benefit
advancement of education 83–4
advancement of religion 86–7
legal requirements of a valid charitable trust 77
meaning and scope 78–9
other heads of charity 87
relief or prevention of poverty 81–2
trust must have exclusively charitable purposes 84–5
purpose trusts
see also **charitable trusts**
anomalous exceptions
animals 102
fox-hunting 103
monuments 102
saying of masses 103
automatic resulting trust
money given for a stated purpose which can no longer be carried out 128–9
surplus of funds after a valid purpose trust has completed its purpose 127–8
general requirements 100
key cases 108
key debates 109
key facts 100
perpetuity rules 101–2
unincorporated associations
overview 103
trust for the members and future members 104–5
trust for the purpose of the association 104

Q

***quia timet* injunctions** 212
***Quistclose* trusts**
modern role of equity 12
resulting trusts 128–9

R

recipient liability 186–7
recreational and similar trusts 92–3
rectification 213
reliance
equity will not suffer a wrong without a remedy 7
estoppel 51
relief of those in need 91
relief or prevention of poverty
meaning and scope 81
'poverty' defined 80–1
public benefit 81–2
trust must have exclusively charitable purposes 82
religion
advancement of religion 85–7
'political purpose' trusts 89–90
saying of masses 103
remedies
covenants to settle 52
equitable remedies
account of profits 213
equity 'will not suffer a wrong without a remedy 214
inadequacy of damages 203
injunctions 206–12
key cases 214
key debates 215
key facts 202
overview 203
rectification 213
rescission 212–13
specific performance 203–6
estoppel 52
key cases 199
key debates 200
key facts 180
maxims of equity
equity sees as done that which ought to be done 10
equity will not suffer a wrong without a remedy 7

modern role of equity 12
overview 198
personal actions against third parties
common law claims 184
defences 185–8
personal actions against trustees
defences 182–3
general principles 181–2
possible routes for a claimant 181
problems with the early common law system 2
proprietary claims
advantages 188–9
tracing 189–98
summary of potential claims in common law 198
summary of potential claims in equity 198
remoteness of vesting 101, 105
removal of trustees
replacement 159–60
retirement 159
remuneration of trustees 160
rescission 212–13
resulting trusts
automatic resulting trust
failure of a contingency 127
failure to dispose of whole beneficial interest 127
money given for a stated purpose which can no longer be carried out 128–9
possible situations 126–7
surplus of funds after a valid purpose trust has completed its purpose 127–8
uncertainty of objects 127
circumstances in which they arise 20
family homes 135–6
presumed resulting trusts
circumstances in which they arise 129–30
rebutting the presumption 131–3
voluntary conveyances 130
role of intention 126
retirement of trustees 159
***Rochefoucauld v Boustead*, rule in** 63–4
***Romalpa* clauses** 190

S

saving of lives *see* **advancement of health or the saving of lives**
science trusts 88–9
search orders
equity will not suffer a wrong without a remedy 7
interim injunctions 210–11
modern role of equity 11
secret commissions 134, 189
secret trusts
acceptance by trustee
key requirements 117
trustee's change his mind 119–20
conceptual uncertainty and inconsistency 122
equity will not permit a statute to be used as an instrument of fraud 10
failure to fulfil key requirements
fully secret trusts 117–18
half secret trusts 118
overview 117
formalities 111
fully secret trusts
communication 114–15
failure to fulfil key requirements 117–18
half secret trusts distinguished 113
half secret trusts
communication 115–17
failure to fulfil key requirements 118
fully secret trusts distinguished 113
justifications
dehors trusts 111–12
fraud theory 111–12
key cases 122–3
key debates 123
key facts 110
key requirements
communication of terms 114
intention 113
proving their existence
burden of proof 118
standard of proof 118–19
unusual questions which may arise
problems with dehors trusts 120–1
secret trusts of land 121
testator's change of mind 120
trustee's change his mind 119–20
self-dealing rule 163–4
settlors
express trusts 17
inter vivos trusts of land 62–3
structure of a trust 17
shares *see* **stocks and shares**
specific performance
defences 205–6

specific performance (*cont.*)
relevant considerations in granting order
personal services 204–5
supervision 204
where damages will be considered inadequate 203–4
sport charities 89
statutory trusts 20
stocks and shares
formalities for transfer 45
'stranger liability' 186–7
***Strong v Bird*, rule in** 47
subject matter, certainty of
beneficial interests 30–1
effect of lack of certainty 31
link with intention 31
overview 28
property held on trust 28–30
'super-injunctions'
general principles 212
modern role of equity 11
surplus funds
dissolution of unincorporated associations 107–8
resulting trusts 127–8

T

taxation
advantages of charitable status 76
benefit of formalities 61
variation of trusts 146
tenancies in common
club members 103–4
fully secret trusts 114–15
testamentary trusts
formalities 61
inter vivos trusts distinguished 17
secret trusts *see* **secret trusts**
statutory trusts 20
tracing
common law proprietary claim 190
equitable proprietary claims 191–2
importance of rules 189
innocent volunteers mixed funds 196–7
innocent volunteers who receive trust property 197–8
presumptions of honesty 193–6
against trustee in breach 192–3
transfers of property
benefiting another with property 43–5
chattels 46
choses in action 45
equitable interests 46
contracts for valuable consideration to assign 65
declarations that interest held for another 68–71
direct assignments 64
directions to trustee to hold for another 65–6
four ways to benefit another person 64
Vandervell exception 67–8
equitable principles to perfect title
covenants to settle 52–3
donatio mortis causa 47–9
estoppel 50–2
'every effort' principle 49
overcoming unconscionability 49–50
rule in *Strong v Bird* 47
general principles 43
key cases 54–6
key debates 57
land 45
money 46
requirement for evidential certainty 54
stocks and shares 45
voluntary conveyances 130
trustees
acceptance of secret trusts 117
advantages of formalities 60
appointment
additional trustees 158
by deed 158
bare trusts 18
communication of secret trusts
fully secret trusts 114–15
half secret trusts 115–17
key requirements 114
trustee's change his mind 119–20
de son tort 186
duties
administration of the trust 161
distributions 172–3
fiduciary duties 161–4
information to beneficiaries 170–2
investments 165–70
key cases 176
key debates 177
overview 161
fiduciary powers 22
fixed and discretionary trusts distinguished 18
importance of three certainties 26
key facts 157
numbers 158

personal actions against
defences 182–3
general principles 181–2
powers
advancement 174–5
maintenance 173–4
powers given to trustees 21–2
protective trusts 18
removal
replacement 159–60
retirement 159
remuneration 160
structure of a trust 17
tracing against trustee in breach 192–3
trusts
categorization
express trusts 17–18
implied trusts 19–21
certainty *see* **certainty**
charitable trusts *see* **charitable trusts**
classification of interests 18–19
defined 17
key cases 23
key debates 24
key facts 16
modern role of equity 11
powers given to trustees 21–2
purpose trusts *see* purpose trusts
secret trusts *see* **secret trusts**
transfers of property 43
variations *see* **variation of trusts**

U

unauthorized profits 21, 162–3, 213
unconscionability
constructive trusts 20, 136, 141
defences available to innocent volunteers 197
implied trusts 65
maxims of equity
equity acts in personam 7
equity follows the law 8
equity will not permit a statute to be used as an instrument of fraud 10
equity will not suffer a wrong without a remedy 7
modern role of equity 10, 12
perfection of transfers 50
recipient liability 187
role of equity 5–6
unincorporated associations
automatic resulting trust 128
dissolution 107–8
gifts
gift for the members subject to their contractual obligations 105–7
outright gifts 103–4
overview 103
purpose trusts
trust for the members and future members 104–5
trust for the purpose of the association 104

V

variation of trusts
with beneficiaries consent 147
court's inherent jurisdiction
generally cautious approach 147
rationale for restrictive approach 149
relevant circumstances 147–9
relevant variations 147
express provisions in trust instrument 146
importance 146
key cases 154–5
key debates 155
key facts 145
overview of methods 146
statutory powers
overview 149
Variation of Trusts Act 1958 150–4
Variation of Trusts Act 1958
'benefit' defined 153
overview 150
relevant beneficiaries 151–3
relevant variations 150–1
settlor's intention 154
vested interests 18–19
voluntary conveyances 130

W

wills *see* **testamentary trusts**

Concentrate **QUESTIONS & ANSWERS**

Revision & study guides
from the **No. 1** legal education publisher

Q&A EQUITY & TRUSTS

Third Edition

Rosalind Malcolm

practise technique › boost your confidence › achieve succes

OXFORD

Concentrate **QUESTIONS & ANSWERS SAMPLE PAGES**

→ **LOOK INSIDE**

Nature of Equity and the Law of Trusts

2

ARE YOU READY?

In order to attempt the questions in this chapter you will need to have covered the following topics:

- The nature of equity
- The development of equity and its relationship to the common law
- The maxims of equity
- The nature of the trust

KEY DEBATES

Debate: The fusion argument.

Have the rules of common law and equity fused? This argument deals with the historical foundations of equity and raises the challenging question as to whether it has fused with common law. The **Judicature Acts 1873** and **1875** are at the heart of the argument insofar as it relates to administrative questions. But of more interest is the substantive side. There is a lot written about this such as: Burrows, 'We do this at Common Law but this in equity' (2002) 22 OJLS 1; Lord Millett, 'Proprietary Restitution' in *Equity in Commercial Law* (Degeling and Edelman, eds), Law Book Co of Australasia, 2005, chapter 12; Worthington, *Equity*, Oxford University Press, 2006, chapter 10; Martin, 'Fusion, fallacy and confusion: a comparative study' [1994] Conv 13—to name just a few. The area requires wide reading.

QUESTION 1

The innate conservatism of English lawyers may have made them slow to recognise that by the **Judicature Act 1873** the two systems of substantive and adjectival law formerly administered by courts of law and courts of equity . . . were fused. As at the confluence of the Rhône and the Saône, it may be possible for a short distance to discern the source from which each part of the combined stream came, but there comes a point at which this ceases to be possible. If Professor Ashburner's fluvial metaphor is to be retained at all, the confluent streams of law and equity have surely mingled now.

(Lord Diplock in ***United Scientific Holdings Ltd* v *Burnley Borough Council*** **[1978] AC 904**)

Discuss.

CAUTION!

- The structure of your answer is critical here to avoid an overly discursive approach. Strict observance of the PEA approach will help to keep your structure tight.
- You need to have covered all the literature in order to engage fully with this question—the answer needs to have full referencing to the various statements made by the judiciary and academics.
- If, when you are in the exam room, this is the first time you have come across the quote, or indeed any quote in a question (it is a key one on this topic), then you may want to consider whether this is the question for you.
- Some students tend to address equity as though it is a 'free-for-all' so don't fall into that trap. When answering any general questions on equity show you understand that it is as rule-bound as the common law!

DIAGRAM ANSWER PLAN

Set out the source of the quotation and the issues in the case

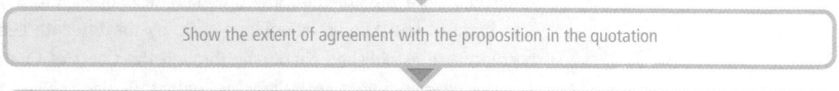

Show the extent of agreement with the proposition in the quotation

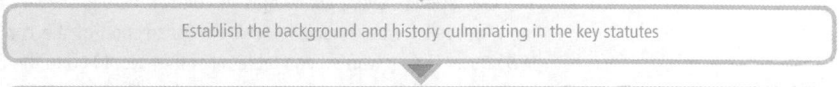

Establish the background and history culminating in the key statutes

Set out the arguments going either way

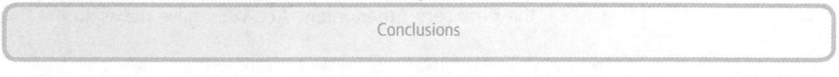

Conclusions

A SUGGESTED ANSWER

The statement by Lord Diplock was accepted unanimously by the judges in the House of Lords.[1] The case concerned the timing of the service of a notice triggering a rent-review clause which had been served late. The question arose as to whether time was of the essence. The **Law of Property Act 1925, s. 41** provides that 'stipulations in a contract, as to time or otherwise, which according to rules of equity are not deemed to be or to have become of the essence of the contract, are also construed and have effect at law in accordance with the same rules'. The section clearly states that a rule of equity is to be adopted within the body of legal rules. Lord Diplock proclaimed that the systems had become fused and no distinction was to be drawn between law and equity.[2]

This view is at the most extreme, yet it is one apparently shared by other eminent judges. Lord Denning, in *Landmarks in the Law*, states that 'the fusion is complete'. Sir George Jessel MR in ***Walsh* v *Lonsdale* (1882) 21 ChD 9**, one of the first cases on this issue to be heard subsequent to the **Judicature Acts 1873** and **1875**, said 'there are not two estates as there were formerly, one estate at common law by reason of the payment of rent from year to year, and an estate in equity under the agreement. There is only one court, and the equity rules prevail in it.' Carnwath LJ concurred in ***Halpern* v *Halpern (No. 2)* [2007] EWCA Civ 291** when relying on the **Senior Courts Act 1981** to conclude that '130 years after the "fusion" of law and equity . . . an argument based on a material difference in the two systems would have faced an uphill task' [70]. The approach of Lord Goff in ***Napier and Ettrick (Lord)* v *Hunter* [1993] AC 713** is in accord with this:[3] 'No doubt our task nowadays is to see the two strands of authority, at law and in equity, moulded into a coherent whole.'

The Development Phase

The difficulty originates from the early development of equity as a separate system from the common law.[4] Intervention by the Lord Chancellor into the common law gradually developed into a separate body of law, known as equity, which, by the fifteenth century, become well established eventually through the Court of Chancery. The two systems were sometimes in conflict. Parties seeking common law relief would need to seek the jurisdiction of the common law courts. If they wanted equitable relief they would go to the Court of Chancery. The common law courts only had limited jurisdiction to grant equitable relief. The **Common Law Procedure Act 1854, s. 79**, gave the common law courts a limited power of granting injunctions; the **Chancery Amendment Act 1858** gave power to the Court of

[1] Start with the source of the quotation. A weakness is to ignore the source of the quote and to go straight into the arguments.

[2] It is good to make reference to the judge in this way to show familiarity with the argument.

[3] Although this looks a bit like listing—often hated by examiners—it actually shows wide reading and support for the proposition made in the quotation.

[4] This paragraph sets out the historical background which helps to give depth and context to the arguments about fusion.